THE
LADY
OF THE
LAKE

and Other Poems

SIR WALTER SCOTT

D1513800

AIRMONT PUBLISHING COMPANY, INC.
22 EAST 60TH STREET · NEW YORK 10022

An Airmont Classic

specially selected for the Airmont Library
from the immortal literature of the world

PUBLISHED SIMULTANEOUSLY IN THE DOMINION OF CANADA
BY THE RYERSON PRESS, TORONTO

PRINTED IN THE UNITED STATES OF AMERICA
BY THE COLONIAL PRESS, INC., CLINTON, MASSACHUSETTS

CONTENTS

THE LADY OF THE LAKE

OF THE

and Other Poems

SIR WALTER SCOTT

Introduction

Walter Scott was born in Edinburgh, of a good Scottish family, on August 15, 1771, and was trained to follow his father's profession of the Law. But although he was admitted to the Bar at the age of twenty-one, and became a Clerk of the Court and Sheriff of Selkirkshire, his dominating interest from childhood was the study of romantic history and legend and the reading and telling of stirring tales of chivalry and romance.

At the age of twelve, following the influential example of Percy's *Reliques of Ancient English Poetry,* he began his own manuscript collection of early ballads. While still at school he exercised the photographic memory that made possible his omnivorously retentive reading and his rapid and copious writing in both verse and prose. The two writers that influenced him most were perfectly suited to his inborn interests and aptitudes—Macpherson's wildly romantic "translations" from the Gaelic of "Ossian" and Spenser's magnificent tapestry of *The Faerie Queene*—and he committed to memory "whole duans of the one and cantos of the other."

The collecting of old ballads was followed by translations

from German romantic poetry and drama, but it was not until 1805 that he published his first original work, *The Lay of the Last Minstrel*. This was followed, in similar subject form and style, and with increasing acclaim, by *Marmion* in 1808 and in 1810 by *The Lady of the Lake,* which he never surpassed and which brought the climax of his reputation as a writer of verse. Scott's seven verse tales and the "Waverley" novels that followed were all distinguished by rapid narrative, crowded and sometimes impeded or interrupted by detail. Against a background of history and legend, fictitious characters and plot provided a more or less important thread for the narrative and a central interest for its development. Its basic theatrical appeal was supported by romantic scenery and innumerable museum pieces of stage property; by the manners and customs of bygone days; by their sports and pastimes, rituals and observances, superstitions, witchcraft and demonology; by maidens in distress and champions—as often as not in disguise—who rescued them from unwanted suitors and won their undying gratitude if not their hand in marriage. The greatest poetry was to come from the greater Romantic poets, but the art and craft of Scott, whether in verse or in prose, was not that of the poet, the prose stylist, or the historian, but that of the teller of stirring tales of action.

To mark the climax of Scott's achievement in verse-narrative, *The Lady of the Lake* has first of all a perfect setting. It brought the attention of artists, tourists, of the reading and the "view-hunting" public to the Trossachs (the modern spelling), the wild and rugged glen or defile between Loch Katrine and Loch Achray, and under the shadow of Ben A'an. The region is now a Mecca for sight-seers rivaled in Scotland for convenience and popularity only by Loch Lomond, and for seekers after literary shrines surpassed nowhere in Scotland, and in Britain only by the Lake District and by Stratford-on-Avon. Today a motor road passes beside Loch Lomond, goes through Glengyle and over the

Brig of Turk, and skirts the three "mighty" lakes—Katrine, Achray, and Vennachar—with a stopover and a launch trip on Loch Katrine. Every turn of the lake and every mile of the highway reveals the accuracy of Scott's eye for topography and terrain, and the six cantos—one for each day of the action—can be followed on a map from Ellen's Isle through Callander to Stirling. Both the details and the main events of the story show equally, in addition, Scott's knowledge of Scottish history, modified only by reasonable license for poet and storyteller. As in the similarly placed novel, *Rob Roy,* the principal families of the locality, their claims and quarrels, their feuds and fealties, are authentic. The portrait of James V is fairly based on the record. It was in fact his custom to go among his people unattended and in disguise, and his liking for humorous deception is attested by two songs, "We'll go no more a-roving" and "The Gaberlunzie Man." Besides its plot, its central characters and their famous duel, and such well-known bravura pieces as the stag-hunt, the story has all the details that Scott knew best how to string like multicolored beads along a storyline of proved and unfailing interest: movement, variety, suspense, danger, adventure, the chase, keen but peaceful rivalry in sports and pastimes, a faithful minstrel, and, to conclude, the hand of a fair damsel from an enchanting if not enchanted isle relinquished by a royal suitor in disguise and won by a faithful and wholly eligible suitor. The facile octosyllabic couplets are relieved from monotony by the Spenserian stanzas that open each canto and close the work, and by interspersed lyrics, ballads, and lays, by a drinking song, and a hymn, and episodes and descriptive passages lend their variety to the narrative.

Scott's history is criticized, ironically, because he was too much a historian to have full rein as a creative writer, and it is forgotten that factual history, as told by his own Dr. Dryasdust, provided the clay rather than the bricks and tile, let alone the walls and battlements and turrets, of

which the framework and structure of his tales were composed. His aim was to lead his readers to history by the
fascination of his stories. In verse as in prose, he was
primarily neither a historian nor a poet, but always a storyteller. In his earlier tales he made use, as did his bards and
minstrels of old, of the devices of meter, rhyme, and figura-
tive and generally heightened language, to carry his readers
and his stories along the rapid road of adventure and suspense. It is tempting, but misleading, to attribute Scott's
decline as a writer of verse merely to his own superiority as
a writer of fiction, to his inferiority to Byron in Byron's
newer and, in its own way, better kind of popular verse,
and to the poetry of the great Romantics, for whom he did
so much to prepare the way but whom he never professed
to emulate. All these played their part, as did also his sense
of his own real destiny, and the success of his moral determination to balance the books of his disastrous adventure
into the business of printing and publishing. Byron and the
Waverley novels have suffered their own undeserved decline,
but they first withdrew Scott's verse from public favor,
and the loss of this, regardless of merit, is seldom easy to
make good.

That Scott cannot compete with Byron in Byron's own
inimitable kind of narrative verse is beside the point. So also
is his inability to match and equal the best, each according
to his own genius, of Wordsworth, Coleridge, Shelley, and
Keats. More relevant, but only by comparison, to his undeserved denigration or neglect, are the looseness, the haste,
the diffuseness, and all-too-frequent second-hand "poetic
diction" borrowed from the poetasters of the previous age
and the jingling meters and easy rhymes of minor "romantics" in his own. The rhetoric admittedly is often contrived
and false, and its trimmings and trappings seem borrowed
for stage effect from the museum or even from the wax-
works. Popular taste is now no more impressed than critical

judgment by such descriptions as that of Ellen's reception at Stirling:

> For her use a menial train
> A rich collation spread in vain.

Nor, probably, were readers in Scott's own first blaze of popularity much impressed by so flat a couplet as

> Awhile the maid the stranger eyed
> And, reassured, at length replied . . .

Incidental blemishes, resulting from a hasty facility, must be measured, not by the perfection of an ode or a sonnet, but by Scott's own purpose and achievement, and his own success in his own way. His virtues were more apparent and his shortcomings less noticeable to his first readers than they are to us, and their judgment may have been better than ours. Scott usually comes nearest to poetry in the songs that are interspersed in both his verse and his novels, but even these, as often as not, are ballads or soldiers' songs— such as we find in *The Lady of the Lake*—and as such are not to be condemned for their failure as lyrics but judged by their success in being what they are and in doing what they were intended to do. By this criterion, the tourists who speed through the Trossachs because of the influence of a writer of whom they have never read a line might well at least begin, if they do not end, their introduction to poetry with the stirring verse of this man whose excesses and short-comings are as easy to disregard as they are to recognize. His virtues, if not sufficient in themselves, are at least a resting place for those who like most of us cannot remain always on the heights. For those who are for the first time on the way to the understanding and enjoyment of greater poetry, he offers a starting point more suitable for begin-ners. For its own beginnings, poetry can be traced back to the retentive memories, the rapid composition, and the stirring recitations of the ballad makers, the minstrels, and the gleemen. They have lost neither their popular nor their literary appeal, and it is in their company that Scott's rapid and picturesque metrical tales of history and legend are deserving of a place.

Dalhousie University   C. L. BENNET

THE
LADY
OF THE
LAKE

The Lady of the Lake and Other Poems

INTRODUCTION TO THE EDITION OF 1830

After the success of *Marmion*, I felt inclined to exclaim with Ulysses in the *Odyssey*—

> Οὗτος μὲν δὴ ἄεθλος ἀάατος ἐκτετέλεσται·
> Νῦν αὖτε σκοπὸν ἄλλον.   *Odys. x. 1. 5.*

"One venturous game my hand has won to-day—
Another, gallants, yet remains to play."

The ancient manners, the habits and customs of the aboriginal race by whom the Highlands of Scotland were inhabited, had always appeared to me peculiarly adapted to poetry. The change in their manners, too, had taken place almost within my own time, or at least I had learned many particulars concerning the ancient state of the Highlands from the old men of the last generation. I had always thought the old Scottish Gael highly adapted for poetical composition. The feuds, and political dissensions, which, half a century earlier, would have rendered the richer and wealthier part of the kingdom indisposed to countenance a poem, the scene of which was laid in the Highlands, were now sunk in the generous compassion which the English, more than any other nation, feel for the misfortunes of an honourable foe. The Poems of Ossian had, by their popularity, sufficiently shown that if writings on Highland subjects were qualified to interest the reader, mere national prejudices were, in the present day, very unlikely to interfere with their success.

I had also read a great deal, seen much, and heard more, of that romantic country, where I was in the habit of spending some time every autumn; and the scenery of Loch Katrine was connected with the recollection of many a dear friend and merry expedition of former days. This poem, the action of which lay among scenes so beautiful, and so deeply imprinted on my recollection, was a labour of love; and it was no less so to recall the manners and incidents introduced. The frequent custom of James IV, and particularly of James V, to walk through their kingdom in disguise, afforded me the hint of an incident, which never fails to be interesting, if managed with the slightest address or dexterity.

I may now confess, however, that the employment, though attended with great pleasure, was not without its doubts and anxieties. A lady, to whom I was nearly related, and with whom I lived, during her whole life, on the most brotherly terms of affection, was residing with me at the time when the work was in progress, and used to ask me what I could possibly do to rise so early in the morning (that happening to be the most convenient time to me for composition). At last I told her the subject of my meditations; and I can never forget the anxiety and affection expressed in her reply. "Do not be so rash," she said, "my dearest cousin. You are already popular—more so, perhaps, than you yourself will believe, or than even I, or other partial friends, can fairly allow to your merit. You stand high—do not rashly attempt to climb higher, and incur the risk of a fall; for, depend upon it, a favourite will not be permitted even to stumble with impunity." I replied to this affectionate expostulation in the words of Montrose—

> "He either fears his fate too much,
>   Or his deserts are small,
> Who dares not put it to the touch
>   To gain or lose it all."

"If I fail," I said, for the dialogue is strong in my recollection, "it is a sign that I ought never to have succeeded, and I will write prose for life; you shall see no change in my temper, nor will I eat a single meal the worse. But if I succeed,

> "Up with the bonnie blue bonnet,
>   The dirk, and the feather, and a'!"

Afterwards, I showed my affectionate and anxious critic the first canto of the poem, which reconciled her to my imprudence. Nevertheless, although I answered thus confidently, with the obstinacy often said to be proper to those who bear my surname, I acknowledge that my confidence was considerably shaken by the warning of her excellent taste and unbiassed friendship. Nor was I much comforted by her retractation of the unfavourable judgment, when I recollected how likely a natural partiality was to effect that change of opinion. In such cases, affection rises like a light on the canvas, improves any favourable tints which it formerly exhibited, and throws its defects into the shade.

I remember that about the same time a friend started in to

"heeze up my hope," like the "sportsman with his cutty gun" in the old song. He was bred a farmer, but a man of powerful understanding, natural good taste, and warm poetical feeling, perfectly competent to supply the wants of an imperfect or irregular education. He was a passionate admirer of field-sports, which we often pursued together.

As this friend happened to dine with me at Ashestiel one day, I took the opportunity of reading to him the first canto of *The Lady of the Lake*, in order to ascertain the effect the poem was likely to produce upon a person who was but too favourable a representative of readers at large. It is, of course, to be supposed that I determined rather to guide my opinion by what my friend might appear to feel, than by what he might think it to say. His reception of my recitation, or prelection, was rather singular. He placed his hand across his brow, and listened with great attention through the whole account of the stag-hunt, till the dogs threw themselves into the lake to follow their master, who embarks with Ellen Douglas. He then started up with a sudden exclamation, struck his hand on the table, and declared, in a voice of censure calculated for the occasion, that the dogs must have been totally ruined by being permitted to take the water after such a severe chase. I own I was much encouraged by the species of reverie which had possessed so zealous a follower of the sports of the ancient Nimrod, who had been completely surprised out of all doubts of the reality of the tale. Another of his remarks gave me less pleasure. He detected the identity of the King with the wandering knight, Fitz-James, when he winds his bugle to summon his attendants. He was probably thinking of the lively, but somewhat licentious, old ballad, in which the denouement of a royal intrigue takes place as follows:

> "He took a bugle frae his side,
>   He blew both loud and shrill,
> And four-and-twenty belted knights
>   Came skipping ower the hill;
> Then he took out a little knife,
>   Let a' his duddies fa',
> And he was the brawest gentleman
>   That was amang them a'.
>   And we'll go no more a-roving," &c. *

This discovery, as Mr. Pepys says of the rent in his camlet cloak, was but a trifle, yet it troubled me; and I was at a good

* "The Jolly Beggar," attributed to King James V. Herd's *Collection*, 1776.

deal of pains to efface any marks by which I thought my secret could be traced before the conclusion, when I relied on it with the same hope of producing effect, with which the Irish post-boy is said to reserve a "trot for the avenue."

I took uncommon pains to verify the accuracy of the local circumstances of this story. I recollect, in particular, that to ascertain whether I was telling a probable tale, I went into Perthshire, to see whether King James could actually have ridden from the banks of Loch Vennachar to Stirling Castle within the time supposed in the Poem, and had the pleasure to satisfy myself that it was quite practicable.

After a considerable delay, *The Lady of the Lake* appeared in May 1810; and its success was certainly so extraordinary as to induce me for the moment to conclude that I had at last fixed a nail in the proverbially inconstant wheel of Fortune, whose stability in behalf of an individual who had so boldly courted her favours for three successive times, had not as yet been shaken. I had attained, perhaps, that degree of public reputation at which prudence, or certainly timidity, would have made a halt, and discontinued efforts by which I was far more likely to diminish my fame than to increase it. But, as the celebrated John Wilkes is said to have explained to his late Majesty, that he himself, amid his full tide of popularity, was never a Wilkite, so I can, with honest truth, exculpate myself from having been at any time a partisan of my own poetry, even when it was in the highest fashion with the million. It must not be supposed that I was either so ungrateful, or so superabundantly candid, as to despise or scorn the value of those whose voice had elevated me so much higher than my own opinion told me I deserved. I felt, on the contrary, the more grateful to the public, as receiving that from partiality to me, which I could not have claimed from merit; and I endeavoured to deserve the partiality, by continuing such exertions as I was capable of for their amusement.

It may be that I did not, in this continued course of scribbling, consult either the interest of the public or my own. But the former had effectual means of defending themselves, and could, by their coldness, sufficiently check any approach to intrusion; and for myself, I had now for several years dedicated my hours so much to literary labour, that I should have felt difficulty in employing myself otherwise; and so, like Dogberry, I gener-ously bestowed all my tediousness on the public, comforting myself with the reflection, that if posterity should think me un-deserving of the favour with which I was regarded by my con-temporaries, "they could not but say I *had* the crown," and had enjoyed for a time that popularity which is so much coveted.

I conceived, however, that I held the distinguished situation I had obtained, however unworthily, rather like the champion of pugilism, on the condition of being always ready to show proofs of my skill, than in the manner of the champion of chivalry, who performs his duties only on rare and solemn occasions. I was in any case conscious that I could not long hold a situation which the caprice, rather than the judgment, of the public, had bestowed upon me, and preferred being deprived of my precedence by some more worthy rival, to sinking into contempt for my indolence, and losing my reputation by what Scottish lawyers call the *negative proscription.* Accordingly, those who choose to look at the Introduction to *Rokeby* . . . will be able to trace the steps by which I declined as a poet to figure as a novelist; as the ballad says, Queen Eleanor sunk at Charing-Cross to rise again at Queenhithe.

It only remains for me to say that, during my short pre-eminence of popularity, I faithfully observed the rules of moderation which I had resolved to follow before I began my course as a man of letters. If a man is determined to make a noise in the world, he is as sure to encounter abuse and ridicule, as he who gallops furiously through a village must reckon on being followed by the curs in full cry. Experienced persons know, that in stretching to flog the latter, the rider is very apt to catch a bad fall; nor is an attempt to chastise a malignant critic attended with less danger to the author. On this principle, I let parody, burlesque, and squibs, find their own level; and while the latter hissed most fiercely, I was cautious never to catch them up, as schoolboys do, to throw them back against the naughty boy who fired them off, wisely remembering that they are, in such cases, apt to explode in the handling. Let me add, that my reign (since Byron has so called it) was marked by some instances of good-nature as well as patience. I never refused a literary person of merit such services in smoothing his way to the public as were in my power: and I had the advantage, rather an uncommon one with our irritable race, to enjoy general favour, without incurring permanent ill-will, so far as is known to me, among any of my contemporaries.

W.S.

Abbotsford, April 1830

The Lady of the Lake

TO THE MOST NOBLE
JOHN JAMES MARQUIS OF ABERCORN
THIS POEM IS INSCRIBED BY THE
AUTHOR

THE SCENE OF THE FOLLOWING POEM IS LAID CHIEFLY IN THE
VICINITY OF LOCH KATRINE, IN THE WESTERN HIGHLANDS OF
PERTHSHIRE. THE TIME OF ACTION INCLUDES SIX DAYS, AND THE
TRANSACTIONS OF EACH DAY OCCUPY A CANTO.

Canto First   THE CHASE

Harp of the North! that mouldering long hast hung
  On the witch-elm that shades Saint Fillan's spring,
And down the fitful breeze thy numbers flung,
  Till envious ivy did around thee cling,
Muffling with verdant ringlet every string,—
  O minstrel Harp, still must thine accents sleep?
'Mid rustling leaves and fountains murmuring,
  Still must thy sweeter sounds their silence keep,
Nor bid a warrior smile, nor teach a maid to weep?

Not thus, in ancient days of Caledon,
  Was thy voice mute amid the festal crowd,
When lay of hopeless love, or glory won,
  Aroused the fearful, or subdued the proud.
At each according pause was heard aloud
  Thine ardent symphony sublime and high!
Fair dames and crested chiefs attention bow'd;
  For still the burden of thy minstrelsy
Was Knighthood's dauntless deed, and Beauty's matchless eye.

O wake once more! how rude soe'er the hand
  That ventures o'er thy magic maze to stray;

O wake once more! though scarce my skill command
   Some feeble echoing of thine earlier lay:
Though harsh and faint, and soon to die away,
   And all unworthy of thy nobler strain,
Yet if one heart throb higher at its sway,
   The wizard note has not been touch'd in vain.
Then silent by no more! Enchantress, wake again!

I

The stag at eve had drunk his fill,
Where danced the moon on Monan's rill,
And deep his midnight lair had made
In lone Glenartney's hazel shade;
But, when the sun his beacon red
Had kindled on Benvoirlich's head,
The deep-mouth'd bloodhound's heavy bay
Resounded up the rocky way,
And faint, from farther distance borne,
Were heard the clanging hoof and horn.

II

As Chief, who hears his warder call,
"To arms! the foemen storm the wall,"
The antler'd monarch of the waste
Sprung from his heathery couch in haste.
But, ere his fleet career he took,
The dew-drops from his flanks he shook;
Like crested leader proud and high,
Toss'd his beam'd frontlet to the sky;
A moment gazed adown the dale,
A moment snuff'd the tainted gale,
A moment listen'd to the cry,
That thicken'd as the chase drew nigh;
Then, as the headmost foes appear'd,
With one brave bound the copse he clear'd,
And, stretching forward free and far,
Sought the wild heaths of Uam-Var.

III

Yell'd on the view the opening pack;
Rock, glen, and cavern, paid them back;
To many a mingled sound at once
The awaken'd mountain gave response.
A hundred dogs bay'd deep and strong,

Clatter'd a hundred steeds along,
Their peal the merry horns rung out,
A hundred voices join'd the shout;
With hark and whoop and wild halloo,
No rest Benvoirlich's echoes knew.
Far from the tumult fled the roe,
Close in her covert cower'd the doe;
The falcon, from her cairn on high,
Cast on the rout a wondering eye,
Till far beyond her piercing ken
The hurricane had swept the glen.
Faint and more faint, its failing din
Return'd from cavern, cliff, and linn,
And silence settled, wide and still,
On the lone wood and mighty hill.

IV

Less loud the sounds of silvan war
Disturb'd the heights of Uam-Var,
And roused the cavern, where, 'tis told,
A giant made his den of old;
For ere that steep ascent was won,
High in his pathway hung the sun,
And many a gallant, stay'd perforce,
Was fain to breathe his faltering horse,
And of the trackers of the deer,
Scarce half the lessening pack was near;
So shrewdly on the mountain side
Had the bold burst their mettle tried.

V

The noble stag was pausing now
Upon the mountain's southern brow,
Where broad extended, far beneath,
The varied realms of fair Menteith.
With anxious eye he wander'd o'er
Mountain and meadow, moss and moor,
And ponder'd refuge from his toil
By far Lochard or Aberfoyle.
But nearer was the copsewood grey,
That waved and wept on Loch-Achray,
And mingled with the pine-trees blue
On the bold cliffs of Benvenue.
Fresh vigour with the hope return'd,
With flying foot the heath he spurn'd,

Held westward with unwearied race,
And left behind the panting chase.

VI

'Twere long to tell what steeds gave o'er,
As swept the hunt through Cambusmore:
What reins were tighten'd in despair,
When rose Benledi's ridge in air;
Who flagg'd upon Bochastle's heath,
Who shunn'd to stem the flooded Teith,—
For twice that day, from shore to shore,
The gallant stag swam stoutly o'er.
Few were the stragglers, following far,
That reach'd the lake of Vennachar;
And when the Brigg of Turk was won,
The headmost horseman rode alone.

VII

Alone, but with unbated zeal,
That horseman plied the scourge and steel;
For jaded now, and spent with toil,
Emboss'd with foam, and dark with soil,
While every gasp with sobs he drew,
The labouring stag strain'd full in view.
Two dogs of black Saint Hubert's breed,
Unmatch'd for courage, breath, and speed.
Fast on his flying traces came,
And all but won that desperate game;
For, scarce a spear's length from his haunch,
Vindictive toil'd the bloodhounds stanch;
Nor nearer might the dogs attain,
Nor farther might the quarry strain.
Thus up the margin of the lake,
Between the precipice and brake,
O'er stock and rock their race they take.

VIII

The Hunter mark'd that mountain high,
The lone lake's western boundary,
And deem'd the stag must turn to bay,
Where that huge rampart barr'd the way;
Already glorying in the prize,
Measured his antlers with his eyes;
For the death-wound and death-halloo,
Muster'd his breath, his whinyard drew;—
But thundering as he came prepared,

With ready arm and weapon bared,
The wily quarry shunn'd the shock,
And turn'd him from the opposing rock;
Then, dashing down a darksome glen,
Soon lost to hound and hunter's ken,
In the deep Trosachs' wildest nook
His solitary refuge took.
There, while close couch'd, the thicket shed
Cold dews and wild-flowers on his head,
He heard the baffled dogs in vain
Rave through the hollow pass amain,
Chiding the rocks that yell'd again.

IX

Close on the hounds the hunter came,
To cheer them on the vanish'd game;
But, stumbling in the rugged dell,
The gallant horse exhausted fell.
The impatient rider strove in vain
To rouse him with the spur and rein,
For the good steed, his labours o'er,
Stretch'd his stiff limbs, to rise no more;
Then, touch'd with pity and remorse,
He sorrow'd o'er the expiring horse:
"I little thought, when first thy rein
I slack'd upon the banks of Seine,
That Highland eagle e'er should feed
On thy fleet limbs, my matchless steed!
Woe worth the chase, woe worth the day,
That costs thy life, my gallant grey!"

X

Then through the dell his horn resounds,
From vain pursuit to call the hounds.
Back limp'd, with slow and crippled pace,
The sulky leaders of the chase;
Close to their master's side they press'd,
With drooping tail and humbled crest;
But still the dingle's hollow throat
Prolong'd the swelling bugle-note.
The owlets started from their dream,
The eagles answer'd with their scream,
Round and around the sounds were cast,
Till echo seem'd an answering blast;
And on the hunter hied his way,
To join some comrades of the day;

Yet often paused, so strange the road,
So wondrous were the scenes it show'd.

XI

The western waves of ebbing day
Roll'd o'er the glen their level way;
Each purple peak, each flinty spire,
Was bathed in floods of living fire.
But not a setting beam could glow
Within the dark ravines below,
Where twined the path in shadow hid,
Round many a rocky pyramid,
Shooting abruptly from the dell
Its thunder-splinter'd pinnacle;
Round many an insulated mass,
The native bulwarks of the pass,
Huge as the tower which builders vain
Presumptuous piled on Shinar's plain.
The rocky summits, plit and rent,
Form'd turret, dome, or battlement,
Or seem'd fantastically set
With cupola or minaret,
Wild crests as pagod ever deck'd,
Or mosque of Eastern architect.
Nor were these earth-born castles bare,
Nor lack'd they many a banner fair;
For, from their shiver'd brows display'd,
Far o'er the unfathomable glade,
All twinkling with the dewdrop sheen,
The brier-rose fell in streamers green,
And creeping shrubs, of thousand dyes,
Waved in the west-wind's summer sighs.

XII

Boon nature scatter'd, free and wild,
Each plant or flower, the mountain's child.
Here eglantine embalm'd the air,
Hawthorn and hazel mingled there;
The primrose pale, and violet flower,
Found in each cliff a narrow bower;
Fox-glove and night-shade, side by side,
Emblems of punishment and pride,
Group'd their dark hues with every stain
The weather-beaten crags retain.
With boughs that quaked at every breath,
Grey birch and aspen wept beneath;

Aloft, the ash and warrior oak
Cast anchor in the rifted rock;
And, higher yet, the pine-tree hung
His shatter'd trunk, and frequent flung,
Where seem'd the cliffs to meet on high,
His boughs athwart the narrow'd sky.
Highest of all, where white peaks glanced,
Where glist'ning streamers waved and danced,
The wanderer's eye could barely view
The summer haven's delicious blue;
So wondrous wild, the whole might seem
The scenery of a fairy dream.

XIII

Onward, amid the copse 'gan peep
A narrow inlet, still and deep,
Affording scarce such breadth of brim
As served the wild duck's brood to swim.
Lost for a space, through thickets veering,
But broader when again appearing,
Tall rocks and tufted knolls their face
Could on the dark-blue mirror trace;
And farther as the hunter stray'd,
Still broader sweep its channels made.
The shaggy mounds no longer stood,
Emerging from entangled wood,
But, wave-encircled, seem'd to float,
Like castle girdled with its moat;
Yet broader floods extending still
Divide them from their parent hill,
Till each, retiring, claims to be
An islet in an inland sea.

XIV

And now, to issue from the glen,
No pathway meets the wanderer's ken,
Unless he climb, with footing nice,
A far projecting precipice.
The broom's tough roots his ladder made,
The hazel saplings lent their aid;
And thus an airy point he won,
Where, gleaming with the setting sun,
One burnish'd sheet of living gold,
Loch Katrine lay beneath him roll'd;
In all her length far winding lay,
With promontory, creek, and bay,

And islands that, empurpled bright,
Floated amid the livelier light,
And mountains, that like giants stand,
To sentinel enchanted land.
High on the south, huge Benvenue
Down to the lake in masses threw
Crags, knolls, and mounds, confusedly hurl'd,
The fragments of an earlier world;
A wildering forest feather'd o'er
His ruin'd sides and summit hoar,
While on the north, through middle air,
Ben-an heaved high his forehead bare.

XV

From the steep promontory gazed
The stranger, raptured and amazed.
And, "What a scene were here," he cried,
"For princely pomp, or churchman's pride!
On this bold brow, a lordly tower;
In that soft vale, a lady's bower;
On yonder meadow, far away,
The turrets of a cloister grey;
How blithely might the bugle-horn
Chide, on the lake, the lingering morn!
How sweet, at eve, the lover's lute
Chime, when the groves were still and mute!
And, when the midnight moon should lave
Her forehead in the silver wave,
How solemn on the ear would come
The holy matins' distant hum,
While the deep peal's commanding tone
Should wake, in yonder islet lone,
A sainted hermit from his cell,
To drop a bead with every knell—
And bugle, lute, and bell, and all,
Should each bewilder'd stranger call
To friendly feast, and lighted hall.

XVI

"Blithe were it then to wander here!
But now,—beshrew yon nimble deer,—
Like that same hermit's, thin and spare,
The copse must give my evening fare;
Some mossy bank my couch must be,
Some rustling oak my canopy.

Yet pass we that; the war and chase
Give little choice of resting-place;—
A summer night, in greenwood spent,
Were but to-morrow's merriment:
But hosts may in these wilds abound,
Such as are better miss'd than found;
To meet with Highland plunderers here
Were worse than loss of steed or deer.
I am alone;—my bugle-strain
May call some straggler of the train;
Or, fall the worst that may betide,
Ere now this falchion has been tried."

XVII

But scarce again his horn he wound,
When lo! forth starting at the sound,
From underneath an aged oak,
That slanted from the islet rock,
A damsel guider of its way,
A little skiff shot to the bay,
That round the promontory steep
Led its deep line in graceful sweep,
Eddying, in almost viewless wave,
The weeping willow-twig to lave,
And kiss, with whispering sound and slow,
The beach of pebbles bright as snow.
The boat had touch'd this silver strand,
Just as the Hunter left his stand,
And stood conceal'd amid the brake,
To view this Lady of the Lake.
The maiden paused, as if again
She thought to catch the distant strain.
With head up-raised, and look intent,
And eye and ear attentive bent,
And locks flung back, and lips apart,
Like monument of Grecian art,
In listening mood, she seem'd to stand,
The guardian Naiad of the strand.

XVIII

And ne'er did Grecian chisel trace
A Nymph, a Naiad, or a Grace
Of finer form, or lovelier face!
What thought the sun, with ardent frown,
Had slightly tinged her cheek with brown;
The sportive toil, which, shot and light,

Had dyed her glowing hue so bright,
Served too in hastier swell to show
Short glimpses of a breast of snow:
What though no rule of courtly grace
To measured mood had train'd her pace;
A foot more light, a step more true,
Ne'er from the health-flower dash'd the dew;
E'en the slight harebell raised its head,
Elastic from her airy tread:
What though upon her speech there hung
The accents of the mountain tongue;
Those silver sounds, so soft, so dear,
The listener held his breath to hear!

XIX

A Chieftain's daughter seem'd the maid;
Her satin snood, her silken plaid,
Her golden brooch, such birth betray'd.
And seldom was a snood amid
Such wild luxuriant ringlets hid,
Whose glossy black to shame might bring
The plumage of the raven's wing;
And seldom o'er a breast so fair,
Mantled a plaid with modest care,
And never brooch the folds combin'd
Above a heart more good and kind.
Her kindness and her worth to spy,
You need but gaze on Ellen's eye;
Not Katrine, in her mirror blue,
Gives back the shaggy banks more true,
Than every free-born glance confess'd
The guileless movements of her breast;
Whether joy danced in her dark eye,
Or woe or pity claim'd a sigh,
Or filial love was glowing there,
Or meek devotion pour'd a prayer,
Or tale of injury call'd forth
The indignant spirit of the North.
One only passion unreveal'd,
With maiden pride the maid conceal'd,
Yet not less purely felt the flame;—
O need I tell that passion's name?

XX

Impatient of the silent horn,
Now on the gale her voice was borne:—

"Father!" she cried; the rocks around
Loved to prolong the gentle sound.
A while she paused, no answer came.
"Malcolm, was thine the blast?" the name
Less resolutely utter'd fell;
The echoes could not catch the swell.
"A stranger I," the Huntsman said,
Advancing from the hazel shade.
The maid, alarm'd, with hasty oar,
Push'd her light shallop from the shore,
And when a space was gain'd between,
Closer she drew her bosom's screen;
(So forth the startled swan would swing,
So turn to prune his ruffled wing.)
Then safe, though flutter'd and amazed,
She paused, and on the stranger gazed.
Not his the form, nor his the eye,
That youthful maidens wont to fly.

XXI

On his bold visage middle age
Had slightly press'd its signet sage,
Yet had not quench'd the open truth
And fiery vehemence of youth;
Forward and frolic glee was there,
The will to do, the soul to dare,
The sparkling glance, soon blown to fire,
Of hasty love, or headlong ire.
His limbs were cast in manly mould,
For hardy sports or contest bold;
And though in peaceful garb array'd,
And weaponless, except his blade,
His stately mien as well implied
A high-born heart, a martial pride,
As if a Baron's crest he wore,
And sheathed in armour trode the shore.
Slighting the petty need he show'd,
He told of his benighted road;
His ready speech flow'd fair and free,
In phrase of gentlest courtesy;
Yet seem'd that tone, and gesture bland,
Less used to sue than to command.

XXII

A while the maid the stranger eyed,
And, reassured, at length replied,

That Highland halls were open still
To wilder'd wanderers of the hill.
"Nor think you unexpected come
To yon lone isle, our desert home;
Before the heath had lost the dew,
This morn, a couch was pull'd for you;
On yonder mountain's purple head
Have ptarmigan and heath-cock bled,
And our broad nets have swept the mere,
To furnish forth your evening cheer."
"Now, by the rood, my lovely maid,
Your courtesy has err'd," he said;
"No right have I to claim, misplaced,
The welcome of expected guest.
A wanderer, here by fortune tost,
My way, my friends, my courser lost,
I ne'er before, believe me, fair,
Have ever drawn your mountain air,
Till on this lake's romantic stand
I found a fay in fairy land!"

XXIII
"I well believe," the maid replied,
As her light skiff approach'd the side,
"I well believe that ne'er before
Your foot has trod Loch Katrine's shore;
But yet, as far as yesternight,
Old Allan-Bane foretold your plight,—
A grey-hair'd sire, whose eye intent
Was on the vision'd future bent.
He saw your steed, a dappled grey,
Lie dead beneath the birchen way;
Painted exact your form and mien,
Your hunting suit of Lincoln green,
That tassell'd horn so gaily gilt,
That falchion's crooked blade and hilt,
That cap with heron plumage trim,
And yon two hounds so dark and grim.
He bade that all should ready be
To grace a guest of fair degree;
But light I held his prophecy,
And deem'd it was my father's horn
Whose echoes o'er the lake were borne."

XXIV
The stranger smiled: "Since to your home
A destined errant-knight I come,

Announced by prophet sooth and old,
Doom'd, doubtless, for achievement bold,
I'll lightly front each high emprise
For one kind glance of those bright eyes.
Permit me, first, the task to guide
Your fairy frigate o'er the tide."
The maid, with smile suppress'd and sly,
The toil unwonted saw him try;
For seldom sure, if e'er before,
His noble hand had grasp'd an oar:
Yet with main strength his strokes he drew,
And o'er the lake the shallop flew;
With heads erect, and whimpering cry,
The hounds behind their passage ply.
Nor frequent does the bright oar break
The dark'ning mirror of the lake,
Until the rocky isle they reach,
And moor their shallop on the beach.

XXV

The stranger view'd the shore around;
'Twas all so close with copsewood bound,
Nor track nor pathway might declare
That human foot frequented there,
Until the mountain-maiden show'd
A clambering unsuspected road,
That winded through the tangled screen,
And open'd on a narrow green,
Where weeping birch and willow round
With their long fibres swept the ground.
Here, for retreat in dangerous hour,
Some chief had framed a rustic bower.

XXVI

It was a lodge of ample size,
But strange of structure and device;
Of such materials, as around
The workman's hand had readiest found;
Loop'd off their boughs, their hoar trunks bared,
And by the hatchet rudely squared.
To give the walls their destined height
The sturdy oak and ash unite;
While moss and clay and leaves combin'd
To fence each crevice from the wind.
The lighter pine-trees, over-head,
Their slender length for rafters spread,

And wither'd heath and rushes dry
Supplied a russet canopy.
Due westward, fronting to the green,
A rural portico was seen,
Aloft on native pillars borne,
Of mountain fir, with bark unshorn,
Where Ellen's hand had taught to twine
The ivy and Idaean vine,
The clematis, the favour'd flower
Which boasts the name of virgin-bower,
And every hardy plant could bear
Loch Katrine's keen and searching air.
An instant in this porch she staid,
And gaily to the stranger said,
"On heaven and on thy lady call,
And enter the enchanted hall!"

XXVII

"My hope, my heaven, my trust must be,
My gentle guide, in following thee."
He cross'd the threshold—and a clang
Of angry steel that instant rang.
To his bold brow his spirit rush'd,
But soon for vain alarm he blush'd
When on the floor he saw display'd,
Cause of the din, a naked blade
Dropp'd from the sheath, that careless flung,
Upon a stag's huge antlers swung;
For all around, the walls to grace,
Hung trophies of the fight or chase:
A target there, a bugle here,
A battle-axe, a hunting-spear,
And broadswords, bows, and arrows store,
With the tusk'd trophies of the boar.
Here grins the wolf as when he died,
And there the wild-cat's brindled hide
The frontlet of the elk adorns,
Or mantles o'er the bison's horns;
Pennons and flags defaced and stain'd,
That blakening streaks of blood retain'd,
And deer-skins, dappled, dun, and white,
With otter's fur and seal's unite,
In rude and uncouth tapestry all,
To garnish forth the silvan hall.

XXVIII

The wondering stranger round him gazed,
And next the fallen weapon raised:
Few were the arms whose sinewy strength
Sufficed to stretch it forth at length;
And as the brand he poised and sway'd,
"I never knew but one," he said,
"Whose stalwart arm might brook to wield
A blade like this in battle-field."
She sigh'd, then smiled and took the word:
"You see the guardian champion's sword;
As light it trembles in his hand,
As in my grasp a hazel wand;
My sire's tall form might grace the part
Of Ferragus or Ascabart;
But in the absent giant's hold
Are women now, and menials old."

XXIX

The mistress of the mansion came,
Mature of age, a graceful dame;
Whose easy step and stately port
Had well become a princely court;
To whom, though more than kindred knew,
Young Ellen gave a mother's due.
Meet welcome to her guest she made,
And every courteous rite was paid
That hospitality could claim,
Though all unask'd his birth and name.
Such then the reverence to a guest,
That fellest foe might join the feast,
And from his deadliest foeman's door
Unquestion'd turn, the banquet o'er.
At length his rank the stranger names,
"The Knight of Snowdoun, James Fitz-James;
Lord of a barren heritage,
Which is brave sires, from age to age,
By their good swords had held with toil;
His sire had fallen in such turmoil,
And he, God wot, was forced to stand
Oft for his right with blade in hand.
This morning, with Lord Moray's train,
He chased a stalwart stag in vain,
Outstripp'd his comrades, miss'd the deer,
Lost his good steed, and wander'd here."

XXX

Fain would the Knight in turn require
The name and state of Ellen's sire.
Well show'd the elder lady's mien,
That courts and cities she had seen;
Ellen, though more her looks display'd
The simple grace of silvan maid,
In speech and gesture, form and face,
Show'd she was come of gentle race.
'Twere strange, in ruder rank to find
Such looks, such manners, and such mind.
Each hint the Knight of Snowdoun gave,
Dame Margaret heard with silence grave;
Or Ellen, innocently gay,
Turn'd all inquiry light away—
"Weird women we! by dale and down
We dwell, afar from tower and town.
We stem the flood, we ride the blast,
On wandering knights our spells we cast;
While viewless minstrels touch the string,
'Tis thus our charmed rhymes we sing."
She sung, and still a harp unseen
Fill'd up the symphony between.

XXXI

SONG

"Soldier, rest! thy warfare o'er,
    Sleep the sleep that knows not breaking;
Dream of battled fields no more,
    Days of danger, nights of waking.
In our isle's enchanged hall,
    Hands unseen thy couch are strewing,
Fairy strains of music fall,
    Every sense in slumber dewing.
Soldier, rest! thy warfare o'er,
Dreams of fighting fields no more:
Sleep the sleep that knows not breaking,
Morn of toil, nor night of waking.

"No rude sound shall reach thine ear,
    Armour's clang, or war-steed champing,
Trump nor pibroch summon here
    Mustering clan, or squadron tramping.

Yet the lark's shrill fife may come
  At the day-break from the fallow,
And the bittern sound his drum,
  Booming from the sedgy shallow.
Ruder sounds shall none be near,
Guards nor warders challenge here,
Here's no war-steed's neigh and champing,
Shouting clans, or squadrons stamping."

XXXII

She paused—then, blushing, led the lay
To grace the stranger of the day.
Her mellow notes awhile prolong
The cadence of the flowing song,
Till to her lips in measured frame
The minstrel verse spontaneous came:—

SONG CONTINUED

"Huntsman, rest! thy chase is done;
  While our slumbrous spells assail ye,
Dream not, with the rising sun,
  Bugles here shall sound reveillé.
Sleep! the deer is in his den;
  Sleep! thy hounds are by thee lying;
Sleep! nor dream in yonder glen,
  How thy gallant steed lay dying.
Huntsman, rest! thy chase is done,
Think not of the rising sun,
For at dawning to assail ye,
Here no bugles sound reveillé."

XXXIII

The hall was clear'd—the stranger's bed
Was there of mountain heather spread,
Where oft a hundred guests had lain,
And dream'd their forest sports again.
But vainly did the heath-flower shed
Its moorland fragrance round his head;
Not Ellen's spell had lull'd to rest
The fever of his troubled breast.
In broken dreams the image rose
Of varied perils, pains, and woes:
His steed now flounders in the brake,
Now sinks his barge upon the lake;
Now leader of a broken host,
His standard falls, his honour's lost.

Then,—from my couch may heavenly might
Chase that worst phantom of the night!—
Again return'd the scenes of youth,
Of confident undoubting truth;
Again his soul he interchanged
With friends whose hearts were long estranged.
They come, in dim procession led,
The cold, the faithless, and the dead;
As warm each hand, each brow as gay,
As if they parted yesterday.
And doubt distracts him at the view—
O were his senses false or true?
Dream'd he of death, or broken vow,
Or is it all a vision now?

XXXIV

At length, with Ellen in a grove
He seem'd to walk, and speak of love;
She listen'd with a blush and sigh,
His suit was warm, his hopes were high.
He sought her yielded hand to clasp,
And a cold gauntlet met his grasp:
The phantom's sex was changed and gone,
Upon its head a helment shone;
Slowly enlarged to giant size,
With darken'd cheek and threatening eyes,
The grisly visage, stern and hoar,
To Ellen still a likeness bore.
He woke, and, panting with affright,
Recall'd the vision of the night.
The hearth's decaying brands were red,
And deep and dusky lustre shed,
Half showing, half concealing, all
The uncouth trophies of the hall.
'Mid those the stranger fix'd his eye,
Where that huge falchion hung on high,
And thoughts on thoughts, a countless throng,
Rush'd, chasing countless thoughts along,
Until, the giddy whirl to cure,
He rose, and sought the moonshine pure.

XXXV

The wild-rose, eglantine, and broom,
Wasted around their rich perfume;
The birch-trees wept in fragrant balm,
The aspens slept beneath the calm;

The silver light, with quivering glance,
Play'd on the water's still expanse:
Wild were the heart whose passion's sway
Could rage beneath the sober ray!
He felt its calm, that warrior guest,
While thus he communed with his breast:
"Why is it, at each turn I trace
Some memory of that exiled race?
Can I not mountain-maiden spy,
But she must bear the Douglas eye?
Can I not view a Highland brand,
But it must match the Douglas hand?
Can I not frame a fever'd dream,
But still the Douglas is the theme?
I'll dream no more; by manly mind
Not even in sleep is will resign'd.
My midnight orisons said o'er,
I'll turn to rest, and dream no more."
His midnight orisons he told,
A prayer with every bead of gold,
Consign'd to heaven his cares and woes,
And sunk in undisturb'd repose,
Until the heath-cock shrilly crew,
And morning dawn'd on Benvenue.

Canto Second   THE ISLAND

I

At morn the black-cock trims his jetty wing,
  'Tis morning prompts the linnet's blithest lay,
All Nature's children feel the matin spring
  Of life reviving with reviving day;
And while yon little bark glides down the bay,
  Wafting the stranger on his way again,
Morn's genial influence roused a minstrel grey,
  And sweetly o'er the lake was heard thy strain,
Mix'd with the sounding harp, O white-hair'd Allan-Bane!

II

SONG

"Not faster yonder rowers' might
  Flings from their oars the spray,

Not faster yonder rippling bright,
That tracks the shallop's course in light,
    Melts in the lake away,
Than men from memory erase
The benefits of former days;
Then, stranger, go! good speed the while,
Nor think again of the lonely isle.
"High place to thee in royal court,
    High place in battled line,
Good hawk and hound for silvan sport,
Where beauty sees the brave resort,
    The honour'd meed be thine!
True be thy sword, thy friend sincere,
They lady constant, kind, and dear,
And lost in love's and friendship's smile
Be memory of the lonely isle.

III

SONG CONTINUED

"But if beneath yon southern sky
    A plaided stranger roam,
Whose drooping crest and stifled sigh,
And sunken cheek and heavy eye,
    Pine for His Highland home;
Then, warrior, then be thin to show
The care that soothes a wanderer's woe;
Remember then thy hap ere while,
A stranger in the lonely isle.

"Or if on life's uncertain main
    Mishap shall mar thy sail;
If faithful, wise, and brave in vain,
Woe, want, and exile thou sustain
    Beneath the fickle gale;
Waste not a sigh on fortune changed,
On thankless courts, or friends estranged,
But come where kindred worth shall smile
To greet thee in the lonely isle."

IV

As died the sounds upon the tide,
The shallop reach'd the mainland side,
And ere his onward way he took,
The stranger cast a lingering look,

Where easily his eye might reach
The Harper on the islet beach,
Reclined against a blighted tree,
As wasted, grey, and worn as he.
To minstrel meditation given,
His reverend brow was raised to heaven,
As from the rising sun to claim
A sparkle of inspiring flame.
His hand, reclined upon the wire,
Seem'd watching the awakening fire;
So still he sate, as those who wait
Till judgment speak the doom of fate;
So still, as if no breeze might dare
To lift one lock of hoary hair;
So still, as life itself were fled,
In the last sound his harp had sped.

V

Upon a rock with lichens wild,
Beside him Ellen sate and smiled.
Smiled she to see the stately drake
Lead forth his fleet upon the lake,
While her vex'd spaniel, from the beach
Bay'd at the prize beyond his reach.
Yet tell me, then, the maid who knows,
Why deepen'd on her cheek the rose?
Forgive, forgive, Fidelity!
Perchance the maiden smiled to see
Yon parting lingerer wave adieu,
And stop and turn to wave anew;
And, lovely ladies, ere your ire
Condemn the heroine of my lyre,
Show me the fair would scorn to spy,
And prize such conquest of her eye!

VI

While yet he loiter'd on the spot,
It seem'd as Ellen mark'd him not;
But when he turn'd him to the glade,
One courteous parting sign she made;
And after, oft the knight would say,
That not when prize of festal day
Was dealt him by the brightest fair
Who e'er wore jewel in her hair,
So highly did his bosom swell,

As at that simple mute farewell.
Now with a trusty mountain-guide,
And his dark stag-hounds by his side,
He parts; the maid, unconscious still,
Watch'd him wind slowly round the hill;
But when his stately form was hid,
The guardian in her bosom chid:
"Thy Malcolm! vain and selfish maid!"
'Twas thus upbraiding conscience said:
"Not so had Malcolm idly hung
On the smooth phrase of southern tongue;
Not so had Malcolm strain'd his eye,
Another step than thine to spy.
Wake, Allan-Bane," aloud she cried,
To the old Minstrel by her side;
"Arouse thee from thy moody dream!
I'll give thy harp heroic theme,
And warm thee with a noble name;
Pour forth the glory of the Græme!"
Scarce from her lip the word had rush'd,
When deep the conscious maiden blush'd;
For of his clan, in hall and bower,
Young Malcolm Græme was held the flower.

VII

The Minstrel waked his harp; three times
Arose the well-known martial chimes,
And thrice their high heroic pride
In melancholy murmurs died.
"Vainly thou bid'st, O noble maid,"
Clasping his wither'd hands, he said,
"Vainly thou bid'st me wake the strain,
Though all unwont to bid in vain.
Alas! than mine a mightier hand
Has turned my harp, my strings has spann'd!
I touch the chords of joy, but low
And mournful answer notes of woe;
And the proud march, which victors tread,
Sinks in the wailing for the dead.
O well for me, if mine alone
That dirge's deep prophetic tone!
If, as my tuneful fathers said,
This harp, which erst Saint Modan sway'd,
Can thus its master's fate foretell,
Then welcome be the minstrel's knell!

VIII

"But ah! dear lady, thus it sigh'd
The eve thy sainted mother died;
And such the sounds which, while I strove
To wake a lay of war or love,
Came marring all the festal mirth,
Appalling me who gave them birth,
And, disobedient to my call,
Wail'd loud through Bothwell's banner'd hall,
Ere Douglases, to ruin driven,
Were exiled from their native heaven.
Oh! if yet worse mishap and woe
My master's house must undergo,
Or aught but weal to Ellen fair
Brood in these accents of despair,
No future bard, sad Harp! shall fling
One short, one final strain shall flow,
Fraught with unutterable woe,
Then shiver'd shall thy fragments lie,
Thy master cast him down and die!"

IX

Soothing she answer'd him, "Assuage,
Mine honour'd friend, the fears of age;
All melodies to thee are known,
That harp has rung, or pipe has blown,
In Lowland vale or Highland glen,
From Tweed to Spey—what marvel, then,
At times, unbidden notes should rise,
Confusedly bound in memory's ties,
Entangling, as they rush along,
The war-march with the funeral song?
Small ground is now for boding fear;
Obscure, but safe, we rest us here.
My sire, in native virtue great,
Resigning lordship, lands, and state,
Not then to fortune more resign'd,
Than yonder oak might give the wind;
The graceful foliage storms may reave,
The noble stem they cannot grieve.
For me,"—she stoop'd, and, looking round,
Pluck'd a blue harebell from the ground,—
"For me, whose memory scarce conveys
An image of more splendid days,
This little flower, that loves the lea,
May well my simple emblem be;

It drinks heaven's dew as blithe as rose
That in the king's own garden grows;
And when I place it in my hair,
Allan, a bard is bound to swear
He ne'er saw a coronet so fair."
Then playfully the chaplet wild
She wreath'd in her dark locks, and smiled.

X

Her smile, her speech, with winning sway,
Wiled the old harper's mood away.
With such a look as hermits throw,
When angels stoop to soothe their woe,
He gazed, till fond regret and pride
Thrill'd to a tear, then thus replied:
"Loveliest and best! thou little know'st
The rank, the honours, thou hast lost!
O might I live to see thee grace,
In Scotland's court, thy birth-right place,
To see my favourite's step advance,
The lightest in the courtly dance,
The cause of every gallant's sigh,
And leading star of every eye,
And theme of every minstrel's art,
The Lady of the Bleeding Heart!"

XI

"Fair dreams are these," the maiden cried,
(Light was her accent, yet she sigh'd;)
"Yet is this mossy rock to me
Worth splendid chair and canopy;
Nor would my footsteps spring more gay
In courtly dance than blithe strathspey,
Nor half so pleased mine ear incline
To royal minstrel's lay as thine.
And then for suitors proud and high,
To bend before my conquering eye,—
Thou, flattering bard! thyself wilt say,
That grim Sir Roderick owns its sway.
The Saxon scourge, Clan-Alpine's pride,
The terror of Loch Lomond's side,
Would, at my suit, thou know'st, delay
A Lennox foray—for a day."

XII

The ancient bard her glee repress'd:
"Ill hast thou chosen theme for jest!

For who, through all this western wild,
Named Black Sir Roderick e'er, and smiled?
In Holy-Rood a knight he slew;
I saw, when back the dirk he drew,
Courtiers give place before the stride
Of the undaunted homicide;
And since, though outlaw'd, hath his hand
Full sternly kept his mountain land.
Who else dared give—ah! woe the day,
That I such hated truth should say—
The Douglas, like a stricken deer,
Disown'd by every noble peer,
Even the rude refuge we have here?
Alas, this wild marauding Chief
Alone might hazard our relief,
And now thy maiden charms expand,
Looks for his guerdon in thy hand;
Full soon may dispensation sought,
To back his suit, from Rome he brought.
Then, though an exile on the hill,
Thy father, as the Douglas, still
Be held in reverence and fear;
And though to Roderick thou'rt so dear,
That thou might'st guide with silken thread,
Slave of thy will, this chieftain dread,
Yet, O loved maid, thy mirth refrain!
They hand is on a lion's mane."

XIII

"Minstrel," the maid replied, and high
Her father's soul glanced from her eye,
"My debts to Roderick's house I know:
All that a mother could bestow,
To Lady Margaret's care I owe,
Since first an orphan in the wild
She sorrow'd o'er her sister's child;
To her brave chieftain son, from ire
Of Scotland's king who shrouds my sire,
A deeper, holier debt is owed;
And, could I pay it with my blood,
Allan! Sir Roderick should command
My blood, my life,—but not my hand.
Rather will Ellen Douglas dwell
A votaress in Maronnan's cell;
Rather through realms beyond the sea,
Seeking the world's cold charity,

Where ne'er was spoke a Scottish word,
And ne'er the name of Douglas heard,
An outcast pilgrim will she rove,
Then wed the man she cannot love.

XIV

"Thou shakest, good friend, thy tresses grey,
That pleading look, what can it say
But what I own?—I grant him brave,
But wild as Bracklinn's thundering wave;
And generous—save vindictive mood,
Or jealous transport, chafe his blood:
I grant him true to friendly band,
As his claymore is to his hand;
But O! that very blade of steel
More mercy for a foe would feel:
I grant him liberal, to fling
Among his clan the wealth they bring,
When back by lake and glen they wind,
And in the Lowland leave behind,
Where once some pleasant hamlet stood,
A mass of ashes slaked with blood.
The hand that for my father fought
I honour, as his daughter ought;
But can I clasp it reeking red,
From peasants slaughter'd in their shed?
No! wildly while his virtues gleam,
They make his passions darker seem,
And flash along his spirit high,
Like lightning o'er the midnight sky.
While yet a child,—and children know,
Instinctive taught, the friend and foe,—
I shudder'd at his brow of gloom,
His shadowy plaid, the sable plume;
A maiden grown, I ill could bear
His haughty mien and lordly air:
But, if thou join'st a suitor's claim,
In serious mood, to Roderick's name,
I thrill with anguish! or, if e'er
A Douglas knew the word, with fear.
To change such odious theme were best;
What think'st thou of our stranger guest?"

XV

"What think I of him?—woe the while
That brought such wanderer to our isle!

Thy father's battle-brand, of yore
For Tine-man forged by fairy lore,
What time he leagued, no longer foes,
His Border spears with Hotspur's bows,
Did, self-unscabbarded, foreshow
The footstep of a secret foe.
If courtly spy hath harbour'd here,
What may we for the Douglas fear?
What for this island, deem'd of old
Clan-Alpine's last and surest hold?
If neither spy nor foe, I pray
What yet may jealous Roderick say?
Nay, wave not thy disdainful head,
Bethink thee of the discord dread
That kindled, when at Beltane game
Thou led'st the dance with Malcolm Græme;
Still, though thy sire the peace renew'd,
Smoulders in Roderick's breast the feud.
Beware!—But Hark, what sounds are these?
My dull ears catch no faltering breeze;
No weeping birch, nor aspens wake,
Nor breath is dimpling in the lake;
Still in the canna's hoary beard;
Yet, by my minstrel faith, I heard—
And hark again! some pipe of war
Sends the bold pibroch from afar."

XVI

Far up the lengthen'd lake were spied
Four darkening specks upon the tide,
That, slow enlarging on the view,
Four mann'd and masted barges grew,
And, bearing downwards from Glengyle,
Steer'd full upon the lonely isle;
The point of Brianchoil they pass'd,
And, to the windward as they cast,
Against the sun they gave to shine
The bold Sir Roderick's banner'd Pine.
Nearer and nearer as they bear,
Spears, pikes, and axes flash in air.
Now might you see the tartans brave,
And plaids and plumage dance and wave:
Now see the bonnets sink and rise,
As his tough oar and rower plies;
See, flashing at each sturdy stroke,
The wave ascending into smoke;

See the proud pipers on the bow,
And mark the gaudy streamers flow
From their loud chanters down, and sweep
The furrow'd bosom of the deep,
As, rushing through the lake amain,
They plied the ancient Highland strain.

XVII

Ever, as on they bore, more loud
And louder rung the pibroch proud.
At first the sound, by distance tame,
Mellow'd along the waters came,
And, lingering long by cape and bay,
Wail'd every harsher note away;
Then bursting bolder on the ear,
The clan's shrill Gathering they could hear;
Those thrilling sounds, that call the might
Of old Clan-Alpine to the fight.
Thick beat the rapid notes, as when
The mustering hundreds shake the glen,
And, hurrying at the signal dread,
The batter'd earth returns their tread.
Then prelude light, of livelier tone,
Express'd their merry marching on,
Ere peal of closing battle rose,
With mingled outcry, shrieks, and blows;
And mimic din of stroke and ward,
As broad sword upon target jarr'd;
And groaning pause, ere yet again,
Condensed, the battle yell'd amain;
The rapid charge, the rallying shout,
Retreat borne headlong into rout,
And bursts of triumph, to declare
Clan-Alpine's conquest—all were there.
Nor ended thus the strain; but slow
Sunk in a moan prolong'd and low,
And changed the conquering clarion swell
For wild lament o'er those that fell.

XVIII

The war-pipes ceased; but lake and hill
Were busy with their echoes still;
And, when they slept, a vocal strain
Bade their hoarse chorus wake again,
While loud a hundred clansmen raise
Their voices in their Chieftain's praise.

Each boatman, bending to his oar,
With measured sweep the burden bore,
In such wild cadence, as the breeze
Makes through December's leafless trees.
The chorus first could Allan know,
"Roderick Vich Alpine, ho! iro!"
And near, and nearer as they row'd,
Distinct the martial ditty flow'd.

XIX

BOAT SONG

"Hail to the Chief who in triumph advances!
  Honour'd and bless'd be the evergreen Pine!
Long may the tree, in his banner that glances,
  Flourish, the shelter and grace of our line!
    Heaven send it happy dew,
    Earth lend it sap anew,
Gayly to bourgeon, and broadly to grow,
    While every Highland glen
    Sends our shout back agen,
Roderigh Vich Alpine dhu, ho! ieroe!

"Ours is no sapling, chance-sown by the fountain,
  Blooming at Beltane, in winter to fade;
When the whirlwind was stripp'd every leaf on the mountain,
  The more shall Clan-Alpine exult in her shade.
    Moor'd in the rifted rock,
    Proof to the tempest's shock,
Firmer he roots him the ruder it blow;
    Menteith and Breadalbane, then,
    Echo his praise agen,
Roderigh Vich Alpine dhu, ho! ieroe!

XX

"Proudly our pibroch has thrill'd in Glen Fruin,
  And Bannochar's groans to our slogan replied;
Glen Luss and Ross-dhu, they are smoking in ruin,
  And the best of Loch Lomond lie dead on her side.
    Widow and Saxon maid
    Long shall lament our raid,
Think of Clan-Alpine with fear and with woe;
    Lennox and Leven-glen
    Shake when they hear agen,
Roderigh Vich Alpine dhu, ho! ieroe!

"Row, vassals, row, for the pride of the Highlands!
   Stretch to your oars, for the evergreen Pine!
O! that the rose-bud that graces yon islands
   Were wreathed in a garland around him to twine!
     O that some seedling gem,
     Worthy such noble stem,
Honour'd and bless'd in their shadow might grow!
     Loud should Clan-Alpine then
     Ring from her deepmost glen,
Roderigh Vich Alpine dhu, ho! ieroe!"

XXI

With all her joyful female band
Had Lady Margaret sought the stand.
Loose on the breeze their tresses flew,
And high their snowy arms they threw,
As echoing back with shrill acclaim,
And chorus wild, the Chieftain's name;
While, prompt to please, with mother's art,
The darling passion of his heart,
The Dane call'd Ellen to the strand,
To greet her kinsman ere he land:
"Come, loiterer, come! a Douglas thou,
And shun to wreathe a victory's brow?"
Reluctantly and slow, the maid
The unwelcome summoning obey'd,
And, when a distant bugle rung,
In the mid-path aside she sprung:
"List, Allan-Bane! From mainland cast,
I hear my father's signal blast.
Be ours," she cried, "the skiff to guide,
And waft him from the mountain side."
Then, like a sunbeam, swift and bright,
She darted to her shallop light,
And, eagerly while Roderick scann'd,
For her dear form, his mother's band,
The islet far behind her lay,
And she had landed in the bay.

XXII

Some feelings are to mortals given,
With less of earth in them than heaven:
And if there be a human tear
From passion's dross refined and clear,
A tear so limpid and so meek,
It would not stain an angel's cheek,

'Tis that which pious fathers shed
Upon a duteous daughter's head!
And as the Douglas to his breast
His darling Ellen closely press'd,
Such holy drops her tresses steep'd,
Though 'twas an hero's eye that weep'd.
Nor while on Ellen's faltering tongue
Her filial welcomes crowded hung,
Mark'd she, that fear (affection's proof)
Still held a graceful youth aloof;
No! not till Douglas named his name,
Although the youth was Malcolm Græme.

XXIII

Allan, with wistful look the while,
Mark'd Roderick landing on the isle;
His master piteously he eyed,
Then gazed upon the Chieftain's pride.
Then dash'd, with hasty hand, away
From his dimm'd eye the gathering spray;
And Douglas, as his hand he laid
On Malcolm's shoulder, kindly said,
"Canst thou, young friend, no meaning spy
In my poor follower's glistening eye?
I'll tell thee:—he recalls the day,
When in my praise he led the lay
O'er the arch'd gate of Bothwell proud,
While many a minstrel answer'd loud,
When Percy's Norman pennon, won
In bloody field, before me shone,
And twice ten knights, the least a name
As mighty as yon Chief may claim,
Gracing my pomp, behind me came.
Yet trust me, Malcolm, not so proud
Was I of all that marshall'd crowd,
Though the waned crescent own'd my might,
And in my train troop'd lord and knight,
Though Blantyre hymn'd her holiest lays,
And Bothwell's bards flung back my praise,
As when this old man's silent tear,
And this poor maid's affection dear,
A welcome give more kind and true,
Than aught my better fortunes knew.
Forgive, my friend, a father's boast,
O! it out-beggars all I lost!"

XXIV

Delightful praise! Like summer rose,
That brighter in the dew-drop glows,
The bashful maiden's cheek appear'd,
For Douglas spoke, and Malcolm heard.
The flush of shame-faced joy to hide,
The hounds, the hawk, her cares divide;
The loved caresses of the maid
The dogs with crouch and whimper paid;
And, at her whistle, on her hand
The falcon took his favourite stand,
Closed his dark wing, relax'd his eye,
Nor, though unhooded, sought to fly.
And, trust, while in such guise she stood,
Like fabled Goddess of the wood,
That if a father's partial thought
O'erweigh'd her worthy and beauty aught,
Well might the lover's judgment fail
To balance with a juster scale;
For with each secret glance he stole,
The fond enthusiast sent his soul.

XXV

Of stature tall, and slender frame,
But firmly knit, was Malcolm Græme.
The belted plaid and tartan hose
Did ne'er more graceful limbs disclose;
His flaxen hair, of sunny hue,
Curl'd closely round his bonnet blue.
Train'd to the chase, his eagle eye
The ptarmigan in snow could spy:
Each pass, by mountain, lake, and heath,
He knew, through Lennox and Menteith;
Vain was the bound of dark-brown doe
When Malcolm bent his sounding bow;
And scarce that doe, though wing'd with fear,
Outstripp'd in speed the mountaineer:
Right up Ben-Lomond could he press,
And not a sob his toil confess.
His form accorded with a mind
Lively and ardent, frank and kind;
A blither heart, till Ellen came,
Did never love nor sorrow tame;
It danced as lightsome in his breast
As play'd the feather on his crest.

Yet friends, who nearest knew the youth,
His scorn of wrong, his zeal for truth,
And bards, who saw his features bold
When kindled by the tales of old,
Said, were that youth to manhood grown,
Not long should Roderick Dhu's renown
Be foremost voiced by mountain fame,
But quail to that of Malcolm Græme.

XXVI

Now back they wend their watery way,
And, "O my sire!" did Ellen say,
"Why urge they chase so far astray?
And why so late return'd? And why"—
The rest was in her speaking eye.
"My child, the chase I follow far,
'Tis mimicry of noble war;
And with that gallant pastime reft
Were all of Douglas I have left.
I met young Malcolm as I stray'd,
Far eastward, in Glenfinlas' shade.
Nor stray'd I safe; for, all around,
Hunters and horsemen scour'd the ground.
This youth, though still a royal ward,
Risk'd life and land to be my guard,
And through the passes of the wood
Guided my steps, not unpursued;
And Roderick shall his welcome make,
Despite old spleen, for Douglas' sake.
Then must he seek Strath-Endrick glen,
Nor peril aught for me agen."

XXVII

Sir Roderick, who to meet them came,
Redden'd at sight of Malcolm Græme,
Yet, not in action, word, or eye,
Fail'd aught in hospitality.
In talk and sport they whiled away
The morning of that summer day;
But at nigh noon a courier light
Held secret parley with the knight,
Whose moody aspect soon declared
That evil were the news he heard.
Deep thought seem'd toiling in his head;
Yet was the evening banquet made,
Ere he assembled round the flame

His mother, Douglas, and the Græme,
And Ellen too; then cast around
His eyes, then fix'd them on the ground,
As studying phrase that might avail
Best to convey unpleasant tale.
Long with his dagger's hilt he play'd,
Then raised his haughty brow, and said:

XXVIII

"Short be my speech; nor time affords,
Nor my plain temper, glozing words.
Kinsman and father—if such name
Douglas vouchsafe to Roderick's claim;
Mine honour'd mother; Ellen—why,
My cousin, turn away thine eye?
And Græme—in whom I hope to know
Full soon a noble friend or foe,
When age shall give thee thy command
And leading in thy native land:
List all!—The King's vindictive pride
Boasts to have tamed the Border-side,
Where chiefs, with hound and hawk who came
To share their monarch's silvan game,
Themselves in bloody toils were snared;
And when the banquet they prepared,
And wide their loyal portals flung,
O'er their own gateway struggling hung.
Loud cries their blood from Meggat's mead,
From Yarrow braes, and banks of Tweed,
Where the lone streams of Ettrick glide,
And from the silver Teviot's side;
The dales, where martial clans did ride,
Are now one sheep-walk, waste and wide.
This tyrant of the Scottish throne,
So faithless and so ruthless known,
Now hither comes; his end the same,
The same pretext of silvan game.
What grace for Highland Chiefs, judge ye
By fate of Border chivalry.
Yet more; amid Glenfinlas green,
Douglas, thy stately form was seen:
This by espial sure I know.
Your counsel! in the streight I show."

XXIX

Ellen and Margaret fearfully
Sought comfort in each other's eye,

Then turn'd their ghastly look, each one,
This to her sire, that to her son.
The hasty colour went and came
In the bold cheek of Malcolm Græme;
But from his glance it well appear'd,
'Twas but for Ellen that he fear'd;
While, sorrowful, but undismay'd,
The Douglas thus his counsel said:—
"Brave Roderick, though the tempest roar,
It may but thunder and pass o'er;
Nor will I here remain an hour,
To draw the lightning on thy bower;
For well thou know'st, at this grey head
The royal bolt were fiercest sped.
For thee, who, at thy King's command,
Canst aid him with a gallant band,
Submission, homage, humbled pride,
Shall turn the Monarch's wrath aside.
Poor remnants of the Bleeding Heart,
Ellen and I will seek, apart,
The refuge of some forest cell,
There, like the hunted quarry, dwell,
Till on the mountain and the moor,
The stern pursuit be pass'd and o'er."

XXX

"No, by mine honour," Roderick said,
"So help me heaven, and my good blade!
No, never! Blasted be yon Pine,
My fathers' ancient crest and mine,
If from its shade in danger part
The lineage of the Bleeding Heart!
Hear me blunt speech: Grant me this maid
To wife, thy counsel to mine aid;
To Douglas, leagued with Roderick Dhu,
Will friends and allies flock enow;
Like cause of doubt, distrust, and grief,
Will bind to us each Western Chief.
When the loud pipes my bridal tell,
The Links of Forth shall hear the knell,
The guards shall start in Stirling's porch;
And, when I light the nuptial torch,
A thousand villages in flames
Shall scare the slumbers of King James!
Nay, Ellen, blench not thus away,
And, mother, cease these signs, I pray;

I meant not all my heat might say.
Small need of inroad, or of fight,
When the sage Douglas may unite
Each mountain clan in friendly band,
To guard the passes of their land,
Till the foil'd king, from pathless glen,
Shall bootless turn him home agen."

XXXI

There are who have, at midnight hour,
In slumber scaled a dizzy tower,
And, on the verge that beetled o'er
The ocean-tide's incessant roar,
Dream'd calmly out their dangerous dream,
Till waken'd by the morning beam;
When, dazzled by the eastern glow,
Such startler cast his glance below,
And saw unmeasured depth around,
And heard unintermitted sound,
And thought the battled fence so frail,
It waved like cobweb in the gale;—
Amid his senses' giddy wheel,
Did he not desperate impulse feel,
Headlong to plunge himself below,
And meet the worst his fears foreshow?
Thus, Ellen, dizzy and astound,
As sudden ruin yawn'd around,
By crossing terrors wildly toss'd,
Still for the Douglas fearing most,
Could scarce the desperate thought withstand,
To buy his safety with her hand.

XXXII

Such purpose dread could Malcolm spy
In Ellen's quivering lip and eye,
And eager rose to speak, but ere
His tongue could hurry forth his fear,
Had Douglas mark'd the hectic strife,
Where death seem'd combating with life;
For to her cheek, in feverish flood,
One instant rush'd the throbbing blood,
Then ebbing back, with sudden sway,
Left its domain as wan as clay.
"Roderick, enough! enough!" he cried,
"'My daughter cannot be thy bride;
Not that the blush to wooer dear,

Nor paleness that of maiden fear.
It may not be; forgive her, Chief,
Nor hazard aught for our relief.
Against his sovereign, Douglas ne'er
Will level a rebellious spear.
'Twas I that taught his youthful hand
To rein a steed and wield a brand;
I see him yet, the princely boy!
Not Ellen more my pride and joy;
I love him still, despite my wrongs,
By hasty wrath, and slanderous tongues.
O seek the grace you well may find,
Without a cause to mine combined."

XXXIII

Twice through the hall the Chieftain strode;
The waving of his tartans broad,
And darken'd brow, where wounded pride
With ire and disappointment vied,
Seem'd, by the torch's gloomy light,
Like the ill Demon of the night,
Stooping his pinions' shadowy sway
Upon the nighted pilgrim's way:
But, unrequited Love! thy dart
Plunged deepest its envenom'd smart,
And Roderick, with thine anguish stung,
At length the hand of Douglas wrung,
While eyes, that mock'd at tears before,
With bitter drops were running o'er.
The death-pangs of long-cherish'd hope
Scarce in that ample breast had scope,
But, struggling with his spirit proud,
Convulsive heaved its chequer'd shroud,
While every sob—so mute were all—
Was heard distinctly through the hall.
The son's despair, the mother's look,
Ill might the gentle Ellen brook;
She rose, and to her side there came,
To aid her parting steps, the Græme.

XXXIV

Then Roderick from the Douglas broke;
As flashes flame through sable smoke,
Kindling its wreaths, long, dark, and low,
To one broad blaze of ruddy glow,
So the deep anguish of despair

Burst, in fierce jealousy, to air.
With stalwart grasp his hand he laid
On Malcolm's breast and belted plaid:
"Back, beardless boy!" he sternly said,
"Back, minion! hold'st thou thus at naught
The lesson I so lately taught?
This roof, the Douglas, and that maid,
Thank thou for punishment delay'd."
Eager as greyhound on his game,
Fiercely with Roderick grappled Græme.
"Perish my name, if aught afford
Its Chieftain safety save his sword!"
Thus as they strove, their desperate hand
Griped to the dagger or the brand,
And death had been—but Douglas rose,
And thrust between the struggling foes
His giant strength:—"Chieftains, forego!
I hold the first who strikes, my foe.
Madmen, forbear your frantic jar!
What! is the Douglas fall'n so far,
His daughter's hand is doom'd the spoil
Of such dishonourable broil?"
Sullen and slowly they unclasp,
As struck with shame, their desperate grasp,
And each upon his rival glared,
With foot advanced, and blade half bared.

XXXV

Ere yet the brands aloft were flung,
Margaret on Roderick's mantle hung,
And Malcolm heard his Ellen's scream,
As falter'd through terrific dream.
Then Roderick plunged in sheath his sword,
And veil'd his wrath in scornful word.
"Rest safe till morning; pity 'twere
Such cheek should feel the midnight air!
Then mayest thou to James Stuart tell
Roderick will keep the lake and fell,
Nor lackey, with his freeborn clan,
The pageant pomp of earthly man.
More would he of Clan-Alpine know,
Thou canst our strength and passes show.
Malise, what ho!"—his henchman came;
"Give our safe-conduct to the Græme."
Young Malcolm answer'd, calm and bold,
"Fear nothing for thy favourite hold;

The spot an angel deigned to grace
Is bless'd, though robers haunt the place.
Thy churlish courtesy for those
Reserve, who fear to be thy foes.
As safe to me the mountain way
At midnight as in blaze of day,
Though with his boldest at his back
Even Roderick Dhu beset the track.
Brave Douglas,—lovely Ellen,—nay,
Nought here of parting will I say.
Earth does not hold a lonesome glen
So secret, but we meet agen.
Chieftain! we too shall find an hour."
He said, and left the silvan bower.

XXXVI

Old Allan follow'd to the strand
(Such was the Douglas's command)
And anxious told, how, on the morn,
The stern Sir Roderick deep had sworn
The Fiery Cross should circle o'er
Dale, glen, and valley, down, and moor.
Much were the peril to the Græme,
From those who to the signal came;
Far up the lake 'twere safest land,
Himself would row him to the strand.
He gave his counsel to the wind,
While Malcolm did, unheeding, bind,
Round dirk and pouch and broadsword roll'd,
His ample plaid in tighten'd fold,
And stripp'd his limbs to such array
As best might suit the watery way;

XXXVII

Then spoke abrupt: "Farewell to thee,
Pattern of old fidelity!"
The Minstrel's hand he kindly press'd,—
"O! could I point a place of rest!
My sovereign holds in ward my land,
My uncle leads my vassal band;
To tame his foes, his friends to aid,
Poor Malcolm has but heart and blade.
Yet, if there be one faithful Græme
Who loves the Chieftain of his name,
Not long shall honour'd Douglas dwell,
Like hunted stag, in mountain cell;

Nor, ere yon pride-swoll'n robber dare—
I may not give the rest to air!
Tell Roderick Dhu, I owed him nought,
Not the poor service of a boat,
To waft me to yon mountain-side."
Then plunged he in the flashing tide.
Bold o'er the flood his head he bore,
And stoutly steer'd him from the shore;
And Allan strain'd his anxious eye,
Far 'mid the lake his form to spy,
Darkening across each puny wave,
To which the moon her silver gave.
Fast as the cormorant could skim,
The swimmer plied each active limb;
Then landing in the moonlight dell,
Loud shouted, of his weal to tell.
The Minstrel heard the far halloo,
And joyful from the shore withdrew.

Canto Third   THE GATHERING

I

Time rolls his ceaseless course. The race of yore,
  Who danced our infancy upon their knee,
And told our marvelling boyhood legends store,
  Of their strange ventures happ'd by land or sea,
How are they blotted from the things that be!
  How few, all weak and wither'd of their force,
Wait on the verge of dark eternity,
  Like stranded wrecks, the tide returning hoarse,
To sweep them from our sight! Time rolls his ceaseless
  course.

Yet live there still who can remember well,
  How, when a mountain chief his bugle blew,
Both field and forest, dingle, cliff, and dell
  And solitary heath, the signal knew;
And fast the faithful clan around him drew,
  What time the warning note was keenly wound,
What time aloft their kindred banner flew,
  While clamorous war-pipes yell'd the gathering sound,
And while the Fiery Cross glanced, like a meteor, round.

II

The summer dawn's reflected hue
To purple changed Loch Katrine blue;
Mildly and soft the western breeze
Just kiss'd the Lake, just stirr'd the trees,
And the pleased lake, like maiden coy,
Trembled but dimpled not for joy;
The mountain-shadows on her breast
Were neither broken nor at rest;
In bright uncertainty they lie,
Like future joys to Fancy's eye.
The water-lily to the light
Her chalice rear'd of silver bright;
The doe awoke, and to the lawn,
Begemm'd with dew-drops, led her fawn;
The grey mist left the mountain side,
The torrent show'd its glistening pride;
Invisible in flecked sky,
The lark sent down her revelry;
The blackbird and the speckled thrush
Good-morrow gave from brake and bush;
In answer coo'd the cushat dove
Her notes of peace, and rest, and love.

III

No thought of peace, no thought of rest,
Assuaged the storm in Roderick's breast.
With sheathed broadsword in his hand,
Abrupt he paced the islet strand,
And eyed the rising sun, and laid
His hand on his impatient blade.
Beneath a rock, his vassals' care
Was prompt the ritual to prepare,
With deep and deathful meaning fraught;
For such Antiquity had taught
Was preface meet, ere yet abroad
The Cross of Fire should take its road.
The shrinking band stood oft aghast
At the impatient glance he cast;—
Such glance the mountain eagle threw,
As, from the cliffs of Benvenue,
She spread her dark sails on the wind,
And, high in middle heaven, reclined,
With her broad shadow on the lake,
Silenced the warblers of the brake.

IV

A heap of wither'd boughs was piled,
Of juniper and rowan wild,
Mingled with shivers from the oak,
Rent by the lightning's recent stroke.
Brian, the Hermit, by it stood,
Barefooted, in his frock and hood.
His grisled beard and matted hair
Obscured a visage of despair;
His naked arms and legs, seam'd o'er,
The scars of frantic penance bore.
That monk, of savage form and face,
The impending danger of his race
Had drawn from deepest solitude,
Far in Benharrow's bosom rude.
Not his the mien of Christian priest,
But Druid's, from the grave released,
Whose harden'd heart and eye might brook
On human sacrifice to look;
And much, 'twas said, of heathen lore
Mix'd in the charms he mutter'd o'er.
The hallow'd creed gave only worse
And deadlier emphasis of curse;
No peasant sought that Hermit's prayer,
His cave the pilgrim shunn'd with care,
The eager huntsman knew his bound,
And in mid chase call'd off his hound;
Or if, in lonely glen or strath,
The desert-dweller met his path,
He pray'd, and sign'd the cross between,
While terror took devotion's mien.

V

Of Brian's birth strange tales were told.
His mother watch'd a midnight fold,
Built deep within a dreary glen,
Where scatter'd lay the bones of men,
In some forgotten battle slain,
And bleach'd by drifting wind and rain.
It might have tamed a warrior's heart,
To view such mockery of his art!
The knot-grass fetter'd there the hand
Which once could burst an iron band;
Beneath the broad and ample bone,
That buckler'd heart to fear unknown,

A feeble and a timorous guest,
The field-fare framed her lowly nest;
There the slow blind-worm left his slime
On the fleet limbs that mock'd at time;
And there, too, lay the lader's skull,
Still wreathed with chaplet, flush'd and full,
For heath-bell with her purple bloom
Supplied the bonnet and the plume.
All night, in this sad glen, the maid
Sate, shrouded in her mantle's shade:
—She said no shepherd sought her side,
No hunter's hand her snood untied;
Yet ne'er again to braid her hair
The virgin snood did Alice wear;
Gone was her maiden glee and sport,
Her maiden girdle all too short,
Nor sought she, from that fatal night,
Or holy church or blessed rite,
But lock'd her secret in her breast,
And died in travail, unconfess'd.

VI

Alone, among his young compeers,
Was Brian from his infant years;
A moody and heart-broken boy,
Estranged from sympathy and joy,
Bearing each taunt which careless tongue
On his mysterious lineage flung.
Whole nights he spent by moonlight pale,
To wood and stream his hap to wail,
Till, frantic, he as truth received
What of his birth the crowd believed,
And sought, in mist and meteor fire,
To meet and know his Phantom Sire!
In vain, to soothe his wayward fate,
The cloister oped her pitying gate;
In vain, the learning of the age
Unclasp'd the sable-letter'd page;
Even in its treasures he could find
Food for the fever of his mind.
Eager he read whatever tells
Of magic, cabala, and spells,
And every dark pursuit allied
To curious and presumptuous pride;
Till with fired brain and nerves o'erstrung,
And heart with mystic horrors wrung,

Desperate he sought Benharrow's den,
And hid him from the haunts of men.

VII

The desert gave him visions wild,
Such as might suit the spectre's child.
Where with black cliffs the torrents toil,
He watch'd the wheeling eddies boil,
Till, from their foam, his dazzled eyes
Beheld the River Demon rise;
The mountain mist took form and limb,
Of noontide hag, or goblin grim;
The midnight wind came wild and dread,
Swell'd with the voices of the dead;
Far on the future battle-heath
His eye beheld the ranks of death:
Thus the lone Seer, from mankind hurl'd,
Shaped forth a disembodied world.
One lingering sympathy of mind
Still bound him to the mortal kind;
The only parent he could claim
Of ancient Alpine's lineage came.
Late had he heard, in prophet's dream,
The fatal Ben-Shie's boding scream;
Sounds, too, had come in midnight blast,
Of charging steeds, careering fast
Along Benharrow's shingly side,
Where mortal horseman ne'er might ride;
The thunderbolt had split the pine;
All augur'd ill to Alpine's line.
He girt his loins, and came to show
The signals of impending woe,
And now stood prompt to bless or ban,
As bade the Chieftain of his clan.

VIII

'Twas all prepared; and from the rock,
A goat, the patriarch of the flock,
Before the kindling pile was laid,
And pierced by Roderick's ready blade.
Patient the sickening victim eyed
The life-blood ebb in crimson tide,
Down his clogg'd beard and shaggy limb,
Till darkness glazed his eyeballs dim.
The grisly priest, with murmuring prayer,
A slender crosslet form'd with care,

A cubit's length in measure due;
The shaft and limbs were rods of yew,
Whose parents in Inch-Cailliach wave
Their shadows o'er Clan-Alpine's grave,
And, answering Lomond's breezes deep,
Soothe many a chieftain's endless sleep.
The Cross, thus form'd, he held on high,
With wasted hand, and haggard eye,
And strange and mingled feelings woke,
While his anathema he spoke:

IX

"Woe to the clansman, who shall view
This symbol of sepulchral yew,
Forgetful that its branches grew
Where weep the heavens their holiest dew
   On Alpine's dwelling low!
Deserter of his Chieftain's trust,
He ne'er shall mingle with their dust,
But, from his sires and kindred thrust,
Each clansman's execration just
   Shall doom him wrath and woe."
He paused;—the word the vassals took,
With forward step and fiery look,
On high their naked brands they shook,
Their clattering targets wildly strook;
   And first in murmur low,
Then, like the billow in his course,
That far to seaward finds his source,
And flings to shore his muster'd force,
Burst, with loud roar, their answer hoarse,
   "Woe to the traitor, woe!"
Ben-an's grey scalp the accents knew,
The joyous wolf from covert drew,
The exulting eagle scream'd afar,—
They knew the voice of Alpine's war.

X

The shout was hush'd on lake and fell,
The monk resumed his mutter'd spell:
Dismal and low its accents came,
The while he scathed the Cross with flame;
And the few words that reach'd the air,
Although the holiest name was there,
Had more of blasphemy than prayer.
But when he shook above the crowd

Its kindled points, he spoke aloud:

"Woe to the wretch who fails to rear
At this dread sign the ready spear!
For, as the flames this symbol sear,
His home, the refuge of his fear,
        A kindred fate shall know;
Far o'er its roof the volumed flame
Clan-Alpine's vengeance shall proclaim,
While maids and matrons on his name
Shall call down wretchedness and shame,
        And infamy and woe."

Then rose the cry of females, shrill
As goss-hawk's whistle on the hill,
Denouncing misery and ill,
Mingled with childhood's babbling trill
        Of curses stammer'd slow;
Answering, with imprecation dread,
"Sunk be his home in embers red!
And cursed be the meanest shed
That e'er shall hide the houseless head,
        We doom to want and woe!"
A sharp and shrieking echo gave,
Coir-Uriskin, thy goblin cave!
And the grey pass where birches wave
        On Beala-nam-bo.

        XI
Then deeper paused the priest anew,
And hard his labouring breath he drew,
While, with set teeth and clenched hand,
And eyes that glow'd like fiery brand,
He meditated curse more dread,
And deadlier, on the clansman's head,
Who, summon'd to his Chieftain's aid,
The signal saw and disobey'd.
The crosslet's points of sparkling wood,
He quenched among the bubbling blood,
And, as again the sign he rear'd,
Hollow and hoarse his voice was heard:
"When flits this Cross from man to man,
Vich-Alpine's summons to his clan,
Burst be the ear that fails to heed!
Palsied the foot that shuns to speed!
May ravens tear the careless eyes,
Wolves make the coward heart their prize!

As sinks that blood-stream in the earth,
So may his heart's-blood drench his hearth!
As dies in hissing gore the spark,
Quench thou his light, Destruction dark,
And be the grace to him denied,
Bought by this sign to all beside!"
He ceased; no echo gave agen
The murmur of the deep Amen.

XII

Then Roderick, with impatient look,
From Brian's hand the symbol took:
"Speed, Malise, speed!" he said, and gave
The crosslet to his henchman brave.
"The muster-place be Lanrick mead—
Instant the time; speed, Malise, speed!"
Like heath-bird, when the hawks pursue,
A barge across Loch Katrine flew;
High stood the henchman on the prow;
So rapidly the barge-men row,
The bubbles, where they launch'd the boat,
Were all unbroken and afloat,
Dancing in foam and ripple still,
When it had near'd the mainland hill;
And from the silver beach's side
Still was the prow three fathom wide,
When lightly bounded to the land
The messenger of blood and brand.

XIII

Speed, Malise, speed! the dun deer's hide
On fleeter foot was never tied.
Speed, Malise, speed! such cause of haste
Thine active sinews never braced.
Bend 'gainst the steepy hill thy breast,
Burst down like torrent from its crest;
With short and springing footstep pass
The trembling bog and false morass;
Across the brook like roebuck bound,
And thread the brake like questing hound;
The crag is high, the scaur is deep,
Yet shrink not from the desperate leap:
Parch'd are thy burning lips and brow,
Yet by the fountain pause not now;
Herald of battle, fate, and fear,
Stretch onward in thy fleet career!

The wounded hind thou track'st not now,
Pursuest not maid through greenwood bough,
Nor pliest thou now thy flying pace,
With rivals in the mountain race;
But danger, death, and warrior deed,
Are in thy course; speed, Malise, speed!

XIV

Fast as the fatal symbol flies,
In arms the huts and hamlets rise;
From winding glen, from upland brown,
They pour'd each hardy tenant down.
Nor slack'd the messenger his pace;
He show'd the sign, he named the place,
And, pressing forward like the wind,
Left clamour and surprise behind.
The fisherman forsook the strand,
The swarthy smith took dirk and brand;
With changed cheer, the mower blithe
Left in the half-cut swath the scythe;
The herds without a keeper stray'd,
The plough was in mid-furrow staid,
The falc'ner toss'd his hawk away,
The hunter left the stag at bay;
Prompt at the signal of alarms,
Each son of Alpine rush'd to arms;
So swept the tumult and affray
Along the margin of Achray.
Alas, thou lovely lake! that e'er
Thy banks should echo sounds of fear!
The rocks, the bosky thickets, sleep
So stilly on thy bosom deep,
The lark's blithe carol, from the cloud,
Seems for the scene too gaily loud.

XV

Speed, Malise, speed! the lake is past,
Duncraggan's huts appear at last,
And peep, like moss-grown rocks, half seen,
Half hidden in the copse so green;
There mayest thou rest, thy labour done,
Their Lord shall speed the signal on.
As stoops the hawk upon his prey,
The henchman shot him down the way.
—What woeful accents load the gale?
The funeral yell, the female wail!

A gallant hunter's sport is o'er,
A valiant warrior fights no more.
Who, in the battle or the chase,
At Roderick's side shall fill his place!—
Within the hall, where torches' ray
Supplies the excluded beams of day,
Lies Duncan on his lowly bier,
And o'er him streams his widow's tear.
His stripling son stands mournful by,
His youngest weeps, but knows not why;
The village maids and matrons round
The dismal coronach resound.

XVI

CORONACH

"He is gone on the mountain,
  He is lost to the forest,
Like a summer-dried fountain,
  When our need was the sorest.
The font, reappearing,
  From the rain-drops shall borrow,
But to us comes no cheering,
  To Duncan no morrow!

"The hand of the reaper
  Takes the ears that are hoary,
But the voice of the weeper
  Wails manhood in glory.
The autumn winds rushing
  Waft the leaves that are searest,
But our flower was in flushing,
  When blighting was nearest.
"Fleet foot on the correi,
  Sage counsel in cumber,
Red hand in the foray,
  How sound is thy slumber!
Like the dew on the mountain,
  Like the foam on the river,
Like the bubble on the fountain,
  Thou art gone, and for ever!"

XVII

See Stumah, who, the bier beside,
His master's corpse with wonder eyed,

Poor Stumah! whom his least halloo
Could send like lightning o'er the dew,
Bristles his crest, and points his ears,
As if some stranger step he hears.
'Tis not a mourner's muffled tread
Who comes to sorrow o'er the dead,
But headlong haste, or deadly fear,
Urge the precipitate career.
All stand aghast:—unheeding all,
The henchman bursts into the hall;
Before the dead man's bier he stood;
Held forth the Cross besmear'd with blood;
"The muster-place is Lanrick mead;
Speed forth the signal! clansmen, speed!"

XVIII

Angus, the heir of Duncan's line,
Sprung forth and seized the fatal sign.
In haste the stripling to his side
His father's dirk and broadsword tied;
But when he saw his mother's eye
Watch him in speechless agony,
Back to her open'd arms he flew,
Press'd on her lips a fond adieu—
"Alas!" she sobb'd, "and yet, be gone,
And speed thee forth, like Duncan's son!"
One look he cast upon the bier,
Dash'd from his eye the gathering tear,
Breathed deep to clear his labouring breast,
And toss'd aloft his bonnet crest,
Then, like the high-bred colt, when, freed,
First he essays his fire and speed,
He vanish'd, and o'er moor and moss
Sped forward with the Fiery Cross.
Suspended was the widow's tear,
While yet his footsteps she could hear;
And when she mark'd the henchman's eye
Wet with unwonted sympathy,
"Kinsman," she said, "his race is run,
That should have sped thine errand on;
The oak has fall'n,—the sapling bough
Is all Duncraggan's shelter now.
Yet trust I well, his duty done,
The orphan's God will guard my son.
And you, in many a danger true,
At Duncan's hest your blades that drew,

To arms, and guard that orphan's head!
Let babes and women wail the dead."
Then weapon-clang, and martial call,
Resounded through the funeral hall,
While from the walls the attendant band
Snatch'd sword and targe, with hurried hand;
And short and flitting energy
Glanced from the mourner's sunken eye,
As if the sounds to warrior dear,
Might rouse her Duncan from his bier.
But faded soon that borrow'd force;
Grief claim'd his right, and tears their course.

XIX

Benledi saw the Cross of Fire,
It glanced like lightning up Strath-Ire;
O'er dale and hill the summons flew,
Nor rest nor pause young Angus knew;
The tear that gather'd in his eye
He left the mountain breeze to dry;
Until, where Teith's young waters roll,
Betwixt him and a wooded knoll,
That graced the sable strath with green,
The chapel of St. Bride was seen.
Swoln was the stream, remote the bridge,
But Angus paused not on the edge;
Though the dark waves danced dizzily,
Though reel'd his sympathetic eye,
He dash'd amid the torrent's roar:
His right hand high the crosslet bore,
His left the pole-axe grasp'd, to guide
And stay his footing in the tide.
He stumbled twice—the foam splash'd high,
With hoarser swell the stream raced by;
And had he fall'n,—for ever there
Farewell Duncraggan's orphan heir!
But still, as if in parting life,
Firmer he grasp'd the Cross of strife,
Until the opposing bank he gain'd,
And up the chapel pathway strain'd.

XX

A blithesome rout, that morning tide,
Had sought the chapel of St. Bride.
Her troth Tombea's Mary gave
To Norman, heir of Armandave.

And, issuing from the Gothic arch,
The bridal now resumed their march.
In rude, but glad procession, came
Bonneted sire and coif-clad dame;
And plaided youth, with jest and jeer,
Which snooded maiden would not hear;
And children, that, unwitting why,
Lent the gay shout their shrilly cry;
And minstrels, that in measures vied
Before the young and bonny bride,
Whose downcast eye and cheek disclose.
The tear and blush of morning rose.
With virgin step, and bashful hand,
She held the 'kerchief's snowy band;
The gallant bridegroom by her side,
Beheld his prize with victor's pride,
And the glad mother in her ear
Was closely whispering word of cheer.

XXI

Who meets them at the churchyard gate?
The messenger of fear and fate!
Haste in his hurried accent lies,
And grief is swimming in his eyes.
All dripping from the recent flood,
Painting and travel-soil'd he stood,
The fatal sign of fire and sword,
Held forth, and spoke the appointed word:
"The muster-place is Lanrick mead;
Speed forth the signal! Norman, speed!"
And must he change so soon the hand,
Just link'd to his by holy band,
For the fell Cross of blood and brand?
And must the day, so blithe that rose,
And promised rapture in the close,
Before its setting hour, divide
The bridegroom from the plighted bride?
O fatal doom! it must! it must!
Clan-Alpine's cause, her Chieftain's trust,
Her summons dread, brook no delay;
Stretch to the race; away! away!

XXII

Yet slow he laid his plaid aside,
And, lingering, eyed his lovely bride,
Until he saw the starting tear

Speak woe he might not stop to cheer;
Then, trusting not a second look,
In haste he sped him up the brook,
Nor backward glanced, till on the heath
Where Lubnaig's lake supplies the Teith.
What in the racer's bosom stirr'd?
The sickening pang of hope deferr'd,
And memory, with a torturing train
Of all his morning visions vain.
Mingled with love's impatience, came
The manly thirst for martial fame;
The stormy joy of mountaineers,
Ere yet they rush upon the spears;
And zeal for Clan and Chieftain burning,
And hope, from well-fought field returning,
With war's red honours on his crest,
To clasp his Mary to his breast.
Stung by such thoughts, o'er bank and brae,
Like fire from flint he glanced away,
While high resolve, and feeling strong,
Burst into voluntary song:—

XXIII

SONG

"The heath this night must be my bed,
The bracken curtain for my head,
My lullaby the warder's tread,
    Far, far from love and thee, Mary;
To-morrow eve, more stilly laid,
My couch may be my bloody plaid,
My vesper song, thy wail, sweet maid!
    It will not waken me, Mary!

"I may not, dare not, fancy now
The grief that clouds thy lovely brow,
I dare not think upon thy vow,
    And all it promised me, Mary.
No fond regret must Norman know;
When bursts Clan-Alpine on the foe,
His heart must be like bended bow,
    His foot like arrow free, Mary.

"A time will come with feeling fraught,
For, if I fall in battle fought,
Thy hapless lover's dying thought

Shall be a thought on thee, Mary.
And if return'd from conquer'd foes,
How blithely will the evening close,
How sweet the linnet sing repose,
    To my young bride and me, Mary!"

XXIV

Not faster o'er thy heathery braes,
Balquidder, speeds the midnight blaze,
Rushing, in conflagration strong,
Thy deep ravines and dells along,
Wrapping thy cliffs in purple glow,
And reddening the dark lakes below;
Nor faster speeds it, nor so far,
As o'er thy heaths the voice of war.
The signal roused to martial coil
The sullen margin of Loch Voil,
Waked still Loch Doine, and to the source
Alarm'd, Balvaig, thy swampy course;
Thence southward turn'd its rapid road
Adown Strath-Gartney's valley broad,
Till rose in arms each man might claim
A portion in Clan-Alpine's name,
From the grey sire, whose trembling hand
Could hardly buckle on his brand,
To the raw boy, whose shaft and bow
Were yet scarce terror to the crow.
Each valley, each sequester'd glen,
Muster'd its little horde of men,
That met as torrents from the height
In Highland dales their streams unite,
Still gathering, as they pour along,
A voice more loud, a tide more strong,
Till at the rendezvous they stood
By hundreds prompt for blows and blood;
Each train'd to arms since life began,
Owning no tie but to his clan,
No oath, but by his chieftain's hand,
No law, but Roderick Dhu's command.

XXV

That summer morn had Roderick Dhu
Survey'd the skirts of Benvenue,
And sent his scouts o'er hill and heath,
To view the frontiers of Menteith.
All backward came with news of truce;

Still lay each martial Græme and Bruce,
In Rednoch courts no horsemen wait,
No banner waved on Cardross gate,
On Duchray's towers no beacon shone,
Nor scared the herons from Loch Con;
All seem'd at peace.—Now, wot ye why
The Chieftain, with such anxious eye,
Ere to the muster he repair,
This western frontier scann'd with care?—
In Benvenue's most darksome cleft,
A fair, though cruel, pledge was left;
For Douglas, to his promise true,
That morning from the isle withdrew,
And in a deep sequester'd dell
Had sought a low and lonely cell.
By many a bard, in Celtic tongue,
Has Coir-nan-Uriskin been sung;
A softer name the Saxons gave,
And call'd the grot the Goblin-cave.

XXVI

It was a wild and strange retreat,
As e'er was trod by outlaw's feet.
The dell, upon the mountain's crest,
Yawn'd like a gash on warrior's breast;
Its trench had staid full many a rock,
Hurl'd by primeval earthquake shock
From Benvenue's grey summit wild,
And here, in random ruin piled,
They frown'd incumbent o'er the spot,
And form'd the rugged silvan grot.
The oak and birch, with mingled shade,
At noontide there a twilight made,
Unless when short and sudden shone
Some straggling beam on cliff or stone,
With such a glimpse as prophet's eye
Gains on thy depth, Futurity.
No murmur waked the solemn still,
Save tinkling of a fountain rill;
But when the wind chafed with the lake,
A sullen sound would upward break,
With dashing hollow voice, that spoke
The incessant war of wave and rock.
Suspended cliffs, with hideous sway,
Seem'd nodding o'er the cavern grey.
From such a den the wolf had sprung,

In such the wild-cat leaves her young;
Yet Douglas and his daughter fair
Sought for a space their safety there.
Grey Superstition's whisper dread
Debarr'd the spot to vulgar tread;
For there, she said, did fays resort,
And satyrs hold their silvan court,
By moonlight tread their mystic maze,
And blast the rash beholder's gaze.

XXVII

Now eve, with western shadows long,
Floated on Katrine bright and strong,
When Roderick, with a chosen few,
Repass'd the heights of Benvenue.
Above the Goblin-cave they go,
Through the wild pass of Beal-nam-bo:
The prompt retainers speed before,
To launch the shallop from the shore,
For cross Loch Katrine lies his way
To view the passes of Achray,
And place his clansmen in array.
Yet lags the chief in musing mind,
Unwonted sight, his men behind.
A single page, to bear his sword,
Alone attended on his lord;
The rest their way through thickets break,
And soon await him by the lake.
It was a fair and gallant sight,
To view them from the neighbouring height,
By the low-levell'd sunbeam's light!
For strength and stature, from the clan
Each warrior was a chosen man,
As even afar might well be seen,
By their proud step and martial mien.
Their feathers dance, their tartans float,
Their targets gleam, as by the boat
A wild and warlike group they stand,
That well became such mountain-strand.

XXVIII

Their Chief, with step reluctant, still
Was lingering on the craggy hill,
Hard by where turn'd apart the road
To Douglas's obscure abode.
It was but with that dawning morn,

That Roderick Dhu had proudly sworn
To drown his love in war's wild roar,
Nor think of Ellen Douglas more;
But he who stems a stream with sand,
And fetters flame with flaxen band,
Has yet a harder task to prove,
By firm resolve to conquer love!
Eve finds the Chief, like restless ghost,
Still hovering near his treasure lost;
For though his haughty heart deny
A parting meeting to the eye,
Still fondly strains his anxious ear,
The accents of her voice to hear,
And inly did he curse the breeze
That waked to sound the rustling trees.
But hark! what mingles in the strain?
It is the harp of Allan-Bane,
That wakes its measure slow and high,
Attuned to sacred minstrelsy.
What melting voice attends the strings?
'Tis Ellen, or an angel, sings.

XXIX

HYMN TO THE VIRGIN

"Ave Maria! maiden mild!
    Listen to a maiden's prayer!
Thou canst hear though from the wild,
    Thou canst save amid despair.
Safe may we sleep beneath thy care,
    Though banish'd, outcast, and reviled;
Maiden! hear a maiden's prayer—
    Mother, hear a suppliant child!
                                Ave Maria!

"Ave Maria! undefiled!
    The flinty couch we now must share
Shall seem with down of eider piled,
    If thy protection hover there.
The murky cavern's heavy air
    Shall breathe of balm if thou hast smiled;
Then, Maiden! hear a maiden's prayer;
    Mother, list a suppliant child!
                                Ave Maria!

"Ave Maria! stainless styled!
    Foul demons of the earth and air,

From this their wonted haunt exiled,
  Shall flee before thy presence fair.
We bow us to our lot of care,
  Beneath thy guidance reconciled;
Hear for a maid a maiden's prayer,
  And for a father hear a child!
                         Ave Maria!"

XXX

Died on the harp the closing hymn.
Unmoved in attitude and limb,
As list'ning still, Clan-Alpine's lord
Stood leaning on his heavy sword,
Until the page, with humble sign,
Twice pointed to the sun's decline.
Then while his plaid he round him cast,
"It is the last time, 'tis the last,"
He mutter'd thrice,—"the last time e'er
That angel voice shall Roderick hear!"
It was a goading thought—his stride
Hied hastier down the mountain-side;
Sullen he flung him in the boat,
And instant 'cross the lake it shot.
They landed in that silvery bay,
And eastward held their hasty way,
Till, with the latest beams of light,
The band arrived on Lanrick height,
Where muster'd, in the vale below,
Clan-Alpine's men in martial show.

XXXI

A various scene the clansmen made;
Some sate, some stood, some slowly stray'd;
But most, with mantles folded round,
Were couch'd to rest upon the ground,
Scarce to be known by curious eye,
From the deep heather where they lie,
So well was match'd the tartan screen
With heath-bell dark and brackens green;
Unless where, here and there, a blade,
Or lance's point, a glimmer made,
Like glow-worm twinkling through the shade.
But when, advancing through the gloom,
They saw the Chieftain's eagle plume,
Their shout of welcome, shrill and wide,

Shook the steep mountain's steady side.
Thrice it arose, and lake and fell
Three times return'd the martial yell;
It died upon Bochastle's plain,
And Silence claim'd her evening reign.

Canto Fourth   THE PROPHECY

I

"The rose is fairest when 'tis budding new,
    And hope is brightest when it dawns from fears;
The rose is sweetest wash'd with morning dew,
    And love is loveliest when embalm'd in tears.
O wilding rose, whom fancy thus endears,
    I bid your blossoms in my bonnet wave,
Emblem of hope and love through future years!"
    Thus spoke young Norman, heir of Armandave,
What time the sun arose on Vennachar's broad wave.

II

Such fond conceit, half said, half sung,
Love prompted to the bridegroom's tongue.
All while he stripp'd the wild-rose spray,
His axe and bow beside him lay,
For on a pass 'twixt lake and wood,
A wakeful sentinel he stood.
Hark! on the rock a footstep rung,
And instant to his arms he sprung.
"Stand, or thou diest!—What, Malise? soon
Art thou return'd from Braes of Doune.
By thy keen step and glance I know,
Thou bring'st us tidings of the foe."
(For while the Fiery Cross hied on,
On distant scout had Malise gone.)
"Where sleeps the Chief?" the henchman said.
"Apart, in yonder misty glade;
To his lone couch I'll be your guide;"
Then call'd a slumberer by his side,
And stirr'd him with his slacken'd bow—
"Up, up, Glentarkin! rouse thee, ho!
We seek the Chieftain; on the track,
Keep eagle watch till I come back."

III

Together up the pass they sped:
"What of the foemen?" Norman said.
"Varying reports from near and far;
This certain, that a band of war
Has for two days been ready boune,
At prompt command, to march from Doune;
King James the while, with princely powers,
Holds revelry in Stirling towers.
Soon will this dark and gathering cloud
Speak on our glens in thunder loud.
Inured to bide such bitter bout,
The warrior's plaid may bear it out;
But, Norman, how wilt thou provide
A shelter for thy bonny bride?"
"What! know ye not that Roderick's care
To the lone isle hath caused repair
Each maid and matron of the clan,
And every child and aged man
Unfit for arms; and given his charge,
Nor skiff nor shallop, boat nor barge,
Upon these lakes shall float at large,
But all beside the islet moor,
That such dear pledge may rest secure?"

IV

" 'Tis well advised; the Chieftain's plan
Bespeaks the father of his clan.
But wherefore sleeps Sir Roderick Dhu
Apart from all his followers true?"
"It is, because last evening-tide
Brian an augury hath tried,
Of that dread kind which must not be
Unless in dread extremity,
The Taghairm call'd; by which, afar,
Our sires foresaw the events of war.
Duncraggan's milk-white bull they slew"—

MALISE

"Ah! well the gallant brute I knew!
The choicest of the prey we had,
When swept our merry-men Gallangad.
His hide was snow, his horns were dark,
His red eye glow'd like fiery spark;
So fierce, so tameless, and so fleet,

Sore did he cumber our retreat,
And kept our stoutest kernes in awe,
Even at the pass of Beal 'maha.
But steep and flinty was the road,
And sharp the hurrying pikemen's goad,
And when we came to Dennan's Row,
A child might scatheless stroke his brow."

V

NORMAN

"That bull was slain: his reeking hide
They stretch'd the cataract beside,
Whose waters their wild tumult toss
Adown the black and craggy boss
Of that huge cliff, whose ample verge
Tradition calls the Hero's Targe.
Couch'd on a shelve beneath its brink,
Close where the thundering torrents sink,
Rocking beneath their headlong sway,
And drizzled by the ceaseless spray,
Midst groan of rock, and roar of stream,
The wizard waits prophetic dream.
Nor distant rests the Chief;—but hush!
See, gliding slow through mist and bush,
The hermit gains yon rock; and stands
To gaze upon our slumbering bands.
Seems he not, Malise, like a ghost,
That hovers o'er a slaughter'd host?
Or raven on the blasted oak,
That, watching while the deer is broke,
His morsel claims with sullen croak?"

MALISE

"Peace! peace! to other than to me,
Thy words were evil augury;
But still I hold Sir Roderick's blade
Clan-Alpine's omen and her aid,
Not aught that, glean'd from heaven or hell,
Yon fiend-begotten monk can tell.
The Chieftain joins him, see; and now,
Together they descend the brow."

VI

And, as they came, with Alpine's lord
The Hermit Monk held solemn word:
"Roderick! it is a fearful strife,
For man endow'd with mortal life,
Whose shroud of sentient clay can still
Feel feverish pang and fainting chill,
Whose eye can stare in stony trance,
Whose hair can rouse like warrior's lance,—
'Tis hard for such to view unfurl'd
The curtain of the future world.
Yet—witness every quaking limb,
My sunken pulse, my eyeballs dim,
My soul with harrowing anguish torn—
This for my Chieftain have I borne!
The shapes that sought my fearful couch,
An human tongue may ne'er avouch;
No mortal man, save he who, bred
Between the living and the dead,
Is gifted beyond nature's law,
Had e'er survived to say he saw.
At length the fateful answer came,
In characters of living flame!
Not spoke in word, nor blazed in scroll,
But borne and branded on my soul—
WHICH SPILLS THE FOREMOST FOEMAN'S LIFE,
THAT PARTY CONQUERS IN THE STRIFE!"

VII

"Thanks, Brian, for thy zeal and care!
Good is thine augury, and fair.
Clan-Alpine ne'er in battle stood,
But first our broadswords tasted blood.
A surer victim still I know,
Self-offer'd to the auspicious blow:
A spy has sought my land this morn,—
No eve shall witness his return!
My followers guard each pass's mouth,
To east, to westward, and to south;
Red Murdoch, bribed to be his guide,
Has charge to lead his steps aside,
Till, in deep path or dingle brown,
He light on those shall bring him down.
—But see who comes his news to show!
Malise! what tidings of the foe?"

VIII

"At Doune, o'er many a spear and glaive
Two Barons proud their banners wave.
I saw the Moray's silver star,
And mark'd the sable pale of Mar."
"By Alpine's soul, high tidings those!
I love to hear of worthy foes.
When move they on?" "To-morrow's noon
Will see them here for battle boune."
"Then shall it see a meeting stern!
But, for the place—say, couldst thou learn
Nought of the friendly clans of Earn?
Strengthen'd by them, we well might bide
The battle on Benledi's side.
Thou couldst not? Well! Clan-Alpine's men
Shall man the Trosachs' shaggy glen;
Within Loch Katrine's gorge we'll fight,
All in our maids' and matrons' sight,
Each for his hearth and household fire,
Father for child, and son for sire,
Lover for maid beloved!—But why—
Is it the breeze affects mine eye?
Or dost thou come, ill-omen'd tear!
A messenger of doubt or fear?
No! sooner may the Saxon lance
Unfix Benledi from his stance,
Than doubt or terror can pierce through
The unyielding heart of Roderick Dhu!
'Tis stubborn as his trusty targe.
Each to his post—all know their charge."
The pibroch sounds, the bands advance,
The broadswords gleam, the banners dance,
Obedient to the Chieftain's glance.
I turn me from the martial roar,
And seek Coir-Uriskin once more.

IX

Where is the Douglas?—he is gone;
And Ellen sits on the grey stone
Fast by the cave, and makes her moan;
While vainly Allan's words of cheer
Are pour'd on her unheeding ear:
"He will return—dear lady, trust!—
With joy return; he will, he must.
Well was it time to seek afar
Some refuge from impending war,

When e'en Clan-Alpine's rugged swarm
Are cow'd by the approaching storm.
I saw their boats with many a light
Floating the live-long yesternight,
Shifting like flashes darted forth
By the red streamers of the north;
I mark'd at morn how close they ride,
Thick moor'd by the lone islet's side,
Like wild-ducks couching in the fen,
When stoops the hawk upon the glen.
Since this rude race dare not abide
The peril on the mainland side,
Shall not thy noble father's care
Some safe retreat for thee prepare?"

X

ELLEN

"No, Allan, no! Pretext so kind
My wakeful terrors could not blind.
When in such tender tone, yet grave,
Douglas a parting blessing gave,
The tear that glisten'd in his eye
Drown'd not his purpose fix'd and high.
My soul, though feminine and weak,
Can image his; e'en as the lake,
Itself disturb'd by slightest stroke,
Reflects the invulnerable rock.
He hears report of battle rife,
He deems himself the cause of strife.
I saw him redden, when the theme
Turn'd, Allan, on thine idle dream
Of Malcolm Græme in fetters bound,
Which I, thou saidst, about him wound.
Think'st thou he trow'd thine omen aught?
Oh no! 'twas apprehensive thought
For the kind youth,—for Roderick too—
(Let me be just) that friend so true;
In danger both, and in our cause!
Minstrel, the Douglas dare not pause.
Why else that solemn warning given,
'If not on earth, we meet in heaven!'
Why else, to Cambus-kenneth's fane,
If eve return him not again,
Am I to hie, and make me known?

Alas! he goes to Scotland's throne,
Buys his friend's safety with his own;
He goes to do—what I had done,
Had Douglas' daughter been his son!"

XI

ALLAN

"Nay, lovely Ellen!—dearest, nay!
If aught should his return delay,
He only named yon holy fane
As fitting place to meet again.
Be sure he's safe; and for the Græme,—
Heaven's blessing on his gallant name!
My vision'd sight may yet prove true,
Nor bode of ill to him or you.
When did my gifted dream beguile?
Think of the stranger at the isle,
And think upon the harpings slow,
That presaged this approaching woe!
Sooth was my prophecy of fear;
Believe it when it augurs cheer.
Would we had left this dismal spot!
Ill luck still haunts a fairy grot.
Of such a wondrous tale I know—
Dear lady, change that look of woe,
My harp was wont thy grief to cheer."

ELLEN

"Well, be it as thou wilt; I hear,
But cannot stop the bursting tear."

The Minstrel tried his simple art,
But distant far was Ellen's heart:

XII

BALLAD

ALICE BRAND

"Merry it is in the good greenwood,
    When the mavis and merle are singing,
When the deer sweeps by, and the hounds are in cry,
    And the hunter's horn is ringing.

" 'O Alice Brand, my native land
   Is lost for love of you;
And we must hold by wood and wold,
   As outlaws wont to do.

" 'O Alice, 'twas all for thy locks so bright,
   And 'twas all for thine eyes so blue,
That on the night of our luckless flight
   Thy brother bold I slew.

" 'Now must I teach to hew the beech
   The hand that held the glaive,
For leaves to spread out lowly bed,
   And stakes to fence our cave.

" 'And for vest of pall, thy fingers small,
   That wont on harp to stray,
A cloak must shear from the slaughter'd deer,
   To keep the cold away.'

" 'O Richard! if my brother died,
   'Twas but a fatal chance;
For darkling was the battle tried,
   And fortune sped the lance.

" 'If pall and vair no more I wear,
   Nor thou the crimson sheen,
As warm, we'll say, is the russet grey,
   As gay the forest-green.

" 'And, Richard, if our lot be hard,
   And lost thy native land,
Still Alice has her own Richard,
   And he his Alice Brand.'

XIII

" 'Tis merry, 'tis merry, in good greenwood,
   So blithe Lady Alice is singing;
On the beech's pride, and oak's brown side,
   Lord Richard's axe is ringing.

"Up spoke the moody Elfin King,
   Who won'd within the hill;
Like wind in the porch of a ruin'd church,
   His voice was ghostly shrill.

" 'Why sounds yon stroke on beech and oak,
   Our moonlight circle's screen?
Or who comes here to chase the deer,
   Beloved of our Elfin Queen?

Or who may dare on wold to wear
  The fairies' fatal green?

" 'Up, Urgan, up! to yon mortal hie,
  For thou wert christen'd man;
For cross or sign thou wilt not fly,
  For mutter'd word or ban.

" 'Lay on him the curse of the wither'd heart,
  The curse of the sleepless eye;
Till he wish and pray that his life would part,
  Nor yet find leave to die.'

XIV

" 'Tis merry, 'tis merry, in good greenwood,
  Though the birds have still'd their singing;
The evening blaze doth Alice raise,
  And Richard is fagots bringing.
"Up Urgan starts, that hideous dwarf,
  Before Lord Richard stands,
And, as he cross'd and bless'd himself,
'I fear not sign,' quoth the grisly elf,
  'That is made with bloody hands.'

"But out then spoke she, Alice Brand,
  That woman, void of fear,—
'And if there's blood upon his hand,
  'Tis but the blood of deer.'

" 'Now loud thou liest, thou bold of mood!
  It cleaves unto his hand,
The stain of thine own kindly blood,
  The blood of Ethert Brand.'

"Then forward stepp'd she, Alice Brand,
  And made the holy sign,—
'And if there's blood on Richard's hand,
  A spotless hand is mine.

" 'And I conjure thee, Demon elf,
  By Him whom Demons fear,
To show us whence thou art thyself,
  And what thine errand here?'

XV

" ' 'Tis merry, 'tis merry, in Fairy-land,
  When fairy birds are singing,
When the court doth ride by their monarch's side,
  With bit and bridle ringing:

" 'And gaily shines the Fairy-land—
    But all is glistening show,
Like the idle gleam that December's beam
    Can dart on ice and snow.

" 'And fading, like that varied gleam,
    Is our inconstant shape,
Who now like knight and lady seem,
    And now like dwarf and ape.
" 'It was between the night and day,
    When the Fairy King has power,
That I sunk down in a sinful fray,
And, 'twixt life and death, was snatch'd away
    To the joyless Elfin bower.

" 'But wist I of a woman bold,
    Who thrice my brow durst sign,
I might regain my mortal mold,
    As fair a form as thine.'

"She cross'd him once, she cross'd him twice,
    That lady was so brave;
The fouler grew his goblin hue,
    The darker grew the cave.

"She cross'd him thrice, that lady bold;
    He rose beneath her hand
The fairest knight on Scottish mold,
    Her brother, Ethert Brand!

"Merry it is in good greenwood,
    When the mavis and merle are singing,
But merrier were they in Dunfermline grey,
    When all the bells were ringing."

XVI

Just as the minstrel sounds were staid,
A stranger climb'd the steepy glade:
His martial step, his stately mien,
His hunting suit of Lincoln green,
His eagle glance remembrance claims:
'Tis Snowdoun's Knight, 'tis James Fitz-James.
Ellen beheld as in a dream,
Then, starting, scarce suppress'd a scream:
"O stranger! in such hour of fear,
What evil hap has brought thee here?"
"An evil hap how can it be,
That bids me look again on thee?

By promise bound, my former guide
Met me betimes this morning tide,
And marshall'd, over bank and bourne,
The happy path of my return."
"The happy path!—what! said he nought
Of war, of battle to be fought,
Of guarded pass?" "No, by my faith!
Nor saw I aught could augur scathe."
"O haste thee, Allan, to the kern,—
Yonder his tartans I discern;
Learn thou his purpose, and conjure
That he will guide the stranger sure!
What prompted thee, unhappy man?
The meanest serf in Roderick's clan
Had not been bribed by love or fear,
Unknown to him to guide thee here."

XVII

"Sweet Ellen, dear my life must be,
Since it is worthy care from thee;
Yet life I hold but idle breath,
When love or honour's weigh'd with death.
Then let me profit by my chance,
And speak my purpose bold at once.
I come to bear thee from a wild,
Where ne'er before such blossom smiled;
By this soft hand to lead thee far
From frantic scenes of feud and war.
Near Bochastle my horses wait;
They bear us soon to Stirling gate.
I'll place thee in a lovely bower,
I'll guard thee like a tender flower"—
"Oh! hush, Sir Knight! 'twere female art,
To say I do not read thy heart;
Too much, before, my selfish ear
Was idly soothed my praise to hear.
That fatal bait hath lured thee back,
In deathful hour, o'er dangerous track;
And how, O how, can I atone
The wreck my vanity brought on!
One way remains—I'll tell him all;
Yes! struggling bosom, forth it shall!
Thou, whose light folly bears the blame,
Buy thine own pardon with thy shame!
But first, my father is a man
Outlaw'd and exiled under ban;

The price of blood is on his head;
With me 'twere infamy to wed.
Still wouldst thou speak? then hear the truth!
Fitz-James, there is a noble youth,
If yet he is! exposed for me
And mine to dread extremity—
Thou hast the secret of my heart;
Forgive, be generous, and depart!"

XVIII

Fitz-James knew every wily train
A lady's fickle heart to gain;
But here he knew and felt them vain.
There shot no glance from Ellen's eye,
To give her steadfast speech the lie;
In maiden confidence she stood,
Though mantled in her cheek the blood,
And told her love with such a sigh
Of deep and hopeless agony,
As death had seal'd her Malcolm's doom,
And she sat sorrowing on his tomb.
Hope vanish'd from Fitz-James's eye,
But not with hope fled sympathy.
He proffer'd to attend her side,
As brother would a sister guide.
"O! little know'st thou Roderick's heart!
Safer for both we go apart.
O haste thee, and from Allan learn,
If thou may'st trust yon wily kern."
With hand upon his forehead laid,
The conflict of his mind to shade,
A parting step or two he made;
Then, as some thought had cross'd his brain,
He paused, and turn'd, and came again.

XIX

"Hear, lady, yet, a parting word!
It chanced in fight that my poor sword
Preserved the life of Scotland's lord.
This ring the grateful Monarch gave,
And bade, when I had boon to crave,
To bring it back, and boldly claim
The recompense that I would name.
Ellen, I am no courtly lord,
But one who lives by lance and sword,
Whose castle is his helm and shield,

His lordship the embattled field.
Who neither reck of state nor land?
What from a prince can I demand,
Ellen, thy hand—the ring is thine;
Each guard and usher knows the sign.
Seek thou the King without delay;
This signet shall secure thy way;
And claim thy suit, whate'er it be,
As ransom of his pledge to me."
He placed the golden circlet on,
Paused, kiss'd her hand, and then was gone.
The aged Minstrel stood aghast,
So hastily Fitz-James shot past.
He join'd his guide, and wending down
The ridges of the mountain brown,
Across the stream they took their way,
That joins Loch Katrine to Achray.

XX

All in the Trosachs' glen was still,
Noontide was sleeping on the hill:
Sudden his guide whoop'd loud and high—
"Murdoch! was that a signal cry?"
He stammer'd forth, "I shout to scare
Yon raven from his dainty fare."
He look'd, he knew the raven's prey—
His own brave steed:—"Ah! gallant grey!
For thee, for me perchance, 'twere well
We ne'er had seen the Trosachs' dell.
Murdoch, move first—but silently;
Whistle or whoop, and thou shalt die!"
Jealous and sullen, on they fared,
Each silent, each upon his guard.

XXI

Now wound the path its dizzy ledge
Around a precipice's edge,
When lo! a wasted female form,
Blighted by wrath of sun and storm,
In tatter'd weeds and wild array,
Stood on a cliff beside the way,
And glancing round her restless eye,
Upon the wood, the rock, the sky,
Seem'd nought to mark, yet all to spy.
Her brow was wreath'd with gaudy broom;
With gesture wild she waved a plume

Of feathers, which the eagles fling
To crag and cliff from dusky wing;
Such spoils her desperate step had sought,
Where scarce was footing for the goat.
The tartan plaid she first descried,
And shriek'd till all the rocks replied;
As loud she laugh'd when near they drew,
For then the Lowland garb she knew;
And then her hands she wildly wrung,
And then she wept, and then she sung.
She sung!—the voice, in better time,
Perchance to harp or lute might chime;
And now, though strain'd and roughen'd, still
Rung wildly sweet to dale and hill:

XXII

SONG

"They bid me sleep, they bid me pray,
    They say my brain is warp'd and wrung;
I cannot sleep on Highland brae,
    I cannot pray in Highland tongue.
But were I now where Allan glides,
Or heard my native Devan's tides,
So sweetly would I rest, and pray
That Heaven would close my wintry day!

" 'Twas thus my hair they bade me braid,
    They made me to the church repair;
It was my bridal morn, they said,
    And my true love would meet me there.
But woe betide the cruel guile,
That drown'd in blood the morning smile!
And woe betide the fairy dream!
I only waked to sob and scream."

XXIII

"Who is this maid? what means her lay?
She hovers o'er the hollow way,
And flutters wide her mantle grey,
As the lone heron spreads his wing,
By twilight, o'er a haunted spring."
" 'Tis Blanche of Devan," Murdoch said,
"A crazed and captive Lowland maid,
Ta'en on the morn she was a bride,

When Roderick foray'd Devan-side.
The gay bridegroom resistance made,
And felt our Chief's unconquer'd blade;
I marvel she is now at large,
But oft she 'scapes from Maudlin's charge.
Hence, brain-sick fool!" He raised his bow:
"Now if thou strik'st her but one blow,
I'll pitch thee from the cliff as far
As ever peasant pitch'd a bar!"
"Thanks, champion, thanks!" the maniac cried,
And press'd her to Fitz-James's side;
"See the grey pennons I prepare
To seek my true-love through the air!
I will not lend that savage groom,
To break his fall, one downy plume!
No! deep amid disjointed stones,
The wolves shall batten on his bones,
And then shall his detested plaid,
By bush and brier in mid-air staid,
Wave forth a banner fair and free,
Meet signal for their revelry."

XXIV

"Hush thee, poor maiden, and be still!"
"O! thou look'st kindly, and I will.
Mine eye has dried and wasted been,
But still it loves the Lincoln green;
And, though mine ear is all unstrung,
Still, still it loves the Lowland tongue.

   " 'For O my sweet William was forester true,
      He stole poor Blanche's heart away!
   His coat it was all of the greenwood hue,
      And so blithely he trill'd the Lowland lay!'

" 'It was not that I meant to tell . . .
But thou art wise and guessest well."
Then, in a low and broken tone,
And hurried note, the song went on.
Still on the Clansman, fearfully,
She fix'd her apprehensive eye;
Then turn'd it on the Knight, and then
Her look glanced wildly o'er the glen.

XXV

   " 'The toils are pitch'd, and the stakes are set,
      Ever sing merrily, merrily;

The bows they bend, and the knives they whet,
   Hunters live so cheerily.

" 'It was a stag, a stag of ten,
   Bearing its branches sturdily;
He came stately down the glen,
   Ever sing hardily, hardily.

" 'It was there he met with a wounded doe,
   She was bleeding deathfully;
She warn'd him of the toils below,
   O, so faithfully, faithfully!

" 'He had an eye, and he could heed,
   Ever sing warily, warily;
He had a foot, and he could speed—
   Hunters watch so narrowly.' "

XXVI

Fitz-James's mind was passion-toss'd,
When Ellen's hints and fears were lost;
But Murdoch's shout suspicion wrought,
And Blanche's song conviction brought.
Not like a stag that spies the snare,
But lion of the hunt aware,
He waved at once his blade on high,
"Disclose thy treachery, or die!"
Forth at full speed the Clansman flew,
But in his race his bow he drew.
The shaft just grazed Fitz-James's crest,
And thrill'd in Blanche's faded breast!
Murdoch of Alpine! prove thy speed,
For ne'er had Alpine's son such need!
With heart of fire, and foot of wind,
The fierce avenger is behind!
Fate judges of the rapid strife—
The forfeit death—the prize is life!
Thy kindred ambush lies before,
Close couch'd upon the heathery moor;
Them couldst thou reach!—it may not be—
Thine ambush'd kin thou ne'er shalt see,
The fiery Saxon gains on thee!
—Resistless speeds the deedly thrust,
As lightning strikes the pine to dust;
With foot and hand Fitz-James must strain,
Ere he can win his blade again.
Bent o'er the fall'n, with falcon eye,

He grimly smiled to see him die;
Then slower wended back his way,
Where the poor maiden bleeding lay.

XXVII

She sate beneath the birchen-tree,
Her elbow resting on her knee;
She had withdrawn the fatal shaft,
And gazed on it, and feebly laugh'd;
Her wreath of broom and feathers grey,
Daggled with blood, beside her lay.
The Knight to stanch the life-stream tried;
"Stranger, it is in vain!" she cried.
"This hour of death has given me more
Of reason's power than years before;
For, as these ebbing veins decay,
My frenzied visions fade away.
A helpless injured wretch I die,
And something tells me in thine eye,
That thou wert mine avenger born.—
Seest thou this tress?—O! still I've worn
This little tress of yellow hair,
Through danger, frenzy, and despair!
It once was bright and clear as thine,
But blood and tears have dimm'd its shine.
I will not tell thee when 'twas shred,
Nor from what guiltless victim's head—
My brain would turn!—but it shall wave
Like plumage on thy helmet brave,
Till sun and wind shall bleach the stain,
And thou wilt bring it me again.—
I waver still. O God! more bright
Let reason beam her parting light!
O! by thy knighthood's honour'd sign,
And for thy life preserved by mine,
When thou shalt see a darksome man,
Who boasts him Chief of Alpine's Clan,
With tartans broad, and shadowy plume,
And hand of blood, and brow of gloom,
Be thy heart bold, thy weapon strong,
And wreak poor Blanche of Devan's wrong!
They watch for thee by pass and fell . . .
Avoid the path . . . O God! . . . farewell."

XXVIII

A kindly heart had brave Fitz-James;
Fast pour'd his eyes at pity's claims;

And now, with mingled grief and ire,
He saw the murder'd maid expire.
"God, in my need, be my relief,
As I wreak this on yonder Chief!"
A lock from Blanche's tresses fair
He blended with her bridegroom's hair;
The mingled braid in blood he dyed,
And placed it on his bonnet-side:
"By Him whose word is truth! I swear,
No other favour will I wear,
Till this sad token I imbrue
In the best blood of Roderick Dhu!
But hark! what means yon faint halloo?
The chase is up; but they shall know,
The stag at bay's a dangerous foe."
Barr'd from the known but guarded way,
Through copse and cliffs Fitz-James must stray,
And oft must change his desperate track,
By stream and precipice turn'd back.
Heartless, fatigued, and faint, at length,
From lack of food and loss of strength,
He couch'd him in a thicket hoar,
And thought his toils and perils o'er:
"Of all my rash adventures past,
This frantic feat must prove the last!
Who e'er so mad but might have guess'd,
That all his Highland hornet's nest
Would muster up in swarms so soon
As e'er they heard of bands at Doune?
Like bloodhounds now they search me out,—
Hark, to the whistle and the shout!—
If farther through the wilds I go,
I only fall upon the foe:
I'll couch me here till evening grey,
Then darkling try my dangerous way."

XXIX

The shades of eve come slowly down,
The woods are wrapt in deeper brown,
The owl awakens from her dell,
The fox is heard upon the fell;
Enough remains of glimmering light
To guide the wanderer's steps aright,
Yet not enough from far to show
His figure to the watchful foe.
With cautious step, and ear awake,

He climbs the crag and threads the brake;
And not the summer solstice, there,
Temper'd the midnight mountain air,
But every breeze, that swept the wold,
Benumb'd his drenched limbs with cold.
In dread, in danger, and alone,
Famish'd and chill'd, through ways unknown,
Tangled and steep, he journey'd on;
Till, as a rock's huge point he turn'd,
A watch-fire close before him burn'd.

XXX

Beside its embers red and clear,
Bask'd in his plaid a mountaineer;
And up he sprung with sword in hand,—
"Thy name and purpose! Saxon, stand!"
"A stranger." "What dost thou require?"
"Rest and a guide, and food and fire.
My life's beset, my path is lost,
The gale has chill'd my limbs with frost."
"Art thou a friend to Roderick?" "No."
"Thou darest not call thyself a foe?"
"'I dare! to him and all the band
He brings to aid his murderous hand."
"Bold words! but, though the beast of game
The privilege of chase may claim,
Though space and law the stag we lend,
Ere hound we slip, or bow we bend,
Who ever reck'd, where, how, or when,
The prowling fox was trapp'd or slain?
Thus treacherous scouts,—yet sure they lie
Who say thou cam'st a secret spy!"
"They do, by heaven! Come Roderick Dhu,
And of his clan the boldest two,
And let me but till morning rest,
I write the falsehood on their crest."
"If by the blaze I mark aright,
Thou bear'st the belt and spur of Knight."
"Then by these tokens mayest thou know
Each proud oppressor's mortal foe."
"Enough, enough; sit down and share
A soldier's couch, a soldier's fare."

XXXI

He gave him of his Highland cheer,
The harden'd flesh of mountain deer;

Dry fuel on the fire he laid,
And bade the Saxon share his plaid.
He tended him like welcome guest,
Then thus his farther speech address'd:
"Stranger, I am to Roderick Dhu
A clansman born, a kinsman true;
Each word against his honour spoke,
Demands of me avenging stroke;
Yet more,—upon thy fate, 'tis said,
A mighty augury is laid.
It rests with me, to wind my horn,—
Thou art with numbers overborne;
It rests with me, here brand to brand,
Worn as thou art, to bid thee stand:
But, not for clan, nor kindred's cause,
Will I depart from honour's laws;
To assail a wearied man were shame,
And stranger is a holy name;
Guidance and rest, and food and fire,
In vain he never must require.
Then rest thee here till dawn of day;
Myself will guide thee on the way,
O'er stock and stone, through watch and ward,
Till past Clan-Alpine's outmost guard,
As far as Coilantogle's ford;
From thence thy warrant is thy sword."
"I take thy courtesy, by heaven,
As freely as 'tis nobly given!"
"Well, rest thee; for the bittern's cry
Sings us the lake's wild lullaby."
With that he shook the gather'd heath,
And spread his plaid upon the wreath;
And the brave foemen, side by side,
Lay peaceful down, like brothers tried,
And slept until the dawning beam
Purpled the mountain and the stream.

Canto Fifth   THE COMBAT

I

Fair as the earliest beam of eastern light,
    When first, by the bewilder'd pilgrim spied,

It smiles upon the dreary brow of night,
  And silvers o'er the torrent's foaming tide,
And lights the fearful path on mountain side,—
  Fair as that beam, although the fairest far,
Giving to horror grace, to danger pride,
  Shine martial Faith, and Courtesy's bright star,
Through all the wreckful storms that cloud the brow of War.

II

That early beam, so fair and sheen,
Was twinkling through the hazel screen,
When, rousing at its glimmer red,
The warriors left their lowly bed,
Look'd out upon the dappled sky,
Mutter'd their soldier matins by,
And then awaked their fire, to steal,
As short and rude, their soldier meal.
That o'er, the Gael around him threw
His graceful plaid of varied hue,
And, true to promise, led the way,
By thicket green and mountain grey.
A wildering path! they winded now
Along the precipice's brow,
Commanding the rich scenes beneath,
The windings of the Forth and Teith,
And all the vales beneath that lie,
Till Stirling's turrets melt in sky;
Then, sunk in copse, their farthest glance
Gain'd not the length of horseman's lance.
'Twas oft so steep, the foot was fain
Assistance from the hand to gain;
So tangled oft, that, bursting through,
Each hawthorn shed her showers of dew,—
That diamond dew, so pure and clear,
It rivals all but Beauty's tear.

III

At length they came where, stern and steep,
The hill sinks down upon the deep.
Here Vennachar in silver flows,
There, ridge on ridge, Benledi rose;
Ever the hollow path twined on,
Beneath steep bank and threatening stone;
An hundred men might hold the post

With hardihood against a host.
The rugged mountain's scanty cloak
Was dwarfish shrubs of birch and oak,
With shingles bare, and cliffs between,
And patches bright of bracken green,
And heather black, that waved so high,
It held the copse in rivalry.
But where the lake slept deep and still,
Dank osiers fringed the swamp and hill;
And oft both path and hill were torn,
Where wintry torrents down had borne,
And heap'd upon the cumber'd land
Its wreck of gravel, rocks, and sand.
So toilsome was the road to trace,
The guide, abating of his pace,
Led slowly through the pass's jaws,
And ask'd Fitz-James, by what strange cause
He sought these wilds, traversed by few,
Without a pass from Roderick Dhu.

                    IV
"Brave Gael, my pass in danger tried,
Hangs in my belt, and by my side;
Yet, sooth to tell," the Saxon said,
"I dreamt not now to claim its aid.
When here, but three days since, I came,
Bewilder'd in pursuit of game,
All seem'd as peaceful and as still
As the mist slumbering on yon hill;
Thy dangerous Chief was then afar,
Nor soon expected back from war.
Thus said, at least, my mountain-guide,
Though deep, perchance, the villain lied."
"Yet why a second venture try?"
"A warrior thou, and ask me why?
Moves our free course by such fix'd cause
As gives the poor mechanic laws?
Enough, I sought to drive away
The lazy hours of peaceful day;
Slight cause will then suffice to guide
A Knight's free footsteps far and wide,—
A falcon flown, a greyhound stray'd,
The merry glance of mountain maid:
Or, if a path be dangerous known,
The danger's self is lure alone."

V

"Thy secret keep, I urge thee not;
Yet, ere again ye sought this spot,
Say, heard ye nought of Lowland war,
Against Clan-Alpine, raised by Mar?"
"No, by my word;—of bands prepared
To guard King James's sports I heard;
Nor doubt I aught, but, when they hear
This muster of the mountaineer,
Their pennons will abroad be flung,
Which else in Doune had peaceful hung."
"Free be they flung! for we were loth
Their silken folds should feast the moth.
Free be they be flung! as free shall wave
Clan-Alpine's pine in banner brave.
But, Stranger, peaceful since you came,
Bewilder'd in the mountain game,
Whence the bold boast by which you show
Vich-Alpine's vow'd and mortal foe?"
"Warrior, but yester-morn, I knew
Nought of thy Chieftain, Roderick Dhu,
Save as an outlaw'd desperate man,
The chief of a rebellious clan,
Who, in the Regent's court and sight,
With ruffian dagger stabb'd a knight:
Yet this alone might from his part
Sever each true and loyal heart."

VI

Wrothful at such arraignment foul
Dark lower'd the clansman's sable scowl.
A space he paused, then sternly said,
"And heard'st thou why he drew his blade?
Heard'st thou that shameful word and blow
Brought Roderick's vengeance on his foe?
What reck'd the Chieftain if he stood
On Highland heath, or Holy-Rood?
He rights such wrong where it is given,
If it were in the court of heaven."
"Still was it outrage;—yet, 'tis true,
Not then claim'd sovereignty his due;
While Albany, with feeble hand,
Held borrow'd truncheon of command,
The young King, mew'd in Stirling tower,
Was stranger to respect and power.
But then, thy Chieftain's robber life!

Winning mean prey by causeless strife,
Wrenching from ruin'd Lowland swain
His herds and harvest reared in vain.
Methinks a soul, like thine, should scorn
The spoils from such foul foray borne."

VII
The Gael beheld him grim the while,
And answer'd with disdainful smile,
"Saxon, from yonder mountain high,
I mark'd thee send delighted eye,
Far to the south and east, where lay,
Extended in succession gay,
Deep waving fields and pastures green,
With gentle slopes and groves between:
These fertile plains, that soften'd vale,
Were once the birthright of the Gael;
The stranger came with iron hand,
And from our fathers reft the land.
Where dwell we now? See, rudely swell
Crag over crag, and fell o'er fell.
Ask we this savage hill we tread,
For fatten'd steer or household bread;
Ask we for flocks these shingles dry,
And well the mountain might reply,—
'To you, as to your sires of yore,
Belong the target and claymore!
I give you shelter in my breast,
Your own good blades must win the rest.'
Pent in this fortress of the North,
Think'st thou we will not sally forth,
To spoil the spoiler as we may,
And from the robber rend the prey?
Ay, by my soul! While on yon plain
The Saxon rears one shock of grain,
While of ten thousand herds there strays
But one along yon river's maze,
The Gael, of plain and river heir,
Shall with strong hand redeem his share.
Where live the mountain Chiefs who hold,
That plundering Lowland field and fold
Is aught but retribution true?
Seek other cause 'gainst Roderick Dhu."

VIII
Answer'd Fitz-James, "And, if I sought,
Think'st thou no other could be brought?

What deem ye of my path waylaid?
My life given o'er to ambuscade?"
"As of a meed to rashness due:
Hadst thou sent warning fair and true—
I seek my hound, or falcon stray'd,
I seek, good faith, a Highland maid—
Free hadst thou been to come and go;
But secret path marks secret foe.
Nor yet, for this, even as a spy,
Hadst thou unheard been doom'd to die,
Save to fulfil an augury."
"Well, let it pass; nor will I now
Fresh cause of enmity avow,
To chafe thy mood and cloud thy brow.
Enough, I am by promise tied
To match me with this man of pride:
Twice have I sought Clan-Alpine's glen
In peace; but when I come agen,
I come with banner, brand, and bow,
As leader seeks his mortal foe.
For love-lorn swain, in lady's bower,
Ne'er panted for the appointed hour,
As I, until before me stand
This rebel Chieftain and his band!"

    IX
"Have, then, thy wish!" He whistled shrill,
And he was answer'd from the hill;
Wild as the scream of the curlew,
From crag to crag the signal flew.
Instant, through copse and heath, arose
Bonnets and spears and bended bows;
On right, on left, above, below,
Sprung up at once the lurking foe;
From shingles grey their lances start,
The bracken bush sends forth the dart,
The rushes and the willow-wand
Are bristling into axe and brand,
And every tuft of broom gives life
To plaided warrior arm'd for strife.
That whistle garrison'd the glen
At once with full five hundred men,
As if the yawning hill to heaven
A subterranean host had given.
Watching their leader's beck and will,
All silent there they stood, and still.

Like the loose crags, whose threatening mass
Lay tottering o'er the hollow pass,
As if an infant's touch could urge
Their headlong passage down the verge,
With step and weapon forward flung,
Upon the mountain-side they hung.
The Mountaineer cast glance of pride
Along Benledi's living side,
Then fix'd his eye and sable brow
Full on Fitz-James—"How say'st thou now?
These are Clan-Alpine's warriors true;
And, Saxon,—I am Roderick Dhu!"

X

Fitz-James was brave. Though to his heart
The life-blood thrill'd with sudden start,
He mann'd himself with dauntless air,
Return'd the Chief his haughty stare,
His back against a rock he bore,
And firmly placed his foot before:
"Come one, come all! this rock shall fly
From its firm base as soon as I."
Sir Roderick mark'd, and in his eyes
Respect was mingled with surprise,
And the stern joy which warriors feel
In foemen worthy of their steel.
Short space he stood, then waved his hand:
Down sunk the disappearing band;
Each warrior vanish'd where he stood,
In broom or bracken, heath or wood;
Sunk brand and spear and bended bow,
In osiers pale and copses low;
It seem'd as if their mother Earth
Had swallow'd up her warlike birth.
The wind's last breath had toss'd in air
Pennon, and plaid, and plumage fair;
The next but swept a lone hill-side,
Where heath and fern were waving wide:
The sun's last glance was glinted back,
From spear and glaive, from targe and jack;
The next, all unreflected, shone
On bracken green and cold grey stone.

XI

Fitz-James look'd round, yet scarce believed
The witness that his sight received;

Such apparition well might seem
Delusion of a dreadful dream.
Sir Roderick in suspense he eyed,
And to his look the Chief replied,
"Fear nought—nay, that I need not say—
But doubt not aught from mine array.
Thou art my guest; I pledged my word
As far as Coilantogle ford:
Nor would I call a clansman's brand
For aid against one valiant hand,
Though on our strife lay every vale
Rent by the Saxon from the Gael.
So move we on; I only meant
To show the reed on which you leant,
Deeming this path you might pursue
Without a pass from Roderick Dhu."
They moved. I said Fitz-James was brave
As ever knight that belted glaive,
Yet dare not say that now his blood
Kept on its wont and temper'd flood,
As, following Roderick's stride, he drew
That seeming lonesome pathway through,
Which yet, by fearful proof, was rife
With lances, that, to take his life,
Waited but signal from a guide
So late dishonour'd and defied.
Ever, by stealth, his eye sought round
The vanish'd guardians of the ground,
And still, from copse and heather deep,
Fancy saw spear and broadsword peep,
And in the plover's shrilly strain,
The signal-whistle heard again,
Nor breathed he free till far behind
The pass was left; for then they wind
Along a wide and level green,
Where neither tree nor tuft was seen,
Nor rush nor bush of broom was near,
To hide a bonnet or a spear.

XII

The Chief in silence strode before,
And reach'd that torrent's sounding shore,
Which, daughter of three mighty lakes,
From Vennachar in silver breaks,
Sweeps through the plain, and ceaseless mines
On Bochastle the mouldering lines,

Where Rome, the Empress of the world,
Of yore her eagle wings unfurl'd.
And here his course the Chieftain staid,
Threw down his target and his plaid,
And to the Lowland warrior said:
"Bold Saxon! to his promise just,
Vich-Alpine has discharged his trust.
This murderous Chief, this ruthless man,
This head of a rebellious clan,
Hath led thee safe, through watch and ward,
Far past Clan-Alpine's outmost guard.
Now man to man, and steel to steel,
A Chieftain's vengeance thou shalt feel.
See here, all vantageless I stand,
Arm'd like thyself with single brand:
For this is Coilantogle ford,
And thou must keep thee with thy sword."

XIII

The Saxon paused: "I ne'er delay'd,
When foeman bade me draw my blade;
Nay, more, brave Chief, I vow'd thy death;
Yet sure thy fair and generous faith,
And my deep debt for life preserved,
A better meed have well deserved:
Can nought but blood our feud atone?
Are there no means?" "No, Stranger, none!
And hear, to fire thy flagging zeal,—
The Saxon cause rests on thy steel;
For thus spoke Fate, by prophet bred
Between the living and the dead:
'Who spills the foremost foeman's life
His party conquers in the strife.'"
"Then, by my word," the Saxon said,
"The riddle is already read.
Seek yonder brake beneath the cliff;
There lies Red Murdoch, stark and stiff.
Thus Fate has solved her prophecy,
Then yield to Fate, and not to me.
To James, at Stirling, let us go,
When, if thou wilt be still his foe,
Or if the King shall not agree
To grant thee grace and favour free,
I plight mine honour, oath, and word,
That, to thy native strengths restored,

With each advantage shalt thou stand,
That aids thee now, to guard thy land."

XIV

Dark lightning flash'd from Roderick's eye:
"Soars thy presumption, then, so high,
Because a wretched kern ye slew,
Homage to name to Roderick Dhu?
He yields not, he, to man nor Fate!
Thou add'st but fuel to my hate:
My clansman's blood demands revenge.
Not yet prepared? By heaven, I change
My thought, and hold thy valour light
As that of some vain carpet knight,
Who ill deserved my courteous care,
And whose best boast is but to wear
A braid of his fair lady's hair."
"I thank thee, Roderick, for the word!
It nerves my heart, it steels my sword;
For I have sworn this braid to stain
In the best blood that warms thy vein.
Now, truce, farewell! and, ruth, begone!
Yet think not that by thee alone,
Proud Chief! Can courtesy be shown;
Though not from copse, or heath, or cairn,
Start at my whistle clansmen stern,
Of this small horn one feeble blast
Would fearful odds against thee cast.
But fear not, doubt not—which thou wilt—
We try this quarrel hilt to hilt."—
Then each at once his falchion drew,
Each on the ground his scabbard threw,
Each look'd to sun, and stream, and plain,
As what he ne'er might see again;
Then foot, and point, and eye opposed,
In dubious strife they darkly closed.

XV

Ill fared it then with Roderick Dhu,
That on the field his targe he threw,
Whose brazen studs and tough bull-hide
Had death so often dash'd aside;
For, train'd abroad his arms to wield,
Fitz-James's blade was sword and shield.
He practised every pass and ward,

To thrust, to strike, to feint, to guard;
While less expert, though stronger far,
The Gael maintain'd unequal war.
Three times in closing strife they stood,
And thrice the Saxon blade drank blood;
No stinted draught, no scanty tide,
The gushing flood the tartans dyed.
Fierce Roderick felt the fatal drain,
And shower'd his blows like wintry rain;
And, as firm rock, or castle-roof,
Against the winter shower is proof,
The foe, invulnerable still,
Foil'd his wild rage by steady skill;
Till, at advantage ta'en, his brand
Forced Roderick's weapon from his hand,
And backward borne upon the lea,
Brought the proud Chieftain to his knee.

XVI

"Now, yield thee, or by Him who made
The world, thy heart's blood dyes my blade!"
"Thy threats, thy mercy, I defy!
Let recreant yield, who fears to die."
Like adder darting from his coil,
Like wolf that dashes through the toil,
Like mountain-cat who guards her young,
Full at Fitz-James's throat he sprung;
Received, but reck'd not of a wound,
And lock'd his arms his foeman round.
Now, gallant Saxon, hold thine own!
No maiden's hand is round thee thrown!
That desperate grasp thy frame might feel
Through bars of brass and triple steel
They tug, they strain! down, down they go,
The Gael above, Fitz-James below.
The Chieftain's gripe his throat compress'd,
His knee was planted in his breast;
His clotted locks he backward threw,
Across his brow his hand he drew,
From blood and mist to clear his sight,
Then gleam'd aloft his dagger bright!
But hate and fury ill supplied
The stream of life's exhausted tide,
And all too late the advantage came,
To turn the odds of deadly game;
For, while the dagger gleam'd on high,

Reel'd soul and sense, reel'd brain and eye.
Down came the blow—but in the heath;
The erring blade found bloodless sheath.
The struggling foe may now unclasp
The fainting Chief's relaxing grasp;
Unwounded from the dreadful close,
But breathless all, Fitz-James arose.

XVII

He falter'd thanks to Heaven for life,
Redeem'd, unhoped, from desperate strife;
Next on his foe his look he cast,
Whose every gasp appear'd his last;
In Roderick's gore he dipt the braid—
"Poor Blanche! thy wrongs are dearly paid:
Yet with thy foe must die, or live,
The praise that Faith and Valour give."
With that he blew a bugle-note,
Undid the collar from his throat,
Unbonneted, and by the wave
Sate down his brow and hands to lave.
Then faint afar are heard the feet
Of rushing steeds in gallop fleet;
The sounds increase, and now are seen
Four mounted squires in Lincoln green;
Two who bear lance, and two who lead,
By loosen'd rein, a saddled steed;
Each onward held his headlong course,
And by Fitz-James rein'd up his horse,
With wonder view'd the bloody spot—
—"Exclaim not, gallants! question not.
You, Herbert and Luffness, alight,
And bind the wounds of yonder knight;
Let the grey palfrey bear his weight,
We destined for a fairer freight,
And bring him on to Stirling straight;
I will before at better speed,
To seek fresh horse and fitting weed.
The sun rides high; I must be boune,
To see the archer-game at noon;
But lightly Bayard clears the lea.
De Vaux and Herries, follow me.

XVIII

"Stand, Bayard, stand!" The steed obey'd,
With arching neck and bended head,

And glancing eye and quivering ear,
As if he loved his lord to hear.
No foot Fitz-James in stirrup staid,
No grasp upon the saddle laid,
But wreath'd his left hand in the mane,
And lightly bounded from the plain,
Turn'd on the horse his armed heel,
And stirr'd his courage with the steel
Bounded the fiery steed in air,
The rider sate erect and fair,
Then like a bolt from steel crossbow
Forth launch'd, along the plain they go.
They dash'd that rapid torrent through,
And up Carhonie's hill they flew;
Still at the gallop prick'd the Knight,
His merry-men follow'd as they might.
Along thy banks, swift Teith! they ride,
And in the race they mock thy tide;
Torry and Lendrick now are past,
And Deanstown lies behind them cast;
They rise, the banner'd towers of Doune,
They sink in distant woodland soon;
Blair-Drummond sees the hoofs strike fire,
They sweep like breeze through Ochtertyre;
They mark just glance and disappear
The lofty brow of ancient Kier;
They bathe their courser's sweltering sides,
Dark Forth! amid thy sluggish tides,
And on the opposing shore take ground,
With plash, with scramble, and with bound.
Right-hand they leave thy cliffs, Craig-Forth!
And soon the bulwark of the North,
Grey Stirling, with her towers and town,
Upon their fleet career look'd down.

XIX

As up the flinty path they strain'd
Sudden his steed the leader rein'd;
A signal to his squire he flung,
Who instant to his stirrup sprung:
"Seest thou, De Vaux, yon woodsman grey,
Who town-ward holds the rocky way,
Of stature tall and poor array?
Mark'st thou the firm, yet active stride,
With which he scales the mountain-side?
Know'st thou from whence he comes, or whom?"

"No, by my word; a burly groom
He seems, who in the field or chase
A baron's train would nobly grace."
"Out, out, De Vaux! can fear supply,
And jealousy, no sharper eye?
Afar, ere to the hill he drew,
That stately form and step I knew;
Like form in Scotland is not seen,
Treads not such step on Scottish green.
'Tis James of Douglas, by Saint Serle!
The uncle of the banish'd Earl.
Away, away to court, to show
The near approach of dreaded foe:
The King must stand upon his guard;
Douglas and he must meet prepared."
Then right-hand wheel'd their steeds, and straight
They won the castle's postern gate.

XX

The Douglas, who had bent his way
From Cambus-Kenneth's abbey grey,
Now, as he climb'd the rocky shelf,
Held sad communion with himself:
"Yes! all is true my fears could frame;
A prisoner lies the noble Græme,
And fiery Roderick soon will feel
The vengeance of the royal steel.
I, only I, can ward their fate;
God grant the ransom come not late!
The Abbess hath her promise given
My child shall be the bride of Heaven;
Be pardon'd one repining tear!
For He who gave her knows how dear,
How excellent—but that is by,
And now my business is to die.
Ye towers! within whose circuit dread
A Douglas by his sovereign bled;
And thou, O sad and fatal mound!
That oft hast heard the death-axe sound,
As on the noblest of the land
Fell the stern headsman's bloody hand,
The dungeon, block, and nameless tomb
Prepare, for Douglas seeks his doom!
But hark! what blithe and jolly peal
Makes the Franciscan steeple reel?
And see! upon the crowded street,

In motley groups what masquers meet!
Banner and pageant, pipe and drum,
And merry morrice-dancers come.
I guess, by all this quaint array,
The burghers hold their sports to-day.
James will be there; he loves such show,
Where the good yeoman bends his bow,
And the tough wrestler foils his foe,
As well as where, in proud career,
The high-born tilter shivers spear.
I'll follow to the Castle-park,
And play my prize; King James shall mark
If age has tamed these sinews stark,
Whose force so oft, in happier days,
His boyish wonder loved to praise."

XXI

The Castle gates were open flung,
The quivering drawbridge rock'd and rung,
And echo'd loud the flinty street
Beneath the coursers' clattering feet,
As slowly down the steep descent
Fair Scotland's King and nobles went,
While all along the crowded way
Was jubilee and loud huzza.
And ever James was bending low
To his white jennet's saddle-bow,
Doffing his cap to city dame,
Who smiled and blush'd for pride and shame.
And well the simperer might be vain;
He chose the fairest of the train.
Gravely he greets each city sire,
Commends each pageant's quaint attire,
Gives to the dancers thanks loud,
And smiles and nods upon the crowd,
Who rend the heavens with their acclaims,
"Long live the Commons' King, King James!"
Behind the King throng'd peer and knight,
And noble dame and damsel bright,
Whose fiery steeds ill brook'd the stay
Of the steep street and crowded way.
But in the train you might discern
Dark lowering brow and visage stern;
There nobles mourn'd their pride restrain'd,
And the mean burgher's joys disdain'd;
And chiefs, who, hostage for their clan,

Were each from home a banish'd man,
There thought upon their own grey tower,
Their waving woods, their feudal power,
And deem'd themselves a shameful part
Of pageant which they cursed in heart.

XXII

Now, in the Castle-park, drew out
Their chequer'd bands the joyous rout.
There morricers, with bell at heel,
And blade in hand, their mazes wheel;
But chief, beside the butts, there stand
Bold Robin Hood and all his band—
Friar Tuck with quarterstaff and cowl,
Old Scathelocke with his surly scowl,
Maid Marion, fair as ivory bone,
Scarlet, and Mutch, and Little John;
Their bugles challenge all that will,
In archery to prove their skill.
The Douglas bent a bow of might;
His first shaft centered in the white,
And when in turn he shot again,
His second split the first in twain.
From the King's hand must Douglas take
A silver dart, the archer's stake;
Fondly he watch'd, with watery eye,
Some answering glance of sympathy;
No kind emotion made reply!
Indifferent as to archer wight,
The monarch gave the arrow bright.

XXIII

Now, clear the ring! for, hand to hand,
The manly wrestlers take their stand.
Two o'er the rest superior rose,
And proud demanded mightier foes,
Nor call'd in vain; for Douglas came.
—For life is Hugh of Larbert lame;
Scarce better John of Alloa's fare,
Whom senseless home his comrades bear.
Prize of the wrestling match, the King
To Douglas gave a golden ring,
While coldly glanced his eye of blue,
As frozen drop of wintry dew.
Douglas would speak, but in his breast
His struggling soul his words suppress'd;

Indignant then he turn'd him where
Their arms the brawny yeomen bare,
To hurl the massive bar in air.
When each his utmost strength had shown,
The Douglas rent an earth-fast stone
From its deep bed, then heaved it high,
And sent the fragment through the sky
A rood beyond the farthest mark.
And still in Stirling's royal park,
The grey-hair'd sires, who know the past,
To strangers point the Douglas-cast,
And moralize on the decay
Of Scottish strength in modern day.

XXIV

The vale with loud applauses rang,
The Ladies' Rock sent back the clang.
The King, with look unmoved, bestow'd
A purse well-fill'd with pieces broad.
Indignant smiled the Douglas proud,
And threw the gold among the crowd,
Who now, with anxious wonder, scan,
And sharper glance, the dark grey man;
Till whispers rose among the throng,
That heart so free, and hand so strong,
Must to the Douglas blood belong;
The old men mark'd, and shook the head,
To see his hair with silver spread;
And wink'd aside, and told each son,
Of feats upon the English done,
Ere Douglas of the stalwart hand
Was exiled from his native land.
The women praised his stately form,
Though wreck'd by many a winter's storm;
The youth with awe and wonder saw
His strength surpassing Nature's law.
Thus judged, as is their wont, the crowd,
Till murmur rose to clamours loud.
But not a glance from that proud ring
Of peers, who circled round the King,
with Douglas held communion kind,
Or call'd the banish'd man to mind;
No, not from those who, at the chase,
Once held his side the honour'd place,
Begirt his board, and, in the field,
Found safety underneath his shield;

For he, whom royal eyes disown,
When was his form to courtiers known!

XXV

The Monarch saw the gambols flag,
And bade let loose a gallant stag,
Whose pride, the holiday to crown,
Two favourite greyhounds should pull down,
That venison free, and Bourdeaux wine,
Might serve the archery to dine.
But Lufra, whom from Douglas' side
Nor bribe nor threat could e'er divide,
The fleetest hound in all the North,
Brave Lufra saw, and darted forth.
She left the royal hounds mid-way,
And dashing on the antler'd prey,
Sunk her sharp muzzle in his flank,
And deep the flowing life-blood drank.
The King's stout huntsman saw the sport
By strange intruder broken short,
Came up, and with his leash unbound,
In anger struck the noble hound.
The Douglas had endured, that morn,
The King's cold look, the nobles' scorn,
And last, and worst to spirit proud,
Had borne the pity of the crowd;
But Lufra had been fondly bred,
To share his board, to watch his bed,
And oft would Ellen Lufra's neck
In maiden glee with garlands deck;
They were such playmates, that with name
Of Lufra, Ellen's image came.
His stifled wrath is brimming high,
In darken'd brow and flashing eye;
As waves before the bark divide,
The crowd gave way before his stride;
Needs but a buffet and no more,
The groom lies senseless in his gore.
Such blow no other hand could deal,
Though gauntleted in glove of steel.

XXVI

Then clamour'd loud the royal train,
And brandish'd swords and staves amain.
But stern the Baron's warning—"Back!
Back, on your lives, ye menial pack!

Beware the Douglas. Yes! behold,
King James! the Douglas, doom'd of old,
And vainly sought for near and far,
A victim to atone the war,
A willing victim, now attends,
Nor craves thy grace but for his friends."
"Thus is my clemency repaid?
Presumptuous lord!" the monarch said;
"Of thy mis-proud ambitious clan,
Thou, James of Bothwell, wert the man,
The only man, in whom a foe
My woman-mercy would not know:
But shall Monarch's presence brook
Injurious blow, and haughty look?
What ho! the Captain of our Guard!
Give the offender fitting ward.
Break off the sports!"—for tumult rose,
And yeomen 'gan to bend their bows.
"Break off the sports!" he said, and frown'd,
"And bid our horsemen clear the ground."

XXVII

Then uproar wild and misarray
Marr'd the fair form of festal day.
The horsemen prick'd among the crowd,
Repell'd by threats and insult loud;
To earth are borne the old and weak,
The timorous fly, the women shriek;
With flint, with shaft, with staff, with bar,
The hardier urge tumultuous war.
At once round Douglas darkly sweep
The royal spears in circle deep,
And slowly scale the pathway steep;
While on the rear in thunder pour
The rabble with disorder'd roar.
With grief the noble Douglas saw
The Commons rise against the law,
And to the leading soldier said,
"Sir John of Hyndford! 'twas my blade
That knighthood on thy shoulder laid;
For that good deed, permit me then
A word with these misguided men.

XXVIII

"Hear, gentle friends! ere yet for me,
Ye break the bands of fealty.

My life, my honour, and my cause,
I tender free to Scotland's laws.
Are these so weak as must require
The aid of your misguided ire?
Or, if I suffer causeless wrong,
Is then my selfish rage so strong,
My sense of public weal so low,
That, for mean vengeance on a foe,
Those cords of love I should unbind,
Which knit my country and my kind?
Oh no! Believe, in yonder tower
It will not soothe my captive hour
To know those spears our foes should dread
For me in kindred gore are red;
To know, in fruitless brawl begun,
For me that mother wails her son;
For me that widow's mate expires;
For me that orphans weep their sires;
That patriots mourn insulted laws,
And curse the Douglas for the cause.
O let your patience ward such ill,
And keep your right to love me still!"

XXIX

The crowd's wild fury sunk again
In tears, as tempests melt in rain.
With lifted hands and eyes, they pray'd
For blessings on his generous head,
Who for his country felt alone,
And prized her blood beyond his own.
Old men, upon the verge of life,
Bless'd him who staid the civil strife;
And mothers held their babes on high,
The self-devoted Chief to spy,
Triumphant over wrongs and ire,
To whom the prattlers owed a sire:
Even the rough soldier's heart was moved;
As if behind some bier beloved,
With trailing arms and drooping head,
The Douglas up the hill he led,
And at the Castle's battled verge,
With sighs resign'd his honour'd charge.

XXX

The offended Monarch rode apart,
With bitter thought and swelling heart,

And would not now vouchsafe again
Through Stirling streets to lead his train.
"O Lennox, who would wish to rule
This changeling crowd, this common fool?
Hear'st thou," he said, "the loud acclaim,
With which they shout the Douglas name?
With like acclaim, the vulgar throat
Strain'd for King James their morning note;
With like acclaim they hail'd the day
When first I broke the Douglas' sway;
And like acclaim would Douglas greet,
If he could hurl me from my seat.
Who o'er the herd would wish to reign,
Fantastic, fickle, fierce, and vain?
Vain as the leaf upon the stream,
And fickle as a changeful dream;
Fantastic as a woman's mood,
And fierce as Frenzy's fever'd blood.
Thou many-headed monster-thing,
O who would wish to be thy king!

XXXI

"But soft! what messenger of speed
Spurs hitherward his panting steed?
I guess his cognizance afar—
What from our cousin, John of Mar?"
"He prays, my liege, your sports keep bound
Within the safe and guarded ground:
For some foul purpose yet unknown—
Most sure for evil to the throne—
The outlaw'd Chieftain, Roderick Dhu,
Has summon'd his rebellious crew;
'Tis said, in James of Bothwell's aid
These loose banditti stand array'd.
The Earl of Mar, this morn, from Doune,
To break their muster march'd, and soon
Your grace will hear of battle fought;
But earnestly the Earl besought,
Till for such danger he provide,
With scanty train you will not ride."

XXXII

"Thou warn'st me I have done amiss;
I should have earlier look'd to this:
I lost it in this bustling day.

Retrace with speed thy former way;
Spare not for spoiling of thy steed,
The best of mine shall be thy meed.
Say to our faithful Lord of Mar,
We do forbid the intended war:
Roderick, this morn, in single fight,
Was made our prisoner by a knight;
And Douglas hath himself and cause
Submitted to our kingdom's laws.
The tidings of their leaders lost
Will soon dissolve the mountain host,
Nor would we that the vulgar feel,
For their Chief's crimes, avenging steel.
Bear Mar our message, Braco: fly!"
He turn'd his steed,—"My liege, I hie,
Yet, ere I cross this lily lawn,
I fear the broadswords will be drawn."
The turf the flying courser spurn'd,
And to his towers the King return'd.

        XXXIII
Ill with King James's mood, that day,
Suited gay feast and minstrel lay;
Soon were dismiss'd the courtly throng,
And soon cut short the festal song.
Nor less upon the sadden'd town
The evening sunk in sorrow down.
The burghers spoke of civil jar,
Of rumour'd feuds and mountain war,
Of Moray, Mar, and Roderick Dhu,
All up in arms:—the Douglas too,
They mourn'd him pent within the hold
"Where stout Earl William was of old,"
And there his word the speaker staid,
And finger on his lip he laid,
Or pointed to his dagger blade.
But jaded horsemen, from the west,
At evening to the Castle press'd;
And busy talkers said they bore
Tidings of fight on Katrine's shore;
At noon the deadly fray begun,
And lasted till the set of sun.
Thus giddy rumour shook the town,
Till closed the Night her pennons brown.

Canto Sixth THE GUARD-ROOM

I

The sun, awakening, through the smoky air
  Of the dark city casts a sullen glance,
Rousing each caitiff to his task of care,
  Of sinful man the sad inheritance;
Summoning revellers from the lagging dance,
  Scaring the prowling robber to his den;
Gilding on battled tower the warder's lance,
  And warning student pale to leave his pen,
And yield his drowsy eyes to the kind nurse of men.

What various scenes, and, O! what scenes of woe,
  Are witness'd by that red and struggling beam!
The fever'd patient, from his pallet low,
  Through crowded hospital beholds its stream;
The ruin'd maiden trembles at its gleam,
  The debtor wakes to thought of gyve and jail,
The love-lorn wretch starts from tormenting dream;
  The wakeful mother, by the glimmering pale,
Trims her sick infant's couch, and soothes his feeble wail.

II

At dawn the towers of Stirling rang
With soldier-step and weapon-clang,
While drums, with rolling note, foretell
Relief to weary sentinel.
Through narrow loop and casement barr'd,
The sunbeams sought the Court of Guard,
And, struggling with the smoky air,
Deaden'd the torches' yellow glare.
In comfortless alliance shone
The lights through arch of blacken'd stone,
And show'd wild shapes in garb of war,
Faces deform'd with beard and scar,
All haggard from the midnight watch,
And fever'd with the stern debauch;
For the oak table's massive board,
Flooded with wine, with fragments stored,
And beakers drain'd, and cups o'er-thrown,
Show'd in what sport the night had flown.
Some, weary, snored on floor and bench;
Some labour'd still their thirst to quench;
Some, chill'd with watching, spread their hands

O'er the huge chimney's dying brands,
While round them, or beside them flung,
At every step their harness rung.

III

These drew not for the fields the sword,
Like tenants of a feudal lord,
Nor own'd the patriarchal claim
Of Chieftain in their leader's name;
Adventurers they, from far who roved,
To live by battle which they loved.
There the Italian's clouded face,
The swarthy Spaniard's there you trace;
The mountain-loving Switzer there
More freely breathed in mountain-air;
The Fleming there despised the soil,
That paid so ill the labourer's toil;
Their rolls show'd French and German name;
And merry England's exiles came,
To share, with ill conceal'd disdain,
Of Scotland's pay the scanty gain.
All brave in arms, well train'd to wield
The heavy halberd, brand, and shield;
In camps licentious, wild, and bold;
In pillage fierce and uncontroll'd;
And now, by holytide and feast,
From rules of discipline released.

IV

They held debate of bloody fray,
Fought 'twixt Loch Katrine and Achray.
Fierce was their speech, and, 'mid their words,
Their hands oft grappled to their swords;
Nor sunk their tone to spare the ear
Of wounded comrades groaning near,
Whose mangled limbs, and bodies gored,
Bore token of the mountain sword,
Though, neighbouring to the Court of Guard,
Their prayers and feverish wails were heard;
Sad burden to the ruffian joke,
And savage oath by fury spoke!
At length up-started John of Brent,
A yeoman from the banks of Trent;
A stranger to respect or fear,
In peace a chaser of the deer,
In host a hardy mutineer,

But still the boldest of the crew,
When deed of danger was to do.
He grieved, that day, their games cut short,
And marr'd the dicer's brawling sport,
And shouted loud, "Renew the bowl!
And, while a merry catch I troll,
Let each the buxom chorus bear,
Like brethren of the brand and spear:—

V

SOLDIER'S SONG

" 'Our vicar still preaches that Peter and Poule
Laid a swinging long curse on the bonny brown bowl,
That there's wrath and despair in the jolly black-jack,
And the seven deadly sins in a flagon of sack;
Yet whoop, Barnaby! off with thy liquor,
Drink upsees out, and a fig for the vicar!

" 'Our vicar he calls it damnation to sip
The ripe ruddy dew of a woman's dear lip,
Says, that Beelzebub lurks in her kerchief so sly,
And Apollyon shoots darts from her merry black eye;
Yet whoop, Jack! kiss Gillian the quicker,
Till she bloom like a rose, and a fig for the vicar!

" 'Our vicar thus preaches—and why should he not?
For the dues of his cure are the placket and pot;
And 'tis right of his office poor laymen to lurch,
Who infringe the domains of our good Mother Church.
Yet whoop, bully-boys! off with your liquor,
Sweet Marjorie's the word, and a fig for the vicar!' "

VI

The warder's challenge, heard without,
Staid in mid-roar the merry shout.
A soldier to the portal went,—
"Here is old Bertram, sirs, of Ghent;
And, beat for jubilee the drum!
A maid and minstrel with him come."
Bertram, a Fleming, grey and scarr'd,
Was entering now the Court of Guard,
A harper with him, and in plaid
All muffled close, a mountain maid,
Who backward shrunk to 'scape the view

Of the loose scene and boisterous crew.
"What news?" they roar'd. "I only know,
From noon till eve we fought with foe,
As wild and as untameable
As the rude mountains where they dwell;
On both sides store of blood is lost,
Nor much success can either boast."
"But whence thy captives, friend? such spoil
As theirs must needs reward thy toil.
Old dost thou wax, and wars grow sharp;
Thou now hast glee-maiden and harp!
Get thee an ape, and trudge the land,
The leader of a juggler band."

VII

"No, comrade; no such fortune mine.
After the fight these sought our line,
That aged harper and the girl,
And, having audience of the Earl,
Mar bade I should purvey them steed,
And bring them hitherward with speed.
Forbear your mirth and rude alarm,
For none shall do them shame or harm."
"Hear ye his boast?" cried John of Brent,
Ever to strife and jangling bent;
"Shall he strike doe beside our lodge,
And yet the jealous niggard grudge
To pay the forester his fee?
I'll have my share, howe'er it be,
Despite of Moray, Mar, or thee."
Bertram his forward step withstood;
And, burning in his vengeful mood,
Old Allan, though unfit for strife,
Laid hand upon his dagger-knife;
But Ellen boldly stepp'd between,
And dropp'd at once the tartan screen:
So, from his morning cloud, appears
The sun of May, through summer tears.
The savage soldiery, amazed,
As on descended angel gazed;
Even hardy Brent, abash'd and tamed,
Stood half admiring, half ashamed.

VIII

Boldly she spoke, "Soldiers, attend!
My father was the soldier's friend;

Cheer'd him in camps, in marches led,
And with him in the battle bled.
Not from the valiant, or the strong,
Should exile's daughter suffer wrong."
Answer'd De Brent, most forward still
In every feat or good or ill—
"I shame me of the part I play'd:
And thou an outlaw's child, poor maid!
An outlaw I by forest laws,
And merry Needwood knows the cause.
Poor Rose—if Rose be living now"—
He wiped his iron eye and brow—
"Must bear such age, I think, as thou.
Hear ye, my mates;—I go to call
The Captain of our watch to hall:
There lies my halberd on the floor;
And he that steps my halberd o'er,
To do the maid injurious part,
My shaft shall quiver in his heart!
Beware loose speech, or jesting rough:
Ye all know John de Brent. Enough."

IX

Their Captain came, a gallant young,
(Of Tullibardine's house he sprung,)
Nor wore he yet the spurs of knight;
Gay with his mien, his humour light,
And, though by courtesy controll'd,
Forward his speech, his bearing bold,
The high-born maiden ill could brook
The scanning of his curious look
And dauntless eye;—and yet, in sooth,
Young Lewis was a generous youth.
But Ellen's lovely face and mien,
Ill suited to the garb and scene,
Might lightly bear construction strange,
And give loose fancy scope to range.
"Welcome to Stirling towers, fair maid!
Come ye to seek a champion's aid,
On palfrey white, with harper hoar,
Like errant damosel of yore?
Does thy high quest a knight require,
Or may the venture suit a squire?"
Her dark eye flash'd; she paused and sigh'd,
"O what have I to do with pride!
Through scenes of sorrow, shame, and strife,

A suppliant for a father's life,
I crave an audience of the King.
Behold, to back my suit, a ring,
The royal pledge of grateful claims,
Given by the Monarch to Fitz-James."

X

The signet-ring young Lewis took,
With deep respect and alter'd look;
And said, "This ring our duties own
And pardon, if to worth unknown,
In semblance mean obscurely veil'd,
Lady, in aught my folly fail'd.
Soon as the day flings wide his gates,
The King shall know what suitor waits.
Please you, meanwhile, in fitting bower
Repose you till his waking hour;
Female attendance shall obey
Your hest, for service or array.
Permit I marshall you the way."
But, ere she followed, with the grace
And open bounty of her race,
She bade her slender purse be shared
Among the soldiers of the guard.
The rest with thanks their guerdon took;
But Brent, with shy and awkward look,
On the reluctant maiden's hold
Forced bluntly back the proffer'd gold—
"Forgive a haughty English heart,
And O forget its ruder part!
The vacant purse shall be my share,
Which in my barret-cap I'll bear,
Perchance, in jeopardy of war,
Where gayer crests may keep afar."
With thanks ('twas all she could) the maid
His rugged courtesy repaid.

XI

When Ellen forth with Lewis went,
Allan made suit to John of Brent:
"My lady safe, O let your grace
Give me to see my master's face!
His minstrel I; to share his doom
Bound from the cradle to the tomb;
Tenth in descent, since first my sires
Waked for his noble house their lyres;

Nor one of all the race was known
But prized its weal above their own.
With the Chief's birth begins our care;
Our harp must soothe the infant heir,
Teach the youth tales of fight, and grace
His earliest feat of field or chase;
In peace, in war, our rank we keep,
We cheer his board, we soothe his sleep,
Nor leave him till we pour our verse,
A doleful tribute! o'er his hearse.
Then let me share his captive lot;
It is my right, deny it not!"
"Little we reck," said John of Brent,
"We Southern men, of long descent;
Nor wot we how a name, a word,
Makes clansmen vassals to a lord:
Yet kind my noble landlord's part,—
God bless the house of Beaudesert!
And, but I loved to drive the deer,
More than to guide the labouring steer,
I had not dwelt an outcast here.
Come, good old Minstrel, follow me;
Thy lord and Chieftain shalt thou see."

XII

Then, from a rusted iron hook,
A bunch of ponderous keys he took,
Lighted a torch, and Allan led
Through grated arch and passage dread;
Portals they pass'd, where, deep within,
Spoke prisoner's moan, and fetters' din;
Through rugged vaults, where, loosely stored,
Lay wheel, and axe, and headsman's sword;
And many an hideous engine grim,
For wrenching joint, and crushing limb,
By artist form'd, who deem'd it shame
And sin to give their work a name.
They halted at a low-brow'd porch,
And Brent to Allan gave the torch,
While bolt and chain he backward roll'd,
And made the bar unhasp its hold.
They enter'd: 'twas a prison-room
Of stern security and gloom,
Yet not a dungeon; for the day
Through lofty gratings found its way,
And rude and antique garniture

Deck'd the sad walls and oaken floor;
Such as the rugged days of old
Deem'd fit for captive noble's hold.
"Here," said De Brent, "thou mayst remain
Till the leech visit him again.
Strict in his charge, the wardens tell,
To tend the noble prisoner well."
Retiring then, the bolt he drew,
And the lock's murmurs growl'd anew.
Roused at the sound, from lowly bed
A captive feebly raised his head;
The wondering Minstrel look'd, and knew
Not his dear lord, but Roderick Dhu!
For, come from where Clan-Apline fought,
They, erring, deem'd the Chief he sought.

XIII

As the tall ship, whose lofty prore
Shall never stem the billows more,
Deserted by her gallant band,
Amid the breakers lies astrand,
So, on his couch, lay Roderick Dhu!
And oft his fever'd limbs he threw
In toss abrupt, as when her sides
Lie rocking in the advancing tides,
That shake her frame with ceaseless beat,
Yet cannot heave her from her seat;
O! how unlike her course at sea!
Or his free step on hill and lea!
Soon as the Minstrel he could scan,
"What of thy lady? of my clan?
My mother? Douglas? tell me all!
Have they been ruin'd in my fall?
Ah, yes! or wherefore art thou here?
Yet speak, speak boldly, do not fear."
(For Allan, who his mood well knew,
Was choked with grief and terror too.)—
"Who fought—who fled? Old man, be brief;
Some might—for they had lost their Chief.
Who basely live? who bravely died?"
"O, calm thee, Chief!" the Minstrel cried,
"Ellen is safe."—"For that, thank Heaven!"
"And hopes are for the Douglas given;
The Lady Margaret, too, is well;
And, for thy clan,—on field or fell,
Has never harp of minstrel told,

Of combat fought so true and bold.
Thy stately Pine is yet unbent,
Though many a goodly bough is rent."

XIV

The Chieftain rear'd his form on high,
And fever's fire was in his eye;
But ghastly, pale, and livid streaks
Chequer'd his swarthy brow and cheeks.
"Hark! Minstrel! I have heard thee play,
With measure bold, on festal day,
In yon lone isle, . . . again where ne'er
Shall harper play, or warrior hear! . . .
That sitrring air that peals on high,
O'er Dermid's race our victory.
Strike it! and then (for well thou canst)
Free from thy minstrel-spirit glanced,
Fling me the picture of the fight
When met my clan the Saxon might.
I'll listen, till my fancy hears
The clang of swords, the crash of spears!
These grates, these walls, shall vanish then,
For the fair field of fighting men,
And my free spirit burst away,
As if it soar'd from battle fray."
The trembling Bard with awe obey'd,
Slow on the harp his hand he laid;
But soon remembrance of the sight
He witness'd from the mountain's height,
With what old Bertram told at night,
Awaken'd the full power of song,
And bore him in career along—
As shallop launch'd on river's tide,
That slow and fearful leaves the side,
But, when it feels the middle stream,
Drives downward swift as lightning's beam:

XV

BATTLE OF BEAL' AN DUINE

"The Minstrel came once more to view
The eastern ridge of Benvenue,
For, ere he parted, he would say
Farewell to lovely Loch Achray:
Where shall he find, in foreign land,

So lone a lake, so sweet a strand!
  There is no breeze upon the fern,
    Nor ripple on the lake;
  Upon her eyry nods the erne,
    The deer has sought the brake;
  The small birds will not sing aloud,
    The springing trout lies still,
  So darkly glooms yon thunder cloud,
  That swathes, as with a purple shroud,
    Benledi's distant hill.
  Is it the thunder's solemn sound
    That mutters deep and dread,
  Or echoes from the groaning ground
    The warrior's measured tread?
  Is it the lightning's quivering glance
    That on the thicket streams,
  Or do they flash on spear and lance
    The sun's retiring beams?
I see the dagger-crest of Mar,
I see the Moray's silver star
Wave o'er the cloud of Saxon war,
That up the lake comes winding far!
  To hero bound for battle-strife,
    Or bard of martial lay,
  'Twere worth ten years of peaceful life,
    One glance at their array!

    XVI
  "Their light-arm'd archers far and near
    Survey'd the tangled ground;
  Their centre ranks, with pike and spear,
    A twilight forest frown'd;
  Their barbed horsemen, in the rear,
    The stern battalia crown'd.
  No cymbal clash'd, no clarion rang,
    Still were the pipe and drum;
  Save heavy tread, and armour's clang,
    The sullen march was dumb.
  There breathed no wind their crests to shake,
    Or wave their flags abroad;
  Scarce the frail aspen seem'd to quake,
    That shadow'd o'er their road.
  Their vaward scouts no tidings bring,
    Can rouse no lurking foe,
  Nor spy a trace of living thing,
    Save when they stirr'd the roe;

The host moves like a deep-sea wave,
  Where rise no rocks its pride to brave,
    High-swelling, dark, and slow.
The lake is pass'd, and now they gain
A narrow and a broken plain,
Before the Trosachs' rugged jaws;
And here the horse and spearmen pause,
While, to explore the dangerous glen,
Dive through the pass the archer-men.

XVII

"At once there rose so wild a yell
Within that dark and narrow dell,
As all the fiends, from heaven that fell,
Had peal'd the banner-cry of hell!
  Forth from the pass in tumult driven,
  Like chaff before the wind of heaven,
    The archery appear;
  For life! for life! their plight they ply—
  And shriek, and shout, and battle-cry,
  And plaids and bonnets waving high,
  And broadswords flashing to the sky,
    Are maddening in the rear.
Onward they drive, in dreadful race,
    Pursuers and pursued;
Before that tide of flight and chase,
How shall it keep its rooted place,
    The spearmen's twilight wood?
'Down, down,' cried Mar, 'your lances down!
    Bear back both friend and foe!'
Like reeds before the tempest's frown,
That serried grove of lances brown
    At once lay levell'd low;
And closely shouldering side to side,
The bristling ranks the onset bide.
'We'll quell the savage mountaineer,
    As their Tinchel cows the game!
They come as fleet as forest deer,
    We'll drive them back as tame.'

XVIII

"Bearing before them, in their course,
The relics of the archer force,
Like wave with crest of sparkling foam,
Right onward did Clan-Alpine come.
  Above the tide, each broadsword bright

Was brandishing like beam of light,
    Each targe was dark below;
And with the ocean's mighty swing,
When heaving to the tempest's wing,
    They hurl'd them on the foe.
I heard the lance's shivering crash,
As when the whirlwind rends the ash,
I heard the broadsword's deadly clang,
As if an hundred anvils rang!
But Moray wheel'd his rearward rank
Of horsemen on Clan-Alpine's flank,
    'My banner-man, advance!
I see,' he cried, 'their columns shake.
Now, gallants! for your ladies' sake,
    Upon them with the lance!'
The horsemen dash'd among the rout,
    As deer break through the broom;
Their steeds are stout, their swords are out,
    They soon make lightsome room.
Clan-Alpine's best are backward borne!
    Where, where was Roderick then?
One blast upon his bugle-horn
    Were worth a thousand men!
And refluent through the pass of fear,
    The battle's tide was pour'd;
Vanish'd the Saxon's struggling spear,
    Vanish'd the mountain-sword.
As Bracklinn's chasm, so black and steep,
    Receives her roaring linn,
As the dark caverns of the deep
    Suck the wild whirlpool in,
So did the deep and darksome pass
Devour the battle's mingled mass:
None linger now upon the plain,
Save those who ne'er shall fight again.

XIX

"Now westward rolls the battle's din,
That deep and doubling pass within.
Minstrel, away, the work of fate
Is bearing on: its issue wait,
Where the rude Trosachs' dread defile
Opens on Katrine's lake and isle.
Grey Benvenue I soon repass'd,
Loch Katrine lay beneath me cast.
    The sun is set; the clouds are met,

    The lowering scowl of heaven
  An inky hue of livid blue
    To the deep lake has given;
Strange gusts of wind from mountain-glen
Swept o'er the lake, then sunk agen.
I heeded not the eddying surge,
Mine eye but saw the Trosachs' gorge,
Mine ear but heard the sullen sound,
Which like an earthquake shook the ground,
And spoke the stern and desperate strife
That parts not but with parting life,
Seeming, to minstrel ear, to toll
The dirge of many a passing soul.
Nearer it comes; the dim-wood glen
The martial flood disgorged agen,
    But not in mingled tide;
The plaided warriors of the North
High on the mountain thunder forth
    And overhang its side;
While by the lake below appears
The dark'ning cloud of Saxon spears.
At weary bay each shatter'd band,
Eyeing their foemen, sternly stand;
Their banners stream like tatter'd sail,
That flings its fragments to the gale,
And broken arms and disarray
Mark'd the fell havoc of the day.

XX

"Viewing the mountain's ridge askance,
The Saxon stood in sullen trance,
Till Moray pointed with his lance,
    And cried—'Behold yon isle!
See! none are left to guard its strand,
But women weak, that wring the hand:
'Tis there of yore the robber band
    Their booty wont to pile;
My purse, with bonnet-pieces store,
To him will swim a bow-shot o'er,
And loose a shallop from the shore.
Lightly we'll tame the war-wolf then,
Lords of his mate, and brood, and den.'
Forth from the ranks a spearman sprung,
On earth his casque and corslet run,
    He plunged him in the wave:
All saw the deed, the purpose knew,

And to their clamours Benvenue
  A mingled echo gave;
The Saxons shout, their mate to cheer,
The helpless females scream for fear,
And yells for rage the mountaineer.
'Twas then, as by the outcry riven,
Pour'd down at once the lowering heaven:
A whirlwind swept Loch Katrine's breast,
Her billows rear'd their snowy crest.
Well for the swimmer swell'd they high,
To mar the Highland marksman's eye;
For round him shower'd, 'mid rain and hail,
The vengeful arrows of the Gael.
In vain; he nears the isle, and lo!
His hand is on a shallop's bow.
Just then a flash of lightning came,
It tinged the waves and strand with flame;
I mark'd Duncraggan's widow'd dame,
Behind an oak I saw her stand,
A naked dirk gleam'd in her hand:
It darken'd; but, amid the moan
Of waves, I heard a dying groan;
Another flash!—the spearman floats
A weltering corse beside the boats,
And the stern matron o'er him stood,
  Her hand and dagger streaming blood.

XXI

" 'Revenge! revenge!' the Saxons cried,
The Gaels' exulting shout replied.
Despite the elemental rage,
Again they hurried to engage;
But, ere they closed in desperate fight,
Bloody with spurring came a knight,
Sprung from his horse, and, from a crag,
Waved 'twixt the hosts a milk-white flag.
Clarion and trumpet by his side
Rung forth a truce-note high and wide,
While, in the Monarch's name, afar
An herald's voice forbade the war,
For Bothwell's lord, and Roderick bold,
Were both, he said, in captive hold."

But here the lay made sudden stand!
The harp escaped the Minstrel's hand!
Oft had he stolen a glance, to spy

How Roderick brook'd his minstrelsy:
At first, the Chieftain, to the chime,
With lifted hand, kept feeble time;
That motion ceased, yet feeling strong
Varied his look as changed the song;
At length, no more his deafen'd ear
The minstrel melody can hear;
His face grows sharp, his hands are clench'd,
As if some pang his heart-strings wrench'd;
Set are his teeth, his facing eye
Is sternly fix'd on vacancy;
Thus, motionless, and moanless, drew
His parting breath, stout Roderick Dhu!
Old Allan-bane look'd on aghast,
While grim and still his spirit pass'd:
But when he saw that life was fled,
He pour'd his wailing o'er the dead:

XXII

LAMENT

"And art thou cold and lowly laid,
Thy foeman's dread, thy people's aid,
Breadalbane's boast, Clan-Alpine's shade!
For thee shall none a requiem say?
For thee, who loved the minstrel's lay,
For thee, of Bothwell's house the stay,
The shelter of her exiled line,
E'en in this prison-house of thine,
I'll wait for Alpine's honour'd Pine!

"What groans shall yonder valleys fill!
What shrieks of grief shall rend yon hill!
What tears of burning rage shall thrill,
When mourns thy tribe thy battles done,
Thy fall before the race was won,
Thy sword ungirt ere set of sun!
There breathes no clansman of thy line,
But would have given his life for thine.
O woe for Alpine's honour'd Pine!

"Sad was thy lot on mortal stage!
The captive thrush may brook the cage,
The prison'd eagle dies for rage.
Brave spirit, do not scorn my strain!

And, when its notes awake again,
Even she, so long beloved in vain,
Shall with my harp her voice combine,
And mix her woe and tears with mine,
To wail Clan-Alpine's honour'd Pine."

XXIII

Ellen the while with bursting heart
Remain'd in lordly bower apart,
Where play'd with many-colour'd gleams,
Through storied pane the rising beams.
In vain on gilded roof they fall,
And lighten'd up a tapestried wall,
And for her use a menial train
A rich collation spread in vain.
The banquet proud, the chamber gay,
Scarce drew one curious glance astray;
Or, if she look'd, 'twas but to say,
With better omen dawn'd the day
In that lone isle, where waved on high
The dun-deer's hide for canopy;
Where oft her noble father shared
The simple meal her care prepared,
While Lufra, crouching by her side
Her station claim'd with jealous pride,
And Douglas, bent on woodland game,
Spoke of the chase to Malcolm Græme,
Whose answer, oft at random made,
The wandering of his thoughts betray'd.
Those who such simple joys have known,
Are taught to prize them when they're gone.
But sudden, see, she lifts her head!
The window seeks with cautious tread.
What distant music has the power
To win her in this woeful hour!
'Twas from a turret that o'erhung
Her latticed bower, the strain was sung:

XXIV

LAY OF THE IMPRISONED HUNTSMAN

"My hawk is tired of perch and hood,
My idle greyhound loathes his food,
My horse is weary of his stall,
And I am sick of captive thrall.

"I wish I were, as I have been,
Hunting the hart in forest green,
With bending bow and bloodhound free,
For that's the life is meet for me.

"I hate to learn the ebb of time
From yon dull steeple's drowsy chime,
Or mark it as the sunbeams crawl,
Inch after inch, along the wall.

"The lark was wont my matins ring,
The sable rook my vespers sing;
These towers, although a king's they be,
Have not a hall of joy for me.

"No more at dawning morn I rise,
And sun myself in Ellen's eyes,
Drive the fleet deer the forest through,
And homeward wend with evening dew;

"A blithesome welcome blithely meet,
And lay my trophies at her feet,
While fled the eve on wing of glee:
That life is lost to love and me!"

XXV

The heart-sick lay was hardly said,
The list'ner had not turn'd her head,
It trickled still, the starting tear,
When light a footstep struck her ear,
And Snowdoun's graceful knight was near.
She turn'd the hastier, lest again
The prisoner should renew his strain.
"O welcome, brave Fitz-James!" she said;
"How may an almost orphan maid
Pay the deep debt"—"O say not so!
To me no gratitude you owe.
Not mine, alas! the boon to give,
And bid thy noble father live;
I can but be thy guide, sweet maid,
With Scotland's king thy suit to aid.
No tyrant he, though ire and pride
May lay his better mood aside.
Come, Ellen, come! 'tis more than time,
He holds his court at morning prime."
With beating heart, and bosom wrung,

As to a brother's arm she clung.
Gently he dried the falling tear,
And gently whisper'd hope and cheer:
Her faltering steps half led, half staid,
Through gallery fair, and high arcade,
Till, at his touch, its wings of pride
A portal arch unfolded wide.

XXVI

Within 'twas brilliant all and light,
A thronging scene of figures bright;
It glow'd on Ellen's dazzled sight,
As when the setting sun has given
Ten thousand hues to summer even,
And from their tissue fancy frames
Aërial knights and fairy dames.
Still by Fitz-James her footing staid;
A few faint steps she forward made,
Then slow her drooping head she raised,
And fearful round the presence gazed;
For him she sought, who own'd this state,
The dreaded prince whose will was fate.
She gazed on many a princely port,
Might well have ruled a royal court;
On many a splendid garb she gazed,
Then turn'd bewilder'd and amazed,
For all stood bare; and, in the room,
Fitz-James alone wore cap and plume.
To him each lady's look was lent;
On him each courtier's eye was bent;
Midst furs, and silks, and jewels sheen,
He stood, in simple Lincoln green,
The centre of the glittering ring.
And Snowdoun's Knight is Scotland's King!

XXVII

As wreath of snow, on mountain-breast,
Slides from the rock that gave it rest,
Poor Ellen glided from her stay,
And at the Monarch's feet she lay;
No word her choking voice commands;
She show'd the ring, she clasp'd her hands.
O! not a moment could he brook,
The generous prince, that suppliant look!
Gently he raised her; and, the while,
Check'd with a glance the circle's smile;

Graceful, but grave, her brow he kiss'd,
And bade her terrors be dismiss'd:
"Yes, fair, the wandering poor Fitz-James
The fealty of Scotland claims.
To him thy woes, thy wishes, bring;
He will redeem his signet ring.
Ask nought for Douglas; yester even,
His prince and he have much forgiven.
Wrong hath he had from slanderous tongue,
I, from his rebel kinsmen, wrong.
We would not, to the vulgar crowd,
Yield what they craved with clamour loud:
Calmly we heard and judged his cause,
Our council aided, and our laws.
I stanch'd thy father's death-feud stern
With stout De Vaux and Grey Glencairn;
And Bothwell's Lord henceforth we own
The friend and bulwark of our Throne.
But, lovely infidel, how now?
What clouds thy misbelieving brow?
Lord James of Douglas, lend thine aid;
Thou must confirm this doubting maid."

XXVIII

Then forth the noble Douglas sprung,
And on his neck his daughter hung.
The Monarch drank, that happy hour,
The sweetest, holiest draught of Power,
When it can say, with godlike voice,
Arise, sad Virtue, and rejoice!
Yet would not James the general eye
On Nature's raptures long should pry;
He stepp'd between—"Nay, Douglas, nay,
Steal not my proselyte away!
The riddle 'tis my right to read,
That brought this happy chance to speed.
Yes, Ellen, when disguised I stray
In life's more low but happier way,
'Tis under name which veils my power,
Nor falsely veils, for Stirling's tower
Of yore the name of Snowdoun claims,
And Normans call me James Fitz-James.
Thus watch I o'er insulted laws,
Thus learn to right the injured cause."
Then, in a tone apart and low,—
"Ah, little traitress! none must know

What idle dream, what lighter thought,
What vanity full dearly bought,
Join'd to thine eye's dark witchcraft, drew
My spell-bound steps to Benvenue,
In dangerous hour, and all but gave
Thy Monarch's life to mountain glaive!"—
Aloud he spoke—"Thou still dost hold
That little talisman of gold,
Pledge of my faith, Fitz-James's ring;
What seeks fair Ellen of the King?"

XXIX

Full well the conscious maiden guess'd
He probed the weakness of her breast;
But, with that consciousness, there came
A lightening of her fears for Græme
And more she deem'd the Monarch's ire
Kindled 'gainst him, who, for her sire,
Rebellious broadsword boldly drew;
And, to her generous feeling true,
She craved the grace of Roderick Dhu.
"Forbear thy suit: the King of kings
Alone can stay life's parting wings:
I know his heart, I know his hand,
Have shared his cheer, and proved his brand:
My fairest earldom would I give
To bid Clan-Alpine's Chieftain live!
Hast thou no other boon to crave?
No other captive friend to save?"
Blushing, she turn'd her from the King,
And to the Douglas gave the ring,
As if she wish'd her sire to speak
The suit that stain'd her glowing cheek.—
"Nay, then, my pledge has lost its force,
And stubborn justice holds her course.
Malcom, come forth!" And at the word,
Down kneel'd the Græme to Scotland's Lord.
"For thee, rash youth, no suppliant sues,
From thee may Vengeance claim her dues,
Who, nurtured underneath our smile,
Hast paid our care by treacherous wile,
And sought, amid thy faithful clan,
A refuge for an outlaw'd man,
Dishonouring thus thy loyal name.
Fetters and warder for the Græme!"
His chain of gold the King unstrung,

The links o'er Malcolm's neck he flung,
Then gently drew the glittering band,
And laid the clasp on Ellen's hand.

Harp of the North, farewell! The hills grow dark,
  On purple peaks a deeper shade descending;
In twilight copse the glow-worm lights her spark,
  The deer, half-seen, are to the covert wending.
Resume thy wizard elm! the fountain lending,
  And the wild breeze, thy wilder minstrelsy;
Thy numbers sweet with nature's vespers blending,
  With distant echo from the fold and lea,
And herd-boy's evening pipe, and hum of housing bee.

Yet once again farewell, thou Minstrel harp!
  Yet once again forgive my feeble sway,
And little reck I of the censure sharp
  May idly cavil at an idle lay.
Much have I owed thy strains on life's long way,
  Through secret woes the world has never known,
When on the weary night dawn'd wearier day,
  And bitterer was the grief devour'd alone.
That I o'erlive such woes, Enchantress! is thine own.

Hark! as my lingering footsteps slow retire,
  Some Spirit of the Air has waked thy string!
'Tis now a seraph bold, with touch of fire,
  'Tis now the brush of Fairy's frolic wing.
Receding now, the dying numbers ring
  Fainter and fainter down the rugged dell,
And now the mountain breezes scarcely bring
  A wandering witch-note of the distant spell—
And now, 'tis silent all!—Enchantress, fare thee well!

Marmion

INTRODUCTION TO THE EDITION OF 1830

What I have to say respecting this poem may be briefly told. In the Introduction to *The Lady of the Last Minstrel*, I have mentioned the circumstances, so far as my literary life is concerned, which induced me to resign the active pursuit of an honourable profession, for the more precarious resources of literature. My appointment to the Sheriffdom of Selkirk called for a change of residence. I left, therefore, the pleasant cottage I had upon the side of the Esk, for the "pleasanter banks of the Tweed," in order to comply with the law, which requires that the Sheriff shall be resident, at least during a certain number of months, within his jurisdiction. We found a delightful retirement, by my becoming the tenant of my intimate friend and cousin-german, Colonel Russell, in his mansion of Ashestiel, which was unoccupied, during his absence on military service in India. The house was adequate to our accommodation, and the exercise of a limited hospitality. The situation is uncommonly beautiful, by the side of a fine river, whose streams are there very favourable for angling, surrounded by the remains of natural woods, and by hills abounding in game. In point of society, according to the heartfelt phrase of Scripture, we dwelt "amongst our own people"; and as the distance from the metropolis was only thirty miles, we were not out of reach of our Edinburgh friends, in which city we spent the terms of the summer and winter Sessions of the Court, that is, five or six months in the year.

An important circumstance had, about the same time, taken place in my life. Hopes had been held out to me from an influential quarter, of a nature to relieve me from the anxiety which I must have otherwise felt, as one upon the precarious tenure of whose own life rested the principal prospects of his family, and especially as one who had necessarily some dependence upon the favour of the public, which is proverbially capricious; though it is but justice to add, that, in my own case, I have not found it so. Mr. Pitt had expressed a wish to my personal friend, the Right Honourable William Dundas, now Lord Clerk Register of Scotland, that some fitting opportunity should be taken to be of service to me; and as my views and wishes pointed to a future rather than an immediate provision, an opportunity of accomplishing this was soon found. One of the Principal Clerks of Session, as they are called (official persons who occupy an important and responsible situation, and enjoy a considerable income), who had served upwards of thirty years, felt himself, from age, and the infirmity of deafness with which it was accompanied, desirous of retiring from his official situation. As the law then stood, such official persons were entitled to bargain with their successors, either for a sum of money, which was usually a considerable one, or for an interest in the emoluments of the office during their life. My predecessor, whose services had been unusually meritorious, stipulated for the emoluments of his office during his life, while I should enjoy the survivorship, on the condition that I discharged the duties of the office in the meantime. Mr. Pitt, however, having died in the interval, his administration was dissolved, and was succeeded by that known by the name of the Fox and Grenville Ministry. My affair was so far completed, that my commission lay in the office subscribed by his Majesty; but, from hurry or mistake the interest of my predecessor was not expressed in it, as had been usual in such cases. Although, therefore, it only required payment of the fees, I could not in honour take out the commission in the present state, since, in the event of my dying before him, the gentleman whom I succeeded must have lost the vested interest which he had stipulated to retain. I had the honour of an interview with Earl Spencer on the subject, and he, in the most handsome manner, gave directions that the commission should issue as originally intended; adding, that the matter having received the royal assent, he regarded only as a claim of justice what he would have willingly done as an act of favour. I never saw Mr. Fox on this, or on any other occasion, and never made any application to him, conceiving that in doing so I might have been supposed to express political opinions contrary to those which I had always professed. In his private capacity, there is no man to whom I would have been more proud to owe an obligation, had I been so distinguished.

By this arrangement I obtained the survivorship of an office, the emoluments of which were fully adequate to my wishes; and as the law respecting the mode of providing for superannuated officers was, about five or six years after, altered from that which admitted the arrangement of assistant and successor, my colleague very handsomely took the opportunity of the alteration, to accept of the retiring annuity provided in such cases, and admitted me to the full benefit of the office.

But although the certainty of succeeding to a considerable

income, at the time I obtained it, seemed to assure me of a quiet harbour in my old age, I did not escape my share of inconvenience from the contrary tides and currents by which we are so often encountered in our journey through life. Indeed, the publication of my next poetical attempt was prematurely accelerated, from one of those unpleasant accidents which can neither be foreseen nor avoided.

I had formed the prudent resolution to endeavour to bestow a little more labour than I had yet done on my productions, and to be in no hurry again to announce myself as a candidate for literary fame. Accordingly, particular passages of a poem, which was finally called *Marmion*, were laboured with a good deal of care, by one by whom much care was seldom bestowed. Whether the work was worth the labour or not, I am no competent judge; but I may be permitted to say, that the period of its composition was a very happy one in my life; so much so, that I remember with pleasure, at this moment, some of the spots in which particular passages were composed. . . .

The misfortunes of a near relation and friend, which happened at this time, led me to alter my prudent determination, which had been to use great precaution in sending this poem into the world; and made it convenient at least, if not absolutely necessary, to hasten its publication. The publishers of *The Lay of the Last Minstrel*, emboldened by the success of that poem, willingly offered a thousand pounds for *Marmion*. The transaction being no secret, afforded Lord Byron, who was then at general war with all who blacked paper, an apology for including me in his satire, entitled "English Bards and Scotch Reviewers." I never could conceive how an arrangement between an author and his publishers, if satisfactory to the persons concerned, could afford matter of censure to any third party. I had taken no unusual or ungenerous means of enhancing the value of my merchandise—I had never higgled a moment about the bargain, but accepted at once what I considered the handsome offer of my publishers. These gentlemen, at least, were not of opinion that they had been taken advantage of in the transaction, which indeed was one of their own framing; on the contrary, the sale of the poem was so far beyond their expectation, as to induce them to supply the Author's cellars with what is always an acceptable present to a young Scottish housekeeper, namely, a hogshead of excellent claret.

The poem was finished in too much haste to allow me an opportunity of softening down, if not removing, some of its most prominent defects. The nature of Marmion's guilt, although similar instances were found, and might be quoted, as existing in feudal times, was nevertheless not sufficiently peculiar to be indicative of the character of the period, forgery being the crime of a commercial, rather than a proud and warlike age. This gross defect ought to have been remedied or palliated. Yet I suffered the tree to lie as it had fallen. I remember my friend, Dr. Leyden, then in the East, wrote me a furious remonstrance on the subject. I have, nevertheless, always been of opinion, that corrections, however in themselves judicious have a bad effect—after publication. An author is never so decidedly condemned as on his own confession, and may long find apologists and partisans, until he gives up his own cause. I was not, therefore, inclined to afford matter for censure out of my own admissions; and, by good fortune, the novelty of the subject, and, if I may say so, some force and vivacity of description, were allowed to atone for many imperfections. Thus the second experiment on the public patience, generally the most perilous—for the public are then most apt to judge with rigour, what in the first instance they had received, perhaps, with imprudent generosity—was in my case decidedly successful. I had the good fortune to pass this ordeal favourably, and the return of sales before me makes the copies amount to thirty-six thousand printed between 1808 and 1825, besides a considerable sale since that period. I shall here pause upon the subject of *Marmion*, and, in a few prefatory words to *The Lady of the Lake*, the last poem of mine which obtained eminent success, I will continue the task which I have imposed on myself respecting the origin of my productions.

ABBOTSFORD, APRIL, 1830

Marmion

Canto First   THE CASTLE

I

Day set on Norham's castled steep,
And Tweed's fair river, broad and deep,
  And Cheviot's mountains lone:
The battled towers, the donjon keep,
The loophole grates, where captives weep,
The flanking walls that round it sweep,
  In yellow lustre shone.
The warriors on the turrets high,
Moving athwart the evening sky,
  Seem'd forms of giant height:
Their armour, as it caught the rays,
Flash'd back again the western blaze,
  In lines of dazzling light.

II

St. George's banner, broad and gay,
Now faded, as the fading ray
  Less bright, and less, was flung;
The evening gale had scarce the power
To wave it on the Donjon Tower,
  So heavily it hung.
The scouts had parted on their search,
  The Castle gates were barr'd;
Above the gloomy portal arch,
Timing his footsteps to a march,
  The Warder kept his guard;
Low humming, as he paced along,
Some ancient Border gathering song.

III

A distant trampling sound he hears;
He looks abroad, and soon appears
O'er Horncliff-hill a plump of spears
  Beneath a pennon gay;
A horseman, darting from the crowd,
Like lightning from a summer cloud,

Spurs on his mettled courser proud,
  Before the dark array.
Beneath the sable palisade,
That clos'd the Castle barricade,
  His bugle horn he blew;
The warder hasted from the wall,
And warn'd the Captain in the hall,
  For well the blast he knew;
And joyfully that knight did call,
To sewer, squire, and seneschal.

IV

"Now broach ye a pipe of Malvoisie,
  Bring pasties of the doe,
And quickly make the entrance free,
And bid my heralds ready be,
And every minstrel sound his glee,
  And all our trumpets blow;
And, from the platform, spare ye not
To fire a noble salvo-shot;
  LORD MARMION waits below!"
Then to the Castle's lower ward
  Sped forty yeomen tall,
The iron-studded gates unbarr'd,
Rais'd the portcullis' ponderous guard,
The lofty palisade unsparr'd
  And let the drawbridge fall.

V

Along the bridge Lord Marmion rode,
Proudly his red-roan charger trode,
His helm hung at the saddlebow;
Well by his visage you might know
He was a stalworth knight, and keen,
And had in many a battle been;
The scar on his brown cheek reveal'd
A token true of Bosworth field;
His eyebrow dark, and eye of fire,
Show'd spirit proud, and prompt to ire;
Yet lines of thought upon his cheek
Did deep design and counsel speak.
His forehead, by his casque worn bare,
His thick mustache, and curly hair,
Coal-black, and grizzled here and there,
  But more through toil than age;
His square-turn'd joints, and strength of limb,

Show'd him no carpet knight so trim,
But in close fight a champion grim,
  In camps a leader sage.

VI

Well was he arm'd from head to heel,
In mail and plate of Milan steel;
But his strong helm, of mighty cost,
Was all with burnish'd gold emboss'd;
Amid the plumage of the crest,
A falcon hover'd on her nest,
With wings outspread, and forward breast;
E'en such a falcon, on his shield,
Soar'd sable in an azure field:
The golden legend bore aright,
Who checks at me, to death is dight.
Blue was the charger's broider'd rein;
Blue ribbons deck'd his arching mane;
The knightly housing's ample fold
Was velvet blue, and trapp'd with gold.

VII

Behind him rode two gallant squires,
Of noble name, and knightly sires;
They burn'd the gilded spurs to claim;
For well could each a war-horse tame,
Could draw the bow, the sword could sway,
And lightly bear the ring away;
Nor less with courteous precepts stor'd,
Could dance in hall, and carve at board,
And frame love-ditties passing rare,
And sing them to a lady fair.

VIII

Four men-at-arms came at their backs,
With halbert, bill, and battle-axe:
They bore Lord Marmion's lance so strong,
And led his sumpter-mules along,
And ambling palfrey, when at need
Him listed ease his battle-steed.
The last and trustiest of the four,
On high his forky pennon bore;
Like swallow's tail, in shape and hue,
Flutter'd the streamer glossy blue,
Where, blazon'd sable, as before,
The towering falcon seem'd to soar.

Last, twenty yeomen, two and two,
In hosen black, and jerkins blue,
With falcons broider'd on each breast,
Attended on their lord's behest.
Each, chosen for an archer good,
Knew hunting-craft by lake or wood;
Each one a six-foot bow could bend,
And far a cloth-yard shaft could send;
Each held a boar-spear tough and strong,
And at their belts their quivers rung.
Their dusty palfreys and array
Show'd they had march'd a weary way.

IX

'Tis meet that I should tell you now,
How fairly arm'd, and order'd how,
  The soldiers of the guard,
With musket, pike, and morion,
To welcome noble Marmion,
  Stood in the Castle-yard:
Minstrels and trumpeters were there;
The gunner held his linstock yare,
  For welcome-shot prepar'd:
Enter'd the train, and such a clang,
As then through all his turrets rang,
  Old Norham never heard.

X

The guards their morrice-pikes advanc'd,
  The trumpets flourish'd brave,
The cannon from the ramparts glanc'd,
  And thundering welcome gave.
A blithe salute, in martial sort,
  The minstrels well might sound,
For, as Lord Marmion cross'd the court,
  He scatter'd angels round.
"Welcome to Norham, Marmion!
  Stout heart, and open hand!
Well dost thou brook thy gallant roan,
  Thou flower of English land!"

XI

Two pursuivants, whom tabarts deck,
With silver scutcheon round their neck,
  Stood on the steps of stone
By which you reach the donjon gate,

And there, with herald pomp and state,
　　They hail'd Lord Marmion:
They hail'd him Lord of Fontenaye,
Of Lutterward, and Scrivelbaye,
　　Of Tamworth tower and town;
And he, their courtesy to requite,
Gave them a chain of twelve marks' weight,
　　All as he lighted down.
"Now, largesse, largesse, Lord Marmion,
　　Knight of the crest of gold!
A blazon'd shield, in battle won,
　　Ne'er guarded heart so bold."

　　XII
They marshall'd him to the Castle-hall,
　　Where the guests stood all aside,
And loudly flourish'd the trumpet-call,
　　And the heralds loudly cried,
"Room, lordings, room for Lord Marmion
　　With the crest and helm of gold!
Full well we know the trophies won
　　In the lists at Cottiswold:
There, vainly Ralph de Wilton stove
　　'Gainst Marmion's force to stand;
To him he lost his lady-love,
　　And to the King his land.
Ourselves beheld the listed field,
　　A sight both sad and fair;
We saw Lord Marmion pierce his shield,
　　And saw his saddle bare;
We saw the victor win the crest
　　He wears with worthy pride;
And on the gibbet-tree, revers'd,
　　His foeman's scutcheon tied.
Place, nobles, or the Falcon-Knight!
　　Room, room, ye gentles gay,
For him who conquer'd in the right,
　　Marmion of Fontenaye!"

　　XIII
Then stepp'd to meet that noble Lord,
　　Sir Hugh the Heron bold,
Baron of Twisell, and of Ford,
　　And Captain of the Hold.
He led Lord Marmion to the deas,
　　Rais'd o'er the pavement high,

And plac'd him in the upper place:
    They feasted full and high:
The whiles a Northern harper rude
Chanted a rhyme of deadly feud,
    How the fierce Thirwalls, and Ridleys all,
        Stout Willimondswick,
        And Hardriding Dick,
    And Hughie of Hawdon, and Will o' the Wall,
    Have set on Sir Albany Featherstonhaugh,
    And taken his life at the Deadman's-shaw.
Scantly Lord Marmion's ear could brook
    The harper's barbarous lay;
Yet much he prais'd the pains he took,
    And well those pains did pay:
For lady's suit, and minstrel's strain,
By knight should ne'er be heard in vain.

                    XIV

"Now, good Lord Marmion," Heron says,
    "Of your fair courtesy,
I pray you bide some little space
    In this poor tower with me.
Here you may keep your arms from rust,
    May breathe your war-horse well;
Seldom hath pass'd a week but giust
    Or feat of arms befell:
The Scots can rein a mettled steed,
    And love to couch a spear;
Saint George! a stirring life they lead,
    That have such neighbours near.
Then stay with us a little space,
    Our northern wars to learn;
I pray you, for your lady's grace!"
    Lord Marmion's brow grew stern.

                    XV

The Captain mark'd his alter'd look,
    And gave a squire the sign;
A mighty wassail-bowl he took,
    And crown'd it high with wine.
"Now pledge me here, Lord Marmion:
    But first I pray thee fair,
Where hast thou left that page of thine,
That us'd to serve thy cup of wine,
    Whose beauty was so rare?
When last in Raby towers we met,

The boy I closely eyed,
And often mark'd his cheeks were wet,
  With tears he fain would hide:
His was no rugged horse-boy's hand,
To burnish shield or sharpen brand,
  Or saddle battle-steed;
But meeter seem'd for lady fair,
To fan her cheek, or curl her hair,
Or through embroidery, rich and rare,
  The slender silk to lead:
His skin was fair, his ringlets gold,
  His bosom—when he sigh'd,
The russet doublet's rugged fold
  Could scarce repel its pride!
Say, hast thou given that lovely youth
  To serve in lady's bower?
Or was the gentle page, in sooth,
  A gentle paramour?"

XVI

Lord Marmion ill could brook such jest;
  He roll'd his kindling eye,
With pain his rising wrath suppress'd,
  Yet made a calm reply:
"That boy thou thought'st so goodly fair,
He might not brook the northern air.
More of his fate if thou wouldst learn,
I left him sick in Lindisfarn:
Enough of him. But, Heron, say,
Why does thy lovely lady gay
Disdain to grace the hall to-day?
Or has that dame, so fair and sage,
Gone on some pious pilgrimage?"
He spoke in covert scorn, for fame
Whisper'd light tales of Heron's dame.

XVII

Unmark'd, at least unreck'd, the taunt,
  Careless the Knight replied,
"No bird, whose feathers gaily flaunt,
  Delights in cage to bide:
Norham is grim and grated close,
Hemm'd in by battlement and fosse,
  And many a darksome tower;
And better loves my lady bright
To sit in liberty and light,

In fair Queen Margaret's bower.
We hold our greyhound in our hand,
  Our falcon on our glove;
But where shall we find leash or band
  For dame that loves to rove?
Let the wild falcon soar her swing,
She'll stoop when she has tis'd her wing."

XVIII

"Nay, if with Royal James's bride
The lovely Lady Heron bide,
Behold me here a messenger,
Your tender greetings prompt to bear;
For, to the Scottish court address'd,
I journey at our King's behest,
And pray you, of your grace, provide
For me, and mine, a trusty guide.
I have not ridden in Scotland since
James back'd the cause of that mock prince,
Warbeck, that Flemish counterfeit,
Who on the gibbet paid the cheat.
Then did I march with Surrey's power,
What time we raz'd old Ayton tower."

XIX

"For such-like need, my lord, I trow,
Norham can find you guides enow;
For here be some have prick'd as far,
On Scottish ground, as to Dunbar;
Have drunk the monks of St. Bothan's ale,
And driven the beeves of Lauderdale;
Harried the wives of Greenlaw's goods,
And given them light to set their hoods."

XX

"Now, in good sooth," Lord Marmion cried,
"Were I in warlike wise to ride,
A better guard I would not lack,
Than your stout forayers at my back;
But, as in form of peace I go,
A friendly messenger, to know
Why through all Scotland, near and far,
Their King is mustering troops for war,
The sight of plundering Border spears
Might justify suspicious fears,

And deadly feud, or thirst of spoil,
Break out in some unseemly broil:
A herald were my fitting guide;
Or friar, sworn in peace to bide;
Or pardoner, or travelling priest,
Or strolling pilgrim, at the least."

XXI

The Captain mus'd a little space,
And pass'd his hand across his face:
"Fain would I find the guide you want,
But ill may spare a pursuivant,
The only men that safe can ride
Mine errands on the Scottish side:
And though a bishop built this fort,
Few holy brethren here resort;
Even our good chaplain, as I ween,
Since our last siege, we have not seen:
The mass he might not sing or say
Upon one stinted meal a-day;
So, safe he sat in Durham aisle,
And pray'd for our success the while.
Our Norham vicar, woe betide,
Is all too well in case to ride;
The priest of Shoreswood—he could rein
The wildest war-horse in your train;
But then, no spearman in the hall
Will sooner swear, or stab, or brawl.
Friar John of Tillmouth were the man:
A blithesome brother at the can,
A welcome guest in hall and bower,
He knows each castle, town and tower,
In which the wine and ale is good,
'Twixt Newcastle and Holy-Rood.
But that good man, as ill befalls,
Hath seldom left our castle walls,
Since, on the vigil of St. Bede,
In evil hour, he cross'd the Tweed,
To teach Dame Alison her creed.
Old Bughtrig found him with his wife;
And John, an enemy to strife,
Sans frock and hood, fled for his life.
The jealous churl hath deeply swore
That, if again he venture o'er,
He shall shrieve penitent no more.

Little he loves such risks, I know;
Yet, in your guard, perchance will go."

XXII

Young Selby, at the fair hall-board,
Carv'd to his uncle and that lord,
And reverently took up the word:
"Kind uncle, woe were we each one,
If harm should hap to brother John.
He is a man of mirthful speech,
Can many a game and gambol teach;
Full well at tables can he play,
And sweep at bowls the stake away.
None can a lustier carol bawl,
The needfullest among us all,
When time hangs heavy in the hall,
And snow comes thick at Christmastide,
And we can neither hunt, nor ride
A foray on the Scottish side.
The vow'd revenge of Bughtrig rude,
May end in worse than loss of hood.
Let Friar John, in safety, still
In chimney-corner snore his fill,
Roast hissing crabs, or flagons swill:
Last night, to Norham there came one,
Will better guide Lord Marmion."
"Nephew," quoth Heron, "by my fay,
Well hast thou spoke; say forth thy say."

XXIII

"Here is a holy Palmer come,
From Salem first, and last from Rome;
One that hath kiss'd the blessed tomb,
And visited each holy shrine
In Araby and Palestine;
On hills of Armenie hath been,
Where Noah's ark may yet be seen;
By that Red Sea, too, hath he trod,
Which parted at the prophet's rod;
In Sinai's wilderness he saw
The Mount, where Israel heard the law,
'Mid thunder-dint, and flashing levin,
And shadows, mists, and darkness, given.
He shows Saint James's cockle-shell;
Of fair Montserrat, too can tell;
    And of that Grot where olives nod,

Where, darling of each heart and eye,
From all the youth of Sicily
 Saint Rosalie retired to God.

XXIV

"To stout Saint George of Norwich merry,
Saint Thomas, too, of Canterbury,
Cuthbert of Durham and Saint Bede,
For his sins' pardon hath he pray'd.
He knows the passes of the North,
And seeks far shrines beyond the Forth;
Little he eats, and long will wake,
And drinks but of the stream or lake.
This were a guide o'er moor and dale;
But, when our John hath quaff'd his ale,
As little as the wind that blows,
And warms itself against his nose,
Kens he, or cares, which way he goes."

XXV

"Gramercy!" quoth Lord Marmion,
"Full loth were I, that Friar John,
That venerable man, for me,
Were placed in fear or jeopardy.
If this same Palmer will me lead
 From hence to Holy-Rood,
Like his good saint, I'll pay his meed,
Instead of cockle-shell, or bead,
 With angels fair and good.
I love such holy ramblers; still
They know to charm a weary hill,
 With song, romance, or lay:
Some jovial tale, or glee, or jest,
Some lying legend, at the least,
 They bring to cheer the way."

XXVI

"Ah! noble sir," young Selby said,
And finger on his lip he laid,
"This man knows much, perchance e'en more
Than he could learn by holy lore.
Still to himself he's muttering,
And shrinks as at some unseen thing.
Last night we listen'd at his cell;
Strange sounds we heard, and, sooth to tell,
He murmur'd on till morn, howe'er

No living mortal could be near.
Sometimes I thought I heard it plain,
As other voices spoke again.
I cannot tell; I like it not;
Friar John hath told us it is wrote
No conscience clear and void of wrong
Can rest awake and pray so long.
Himself still sleeps before his beads
Have mark'd ten aves, and two creeds."

XXVII

"Let pass," quoth Marmion; "by my fay,
This man shall guide me on my way,
Although the great arch-fiend and he
Had sworn themselves of company.
So please you, gentle youth, to call
This Palmer to the Castle-hall."
The summon'd Palmer came in place;
His sable cowl o'erhung his face;
In his black mantle was he clad,
With Peter's keys, in cloth of red,
    On his broad shoulders wrought;
The scallop shell his cap did deck;
The crucifix around his neck
    Was from Loretto brought;
His sandals were with travel tore;
Staff, budget, bottle, scrip, he wore;
The faded palm-branch in his hand
Show'd pilgrim from the Holy Land.

XXVIII

Whenas the Palmer came in hall,
Nor lord, nor knight, was there more tall,
Or had a statelier step withal,
    Or look'd more high and keen;
For no saluting did he wait,
But strode across the hall of state.
And fronted Marmion where he sate,
    As he his peer had been.
But his gaunt frame was worn with toil;
His cheek was sunk, alas the while!
And when he struggled at a smile,
    His eye look'd haggard wild:
Poor wretch! the mother that him bare,
If she had been in presence there,
In his wan face, and sun-burn'd hair,

She had not known her child.
Danger, long travel, want, or woe,
Soon change the form that best we know;
For deadly fear can time outgo,
 And blanch at once the hair;
Hard toil can roughen form and face,
And want can quench the eye's bright grace,
Nor does old age a wrinkle trace
 More deeply than despair.
Happy whom none of these befall,
But this poor Palmer knew them all.

XXIX

Lord Marmion then his boon did ask;
The Palmer took on him the task,
So he would march with morning tide,
To Scottish court to be his guide.
"But I have solemn vows to pay,
And may not linger by the way,
 To fair St. Andrews bound,
Within the ocean-cave to pray,
Where good Saint Rule his holy lay,
From midnight to the dawn of day,
 Sung to the billows' sound;
Thence to Saint Fillan's blessed well,
Whose spring can frenzied dreams dispel,
 And the craz'd brain restore:
Saint Mary grant that cave or spring
Could back to peace my bosom bring,
 Or bid it throb no more!"

XXX

And now the midnight draught of sleep,
Where wine and spices richly steep,
In massive bowl of silver deep,
 The page presents on knee.
Lord Marmion drank a fair good rest,
The Captain pledg'd his noble guest,
The cup went through among the rest,
 Who drain'd it merrily;
Alone the Palmer pass'd it by,
Though Selby press'd him courteously.
This was a sign the feast was o'er;
It hush'd the merry wassail roar,
 The minstrels ceas'd to sound.
Soon in the castle nought was heard,

But the slow footstep of the guard,
   Pacing his sober round.

XXXI

With early dawn Lord Marmion rose:
And first the chapel doors unclose;
Then, after morning rites were done
(A hasty mass from Friar John)
And knight and squire had broke their fast
On rich substantial repast,
Lord Marmion's bugles blew to horses;
Then came the stirrup-cup in course:
Between the Baron and his host
No point of courtesy was lost;
High thanks were by Lord Marmion paid,
Solemn excuse the Captain made,
Till, filing from the gate, had pass'd
That noble train, their Lord the last.
Then loudly rung the trumpet call;
Thunder'd the cannon from the wall,
   And shook the Scottish shore;
Around the castle eddied slow,
Volumes of smoke as white as snow,
   And hid its turrets hoar;
Till they roll'd forth upon the air,
And met the river breezes there,
Which gave again the prospect fair.

Canto Second   THE CONVENT

I

The breeze, which swept away the smoke
   Round Norham Castle roll'd,
When all the loud artillery spoke,
With lightning-flash, and thunder-stroke,
   As Marmion left the Hold,—
It curl'd not Tweed alone, that breeze,
For, far upon Northumbrian seas,
   It freshly blew, and strong,
Where, from high Whitby's cloister'd pile,
Bound to Saint Cuthbert's Holy Isle,
   It bore a bark along.

Upon the gale she stoop'd her side,
And bounded o'er the swelling tide,
  As she were dancing home:
The merry seamen laugh'd to see
Their gallant ship so lustily
  Furrow the green sea-foam.
Much joy'd they in their honour'd freight;
For, on the deck, in chair of state,
The Abbess of Saint Hilda plac'd,
With five fair nuns, the galley grac'd.

    II

'Twas sweet to see these holy maids,
Like birds escaped to greenwood shades,
  Their first flight from the cage,
How timid, and how curious too,
For all to them was strange and new,
And all the common sights they view
  Their wonderment engage.
One eyed the shrouds and swelling sail,
  With many a benedicite;
One at the rippling surge grew pale,
  And would for terror pray;
Then shriek'd, because the sea-dog, nigh,
His round black head, and sparkling eye,
  Rear'd o'er the foaming spray;
And one would still adjust her veil,
Disorder'd by the summer gale,
Perchance lest some more worldly eye
Her dedicated charms might spy;
Perchance, because such action grac'd
Her fair-turn'd arm and slender waist.
Light was each simple bosom there,
Save two, who ill might pleasure share,
The Abbess and the Novice Clare.

    III

The Abbess was of noble blood,
But early took the veil and hood,
Ere upon life she cast a look,
Or knew the world that she forsook.
Fair too she was, and kind had been
As she was fair, but ne'er had seen
For her a timid lover sigh,
Nor knew the influence of her eye.
Love, to her ear, was but a name,

Combined with vanity and shame;
Her hopes, her fears, her joys, were all
Bounded within the cloister wall:
The deadliest sin her mind could reach,
Was of monastic rule the breach;
And her ambition's highest aim
To emulate Saint Hilda's fame.
For this she gave her ample dower,
To raise the convent's eastern tower;
For this, with carving rare and quaint,
She deck'd the chapel of the saint,
And gave the relic-shrine of cost,
With ivory and gems emboss'd.
The poor her Convent's bounty blest,
The pilgrim in its halls found rest.

IV

Black was her garb, her rigid rule
Reform'd on Benedictine school;
Her cheek was pale, her form was spare;
Vigils, and penitence austere,
Had early quench'd the light of youth,
But gentle was the dame, in sooth;
Though, vain of her religious sway,
She loved to see her maids obey,
Yet nothing stern was she in cell,
And the nuns loved their Abbess well.
Sad was this voyage to the dame:
Summon'd to Lindisfarne, she came,
There, with Saint Cuthbert's Abbot old,
And Tynemouth's Prioress, to hold
A chapter of Saint Benedict
For inquisition stern and strict
On two apostates from the faith,
And, if need were, to doom to death.

V

Nought say I here of Sister Clare,
Save this, that she was young and fair;
As yet a novice unprofess'd,
Lovely and gentle, but distress'd.
She was betroth'd to one now dead,
Or worse, who had dishonour'd fled.
Her kinsmen bade her give her hand
To one, who lov'd her for her land:
Herself, almost heart-broken now,

Was bent to take the vestal vow,
And shroud, within Saint Hilda's gloom,
Her blasted hopes and wither'd bloom.

VI

She sate upon the galley's prow,
And seem'd to mark the waves below;
Nay, seem'd, so fix'd her look and eye,
To count them as they glided by.
She saw them not—'twas seeming all;
Far other scene her thoughts recall,—
A sun-scorch'd desert, waste and bare,
Nor waves, nor breezes, murmur'd there;
There saw she where some careless hand
O'er a dead corpse had heap'd the sand
To hide it—till the jackals come
To tear it from the scanty tomb.
See what a woful look was given
As she raised up her eyes to heaven!

VII

Lovely, and gentle, and distress'd—
These charms might tame the fiercest breast:
Harpers have sung, and poets told,
That he, in fury uncontroll'd,
The shaggy monarch of the wood,
Before a virgin, fair and good,
Hath pacified his savage mood.
But passions in the human frame
Oft put the lion's rage to shame:
And jealousy, by dark intrigue,
With sordid avarice in league,
Had practis'd with their bowl and knife
Against the mourner's harmless life.
This crime was charg'd 'gainst those who lay
Prison'd in Cuthbert's islet grey.

VIII

And now the vessel skirts the strand
Of mountainous Northumberland;
Towns, towers, and halls, successive rise,
And catch the nuns' delighted eyes.
Monk-Wearmouth soon behind them lay,
And Tynemouth's priory and bay;
They mark'd, amid her trees, the hall
Of lofty Seaton-Delaval;

They saw the Blythe and Wansbeck floods
Rush to the sea through sounding woods;
They pass'd the tower of Widderington,
Mother of many a valiant son;
At Coquet-isle their beads they tell
To the good Saint who own'd the cell;
Then did the Alne attention claim,
And Warkworth, proud of Percy's name;
And next, they cross'd themselves, to hear
The whitening breakers sound so near,
Where, boiling through the rocks, they roar,
On Dunstanborough's cavern'd shore;
Thy tower, proud Bamborough, mark'd they there,
King Ida's castle, huge and square,
From its tall rock look grimly down,
And on the swelling ocean frown;
Then from the coast they bore away,
And reach'd the Holy Island's bay.

IX
The tide did now its flood-mark gain,
And girdled in the Saint's domain:
For, with the flow and ebb, its style
Varies from continent to isle;
Dry shod, o'er sands, twice every day,
The pilgrims to the shrine find way;
Twice every day, the waves efface
Of staves and sandall'd feet the trace.
As to the port the galley flew,
Higher and higher rose to view
The Castle with its battled walls,
The ancient Monastery's halls,
A solemn, huge, and dark-red pile,
Plac'd on the margin of the isle.

X
In Saxon strength that Abbey frown'd,
With massive arches broad and round,
    That rose alternate, row and row,
On ponderous columns, short and low,
    Built ere the art was known,
By pointed aisle, and shafted stalk,
The arcades of an alley'd walk
    To emulate in stone.
On the deep walls, the heathen Dane
Had pour'd his impious rage in vain;

And needful was such strength to these
Expos'd to the tempestuous seas,
Scourg'd by the winds' eternal sway,
Open to rovers fierce as they,
Which could twelve hundred years withstand
Winds, waves, and northern pirates' hand.
Not but that portions of the pile,
Rebuilded in a later style,
Show'd where the spoiler's hand had been;
Not but the wasting sea-breeze keen
Had worn the pillar's carving quaint,
And moulder'd in his niche the saint,
And rounded, with consuming power,
The pointed angles of each tower;
Yet still entire the Abbey stood,
Like veteran, worn, but unsubdu'd.

XI

Soon as they near'd his turrets strong,
The maidens rais'd Saint Hilda's song,
  And with the sea-wave and the wind,
   Their voices, sweetly shrill, combin'd,
    And made harmonious close;
  Then, answering from the sandy shore,
  Half-drown'd amid the breakers' roar,
   According chorus rose:
Down to the haven of the Isle,
The monks and nuns in order file,
  From Cuthbert's cloisters grim;
Banner, and cross, and relics there,
To meet Saint Hilda's maids, they bare;
And, as they caught the sounds on air,
  They echo'd back the hymn.
The islanders, in joyous mood,
Rush'd emulously through the food,
  To hale the bark to land;
Conspicuous by her veil and hood,
Signing the cross, the Abbess stood,
  And bless'd them with her hand.

XII

Suppose we now the welcome said,
Suppose the Convent banquet made:
  All through the holy dome,
Through cloister, aisle, and gallery,
Wherever vestal maid might pry,

Nor risk to meet unhallow'd eye,
    The stranger sisters roam,—
Till fell the evening damp with dew,
And the sharp sea-beeeze coldly blew,
For there, even summer night is chill.
Then, having stray'd and gaz'd their fill,
    They clos'd around the fire;
And all, in turn, essay'd to paint
The rival merits of their saint,
    A theme that ne'er can tire
A holy maid; for, be it known,
That their saint's honour is their own.

XIII

Then Whitby's nuns exulting told,
How to their house three Barons bold
    Must menial service do;
While horns blow out a note of shame,
And monks cry " 'Fye upon your name!
In wrath, for loss of silvan game,
    Saint Hilda's priest ye slew.'
This, on Ascension-day, each year,
While labouring on our harbour-pier,
Must Herbert, Bruce, and Percy hear."
They told how in their convent-cell
A Saxon princess once did dwell,
    The lovely Edelfled;
And how, of thousand snakes, each one
Was chang'd into a coil of stone,
    When holy Hilda pray'd;
Themselves, within their holy bound,
Their stony folds had often found.
They told how sea-fowls' pinions fail,
As over Whitby's towers they sail,
And, sinking down, with flutterings faint,
They do their homage to the saint.

XIV

Nor did Saint Cuthbert's daughters fail
To vie with these in holy tale;
His body's resting-place, of old,
How oft their patron chang'd, they told;
How, when the rude Dane burn'd their pile,
The monks fled forth from Holy Isle;
O'er northern mountain, marsh, and moor,
From sea to sea, from shore to shore,

Seven years Saint Cuthbert's corpse they bore.
　They rested them in fair Melrose;
　　But though, alive, he lov'd it well,
　Not there his relics might repose;
　　For, wondrous tale to tell!
　In his stone-coffin forth he rides,
　A ponderous bark for river tides,
　Yet light as gossamer it glides,
　　Downward to Tilmouth cell.
Nor long was his abiding there,
For southward did the saint repair;
Chester-le-Street, and Rippon, saw
His holy corpse, ere Wardilaw
　Hail'd him with joy and fear;
And, after many wanderings past,
He chose his lordly seat at last,
Where his cathedral, huge and vast,
　Looks down upon the Wear:
　There, deep in Durham's Gothic shade,
His relics are in secret laid;
　But none may know the place,
Save of his holiest servants three,
Deep sworn to solemn secrecy,
　Who share that wondrous grace.

XV

Who may his miracles declare!
Even Scotland's dauntless king, and heir,
　(Although with them they led
Galwegians, wild as ocean's gale,
And Lodon's knights, all sheath'd in mail,
And the bold men of Teviotdale)
　Before his standard fled.
'Twas he, to vindicate his reign,
Edg'd Alfred's falchion on the Dane,
And turn'd the Conqueror back again,
When, with his Norman bowyer band,
He came to waste Northumberland.

XVI

But fain Saint Hilda's nuns would learn
If, on a rock, by Lindisfarne,
Saint Cuthbert sits, and toils to frame
The sea-born beads that bear his name:
Such tales had Whitby's fishers told,
And said they might his shape behold,

And hear his anvil sound;
A deaden'd clang, a huge dim form,
Seen but, and heard, when gathering storm
    And night were closing round.
But this, as tale of idle fame,
The nuns of Lindisfarne disclaim.

    XVII

While round the fire such legends go,
Far different was the scene of woe,
Where, in a secret aisle beneath,
Council was held of life and death.
    It was more dark and lone that vault,
        Than the worst dungeon cell:
    Old Colwulf built it, for his fault,
        In penitence to dwell,
When he, for cowl and beads, laid down
The Saxon battle-axe and crown.
This den, which, chilling every sense
    Of feeling, hearing, sight,
Was call'd the Vault of Penitence,
    Excluding air and light,
Was, by the prelate Sexhelm, made
A place of burial for such dead,
As, having died in mortal sin,
Might not be laid the church within.
'Twas now a place of punishment;
Whence if so loud a shriek were sent
    As reach'd the upper air,
The hearers bless'd themselves, and said
The spirits of the sinful dead
    Bemoan'd their torments there.

    XVIII

But though, in the monastic pile,
Did of this penitential aisle
    Some vague tradition go,
Few only, save the Abbot, knew
Where the place lay; and still more few
Were those who had from him the clew
    To that dread vault to go.
Victim and executioner
Were blindfold when transported there.
In low dark rounds the arches hung,
From the rude rock the side-walls sprung;
The grave-stones, rudely sculptur'd o'er,

Half sunk in earth, by time half wore,
Were all the pavement of the floor;
The mildew-drops fell one by one,
With tinkling plash, upon the stone.
A cresset, in an iron chain,
Which served to light this drear domain,
With damp and darkness seem'd to strive,
As if it scarce might keep alive;
And yet it dimly serv'd to show
The awful conclave met below.

XIX

There, met to doom in secrecy,
Were plac'd the heads of convents three—
All servants of Saint Benedict,
The statutes of whose order strict
    On iron table lay;
In long black dress, on seats of stone,
Behind were these three judges shown
    By the pale cresset's ray:
The Abbess of Saint Hilda's there,
Sat for a space with visage bare,
Until, to hide her bosom's swell,
And tear-drops that for pity fell,
    She closely drew her veil:
Yon shrouded figure, as I guess,
By her proud mien and flowing dress,
Is Tynemouth's haughty Prioress,
    And she with awe looks pale:
And he, that Ancient Man, whose sight
Has long been quench'd by age's night,
Upon whose wrinkled brow alone,
Nor ruth, nor mercy's trace, is shown,
    Whose look is hard and stern,—
Saint Cuthbert's Abbot is his style;
For sanctity call'd, through the isle,
    The Saint of Lindisfarne.

XX

Before them stood a guilty pair;
But, though an equal fate they share,
Yet one alone deserves our care.
Her sex a page's dress belied;
The cloak and doublet, loosely tied,
Obscur'd her charms, but could not hide.

Her cap down o'er her face she drew;
   And, on her doublet breast,
She tried to hide the badge of blue,
   Lord Marmion's falcon crest.
But, at the Prioress' command,
A Monk undid the silken band
   That tied her tresses fair,
And rais'd the bonnet from her head,
And down her slender form they spread,
   In ringlets rich and rare.
Constance de Beverley they know,
Sister profess'd of Fontevraud,
Whom the Church number'd with the dead,
For broken vows, and convent fled.

                    XXI
When thus her face was given to view,
(Although, so pallid was her hue,
   It did a ghastly contrast bear
To those bright ringlets glistering fair)
Her look compos'd, and steady eye,
Bespoke a matchless constancy;
And there she stood so calm and pale,
That, but her breathing did not fail,
And motion slight of eye and head,
And of her bosom, warranted
That neither sense nor pulse she lacks,
You might have thought a form of wax,
Wrought to the very life, was there;
So still she was, so pale, so fair.

                    XXII
Her comrade was a sordid soul,
   Such as does murder for a meed;
Who, but of fear, knows no control,
Because his conscience, sear'd and foul,
   Feels not the import of his deed;
One whose brute-feeling ne'er aspires
Beyond his own more brute desires.
Such tools the Tempter ever needs,
To do the savagest of deeds;
For them no vision'd terrors daunt,
Their nights no fancied spectres haunt,
One fear with them, of all most base,
The fear of death, alone finds place.
This wretch was clad in frock and cowl,

And sham'd not loud to moan and howl,
His body on the floor to dash,
And crouch, like hound beneath the lash;
While his mute partner, standing near,
Waited her doom without a tear.

XXIII

Yet well the luckless wretch might shriek,
Well might her paleness terror speak!
For there were seen in that dark wall,
Two niches narrow, deep and tall:
Who enters at such grisly door,
Shall ne'er, I ween, find exit more.
In each a slender meal was laid,
Of roots, of water, and of bread:
By each, in Benedictine dress,
Two haggard monks stood motionless;
Who, holding high a blazing torch,
Show'd the grim entrance of the porch:
Reflecting back the smoky beam,
The dark-red walls and arches gleam
Hewn stones and cement were display'd,
And building tools in order laid.

XXIV

These executioners were chose,
As men who were with mankind foes,
And, with despite and envy fir'd,
Into the cloister had retir'd;
  Or who, in desperate doubt of grace,
  Strove, by deep penance, to efface
    Of some foul crime the stain;
  For, as the vassals of her will,
  Such men the Church selected still,
  As either joy'd in doing ill,
    Or thought more grace to gain,
If, in her cause, they wrestled down
Feelings their nature strove to own.
By strange device were they brought there,
They knew not how, nor knew not where.

XXV

And now that blind old Abbot rose,
  To speak the Chapter's doom,
On those the wall was to enclose,
  Alive, within the tomb;

But stopp'd, because that woful Maid,
Gathering her powers, to speak essay'd.
Twice she essay'd, and twice in vain;
Her accents might no utterance gain;
Nought but imperfect murmurs slip
From her convuls'd and quivering lip;
   'Twixt each attempt all was so still,
You seem'd to hear a distant rill;
    'Twas ocean's swells and falls;
For though this vault of sin and fear
Was to the sounding surge so near,
A tempest there you scarce could hear,
   So massive were the walls.

XXVI

At length, an effort sent apart
The blood that curdled to her heart,
   And light came to her eye,
And colour dawn'd upon her cheek,
A hectic and a flutter'd streak,
Like that left on the Cheviot peak,
   By Autumn's stormy sky;
And when her silence broke at length,
Still as she spoke she gather'd strength,
   And arm'd herself to bear.
It was a fearful sight to see
Such high resolve and constancy
   In form so soft and fair.

XXVII

"I speak not to implore your grace,—
Well know I, for one minute's space
   Successless might I sue:
Nor do I speak your prayers to gain;
For if a death of lingering pain,
To cleanse my sins, be penance vain,
   Vain are your masses too.
I listen'd to a traitor's tale,
I left the convent and the veil;
For three long years I bow'd my pride,
A horse-boy in his train to ride;
And well my folly's meed he gave,
Who forfeited, to be his slave,
All here, and all beyond the grave.
He saw young Clara's face more fair,
He knew her of broad lands the heir,

Forgot his vows, his faith forswore,
And Constance was belov'd no more.
  'Tis an old tale, and often told;
    But did my fate and wish agree,
  Ne'er had been read, in story old,
  Of maiden true betray'd for gold,
    That lov'd or was aveng'd, like me!

    XXVIII

"The King approv'd his favourite's aim;
In vain a rival barr'd his claim,
  Whose fate with Clare's was plight,
For he attaints that rival's fame
With treason's charge—and on they came,
  In mortal lists to fight.
    Their oaths are said,
    Their prayers are pray'd,
    Their lances in the rest are laid,
  They meet in mortal shock;
And, hark! the throng, with thundering cry,
Shout 'Marmion, Marmion! to the sky,
  De Wilton to the block!'
Say ye, who preach Heaven shall decide
When in the lists two champions ride,
  Say, was Heaven's justice here?
When, loyal in his love and faith,
Wilton found overthrow or death
  Beneath a traitor's spear?
How false the charge, how true he fell,
This guilty packet best can tell."
Then drew a packet from her breast,
Paus'd, gather'd voice, and spoke the rest.

    XXIX

"Still was false Marmion's bridal staid;
To Whitby's convent fled the maid,
  The hated match to shun.
'Ho! shifts she thus?' King Henry cried;
'Sir Marmion, she shall be thy bride
  If she were sworn a nun.'
One way remain'd—the King's command
Sent Marmion to the Scottish land:
I linger'd here, and rescue plann'd
  For Clara and for me:
This caitiff Monk, for gold, did swear
He would to Whitby's shrine repair,

And, by his drugs, my rival fair
  A saint in heaven should be.
But ill the dastard kept his oath,
Whose cowardice has undone us both.

XXX

"And now my tongue the secret tells
Not that remorse my bosom swells,
But to assure my soul that none
Shall ever wed with Marmion.
Had fortune my last hope betray'd,
This packet, to the King convey'd,
Had given him to the headsman's stroke,
Although my heart that instant broke.
Now, men of death, work forth your will,
For I can suffer, and be still;
And come he slow, or come he fast,
It is but Death who comes at last.

XXXI

"Yet dread me, from my living tomb,
Ye vassal slaves of bloody Rome!
If Marmion's late remorse should wake,
Full soon such vengeance will he take,
That you should wish the fiery Dane
Had rather been your guest again.
Behind, a darker hour ascends!
The altars quake, the crosier bends,
The ire of a despotic King
Rides forth upon destruction's wing;
Then shall these vaults, so strong and deep
Burst open to the sea-winds' sweep;
Some traveller then shall find my bones
Whitening amid disjointed stones,
And, ignorant of priests' cruelty,
Marvel such relics here should be."

XXXII

Fix'd was her look, and stern her air:
Back from her shoulders stream'd her hair;
The locks, that wont her brow to shade,
Star'd up erectly from her head;
Her figure seem'd to rise more high;
Her voice, despair's wild energy
Had given a tone of prophecy.

Appall'd the astonish'd conclave sate;
With stupid eyes, the men of fate
Gaz'd on the light inspired form,
And listen'd for the avenging storm;
The judges felt the victim's dread;
No hand was mov'd, no word was said,
Till thus the Abbot's doom was given,
Raising his sightless balls to heaven:—
"Sister, let thy sorrows cease;
Sinful brother, part in peace!"
    From that dire dungeon, place of doom,
    Of execution too, and tomb,
        Pac'd forth the judges three;
    Sorrow it were, and shame, to tell
    The butcher-work that there befell,
    When they had glided from the cell
        Of sin and misery.

XXXIII

An hundred winding steps convey
That conclave to the upper day;
But, ere they breath'd the fresher air,
They heard the shriekings of despair,
    And many a stifled groan:
With speed their upward way they take,
(Such speed as age and fear can make)
And cross'd themselves for terror's sake,
    As hurrying, tottering on:
Even in the vesper's heavenly tone,
They seem'd to hear a dying groan,
And bade the passing knell to toll
For welfare of a parting soul.
Slow o'er the midnight wave it swung,
Northumbrian rocks in answer rung;
To Warkworth cell the echoes roll'd,
His beads the wakeful hermit told,
The Bamborough peasant rais'd his head,
But slept ere half a prayer he said;
So far was heard the mighty knell,
The stag sprung up on Cheviot Fell,
Spread his broad nostril to the wind,
Listed before, aside, behind,
Then couch'd him down beside the hind,
And quak'd among the mountain fern,
To hear that sound so dull and stern.

Canto Third THE HOSTEL, OR INN

I

The livelong day Lord Marmion rode:
The mountain path the Palmer show'd,
By glen and streamlet winded still,
Where stunted birches hid the rill.
They might not choose the lowland road,
For the Merse forayers were abroad,
Who, fir'd with hate and thirst of prey,
Had scarcely fail'd to bar their way.
Oft on the trampling band, from crown
Of some tall cliff, the deer look'd down;
On wing of jet, from his repose
In the deep heath, the black-cock rose;
Sprung from the gorse the timid roe,
Nor waited for the bending bow;
And when the stony path began,
By which the naked peak they wan,
Up flew the snowy ptarmigan.
The noon had long been pass'd before
They gain'd the height of Lammermoor;
Thence winding down the northern way,
Before them, at the close of day,
Old Gifford's towers and hamlet lay.

II

No summons calls them to the tower,
To spend the hospitable hour.
To Scotland's camp the lord was gone:
His cautious dame, in bower alone,
Dreaded her castle to unclose,
So late, to unknown friends or foes.
  On through the hamlet as they pac'd,
  Before a porch, whose front was grac'd
  With bush and flagon trimly plac'd,
    Lord Marmion drew his rein;
  The village inn seem'd large, though rude;
  Its cheerful fire and hearty food
    Might well relieve his train.
Down from their seats the horsemen sprung,
With jingling spurs the court-yard rung;
They bind their horses to the stall,

For forage, food, and firing call,
And various clamour fills the hall:
Weighing the labour with the cost,
Toils everywhere the bustling host.

III

Soon, by the chimney's merry blaze,
Through the rude hostel might you gaze;
Might see, where, in dark nook aloof,
The rafters of the sooty roof
    Bore wealth of winter cheer;
Of sea-fowl dried, and solands store,
And gammons of the tusky boar,
    And savoury haunch of deer.
The chimney arch projected wide;
Above, around it, and beside,
    Were tools for housewives' hand;
Nor wanted, in that martial day,
The implements of Scottish fray,
    The buckler, lance, and brand.
Beneath its shade, the place of state,
On oaken settle Marmion sate,
And view'd around the blazing hearth.
His followers mix in noisy mirth;
Whom with brown ale, in jolly tide,
From ancient vessels ranged aside,
Full actively their host supplied.

IV

Theirs was the glee of martial breast,
And laughter theirs at little jest;
And oft Lord Marmion deign'd to aid,
And mingle in the mirth they made;
For though, with men of high degree,
The proudest of the proud was he,
Yet, train'd in camps, he knew the art
To win the soldier's hardy heart.
They love a captain to obey,
Boisterous as March, yet fresh as May;
With open hand, and brow as free,
Lover of wine and minstrelsy;
Even the first to scale a tower,
As venturous in a lady's bower:
Such buxom chief shall lead his host
From India's fires to Zembla's frost.

V

Resting upon his pilgrim staff,
  Right opposite the Palmer stood;
His thin dark visage seen but half,
  Half hidden by his hood.
Still fix'd on Marmion was his look,
Which he, who ill such gaze could brook,
  Strove by a frown to quell;
But not for that, though more than once
Full met their stern encountering glance,
  The Palmer's visage fell.

VI

By fits less frequent from the crowd
Was heard the burst of laughter loud;
For still, as squire and archer star'd
On that dark face and matted beard,
  Their glee and game declin'd.
All gaz'd at length in silence drear,
Unbroke, save when in comrade's ear
Some yeoman, wondering in his fear,
  Thus whisper'd forth his mind:—
"Saint Mary! saw'st thou e'er such sight?
How pale his cheek, his eye how bright,
Whene'er the firebrand's fickle light
  Glances beneath his cowl!
Full on our lord he sets his eye;
For his best palfrey, would not I
  Endure that sullen scowl."

VII

But Marmion, as to chase the awe
Which thus had quell'd their hearts who saw
The ever-varying fire-light show
That figure stern and face of woe,
  Now call'd upon a squire:
"Fitz-Eustace, know'st thou not some lay,
To speed the lingering night away?
  We slumber by the fire."

VIII

"So please you," thus the youth rejoin'd,
"Our choicest minstrel's left behind.
Ill may we hope to please your ear,
Accustom'd Constant's strains to hear.
The harp full deftly can he strike,

And wake the lover's lute alike;
To dear Saint Valentine, no thrush
Sings livelier from a spring-tide bush,
No nightingale her love-lorn tune
More sweetly warbles to the moon.
Woe to the cause, whate'er it be,
Detains from us his melody,
Lavish'd on rocks, and billows stern,
Or duller monks of Lindisfarne.
Now must I venture, as I may,
To sing his favourite roundelay."

IX

A mellow voice Fitz-Eustace had,
The air he chose was wild and sad;
Such have I heard, in Scottish land,
Rise from the busy harvest band,
When falls before the mountaineer,
On Lowland plains, the ripen'd ear.
Now one shrill voice the notes prolong,
Now a wild chorus swells the song:
Oft have I listen'd, and stood still,
As it came soften'd up the hill,
And deem'd it the lament of men
Who languish'd for their native glen;
And thought how sad would be such sound
On Susquehana's swampy ground,
Kentucky's wood-encumber'd brake,
Or wild Ontario's boundless lake,
Where heart-sick exiles, in the strain,
Recall'd fair Scotland's hills again!

X

SONG

"Where shall the lover rest,
    Whom the fates sever
From his true maiden's breast,
    Parted for ever?
Where, through groves deep and high,
    Sounds the far billow,
Where early violets die,
    Under the willow.

Chorus

Eleu loro, &c.   Soft shall be his pillow.

"There, through the summer day,
    Cool streams are laving;
There, while the tempests sway,
    Scarce are boughs waving;
There, thy rest shalt thou take,
    Parted for ever,
Never again to wake,
    Never, O never!

Chorus

Eleu loro, &c.   Never, O never!

XI

"Where shall the traitor rest,
    He, the deceiver,
Who could win maiden's breast,
    Ruin, and leave her?
In the lost battle,
    Borne down by the flying,
Where mingles war's rattle
    With groans of the dying.

Chorus

Eleu loro, &c.   There shall he be lying.

"Her wing shall the eagle flap
    O'er the false-hearted;
His warm blood the wolf shall lap,
    Ere life be parted.
Shame and dishonour sit
    By his grave ever;
Blessing shall hallow it,
    Never, O never!

Chorus

Eleu loro, &c.   Never, O never!"

XII

It ceased, the melancholy sound;
And silence sunk on all around.
The air was sad; but sadder still
    It fell on Marmion's ear,

And plain'd as if disgrace and ill,
  And shameful death, were near.
He drew his mantle past his face,
  Between it and the band,
And rested with his head a space,
  Reclining on his hand.
His thoughts I scan not; but I ween,
That, could their import have been seen,
The meanest groom in all the hall,
That e'er tied courser to a stall,
Would scarce have wish'd to be their prey,
For Lutterward and Fontenaye.

XIII

High minds, of native pride and force,
Most deeply feel thy pangs, Remorse!
Fear, for their scourge, mean villains have;
Thou art the torturer of the brave
Yet fatal strength they boast to steel
Their minds to bear the wounds they feel,
Even while they writhe beneath the smart
Of civil conflict in the heart.
For soon Lord Marmion raised his head,
And, smiling, to Fitz-Eustace said—
"Is it not strange, that, as ye sung,
Seem'd in mine ear a death-peal rung,
Such as in nunneries they toll
For some departing sister's soul?
  Say, what may this protend?"
Then first the Palmer silence broke
(The livelong day he had not spoke)—
  "The death of a dear friend."

XIV

Marmion, whose steady heart and eye
Ne'er changed in worst extremity;
Marmion, whose soul could scantly brook,
Even from his King, a haughty look;
Whose accent of command controll'd,
In camps, the boldest of the bold—
Thought, look, and utterance fail'd him now,
Fall'n was his glance, and flush'd his brow:
  For either in the tone,
Or something in the Palmer's look,
So full upon his conscience strook,
  That answer he found none.

Thus oft it haps, that when within
They shrink at sense of secret sin,
   A feather daunts the brave;
A fool's wild speech confounds the wise,
And proudest princes vail their eyes
   Before their meanest slave.

XV

Well might he falter! By his aid
Was Constance Beverley betray'd.
Not that he augur'd of the doom,
Which on the living closed the tomb;
But, tired to hear the desperate maid
Threaten by turns, beseech, upbraid;
And wroth, because in wild despair,
She practis'd on the life of Clare;
Its fugitive the Church he gave,
Though not a victim, but a slave;
And deem'd restraint in convent strange
Would hide her wrongs, and her revenge.
Himself, proud Henry's favourite peer,
Held Romish thunders idle fear,
Secure his pardon he might hold,
For some slight mulct of penance-gold.
Thus judging, he gave secret way,
When the stern priests surpris'd their prey.
His train but deem'd the favourite page
Was left behind, to spare his age;
Or other if they deem'd, none dar'd
To mutter what he thought and heard:
Woe to the vassal, who durst pry
Into Lord Marmion's privacy!

XVI

His conscience slept—he deem'd her well,
And safe secured in distant cell;
But, waken'd by her favourite lay,
And that strange Palmer's boding say,
That fell so ominous and drear
Full on the object of his fear
To aid remorse's venom'd throes,
Dark tales of convent-vengeance rose;
And Constance, late betray'd and scorn'd,
All lovely on his soul return'd;
Lovely as when, at treacherous call,
She left her convent's peaceful wall,

Crimson'd with shame, with terror mute,
Dreading alike escape, pursuit,
Till love, victorious o'er alarms,
Hid fears and blushes in his arms.

XVII

"Alas!" he thought, "how changed that mien!
How changed these timid looks have been,
Since years of guilt, and of disguise,
Have steel'd her brow, and arm'd her eyes!
No more of virgin terror speaks
The blood that mantles in her cheeks;
Fierce, and unfeminine, are there,
Frenzy for joy, for grief despair;
And I the cause—for whom were given
Her peace on earth, her hopes in heaven!
Would," thought he, as the picture grows,
"I on its stalk had left the rose!
Oh, why should man's success remove
The very charms that wake his love!
Her convent's peaceful solitude
Is now a prison harsh and rude;
And, pent within the narrow cell,
How will her spirit chafe and swell!
How brook the stern monastic laws!
The penance how—and I the cause!
Vigil and scourge—perchance even worse!"
And twice he rose to cry, "To horse!"
And twice his Sovereign's mandate came,
Like damp upon a kindling flame;
And twice he thought, "Gave I not charge
She should be safe, though not at large?
They durst not, for their island, shred
One golden ringlet from her head."

XVIII

While thus in Marmion's bosom strove
Repentance and reviving love,
Like whirlwinds, whose contending sway
I've seen Loch Vennachar obey,
Their Host the Palmer's speech had heard,
And, talkative, took up the word:
"Ay, reverend Pilgrim, you, who stray
From Scotland's simple land away,
    To visit realms afar,
Full often learn the art to know

Of future weal, or future woe,
　　By word, or sign, or star;
Yet might a knight his fortune hear,
If, knight-like, he despises fear,
Not far from hence;—if fathers old
Aright our hamlet legend told."
These broken words the menials move
(For marvels still the vulgar love);
And, Marmion giving license cold,
His tale the host thus gladly told:—

XIX

THE HOST'S TALE

"A Clerk could tell what years have flown
Since Alexander fill'd our throne
(Third monarch of that warlike name),
And eke the time when here he came
To seek Sir Hugo, then our lord:
A braver never drew a sword;
A wiser never, at the hour
Of midnight, spoke the word of power:
The same, whom ancient records call
The founder of the Goblin-Hall.
I would, Sir Knight, your longer stay
Gave you that cavern to survey.
Of lofty roof, and ample size,
Beneath the castle deep it lies:
To hew the living rock profound,
The floor to pave, the arch to round,
There never toil'd a mortal arm;
It all was wrought by word and charm;
And I have heard my grandsire say,
That the wild clamour and affray
Of those dread artisans of hell,
Who labour'd under Hugo's spell,
Sounded as loud as ocean's war
Among the caverns of Dunbar.

XX

"The King Lord Gifford's castle sought,
Deep labouring with uncertain thought;
Even then he muster'd all his host,
To meet upon the western coast:

For Norse and Danish galleys plied
Their oars within the frith of Clyde.
There floated Haco's banner trim,
Above Norweyan warriors grim,
Savage of heart, and large of limb;
Threatening both continent and isle,
Bute, Arran, Cunninghame, and Kyle.
Lord Gifford, deep beneath the ground,
Heard Alexander's bugle sound,
And tarried not his garb to change,
But, in his wizard habit strange,
Came forth,—a quaint and fearful sight;
His mantle lined with fox-skins white;
His high and wrinkled forehead bore
A pointed cap, such as of yore
Clerks say that Pharaoh's Magi wore:
His shoes were mark'd with cross and spell,
Upon his breast a pentacle;
His zone, of virgin parchment thin,
Or, as some tell, of dead man's skin,
Bore many a planetary sign,
Combust, and retrograde, and trine;
And in his hand he held prepar'd,
A naked sword without a guard.

XXI

"Dire dealings with the fiendish race
Had mark'd strange lines upon his face;
Vigil and fast had worn him grim,
His eyesight dazzled seem'd and dim,
As one unus'd to upper day;
Even his own menials with dismay
Beheld, Sir Knight, the grisly Sire,
In his unwonted wild attire;
Unwonted, for traditions run,
He seldom thus beheld the sun.
'I know,' he said—his voice was hoarse,
And broken seem'd its hollow force,—
'I know the cause, although untold,
Why the King seeks his vassal's hold:
Vainly from me my liege would know
His kingdom's future weal or woe;
But yet, if strong his arm and heart,
His courage may do more than art.

XXII

" 'Of middle air the demons proud,
Who ride upon the racking cloud,
Can read, in fix'd or wandering star,
The issue of events afar;
But still their sullen aid withhold,
Save when by mightier force controll'd.
Such late I summon'd to my hall;
And though so potent was the call
That scarce the deepest nook of hell
I deem'd a refuge from the spell,
Yet, obstinate in silence still,
The haughty demon mocks my skill.
But thou—who little know'st thy might,
As born upon that blessed night
When yawning graves, and dying groan,
Proclaim'd hell's empire overthrown—
With untaught valour shalt compel
Response denied to magic spell.'
'Gramercy,' quoth our Monarch free,
'Place him but front to front with me,
And, by this good and honour'd brand,
The gift of Cœur-de-Lion's hand,
Soothly I swear, that, tide what tide,
The demon shall a buffet bide.'
His bearing bold the wizard view'd,
And thus, well pleas'd, his speech renew'd:—
'There spoke the blood of Malcolm!—mark:
Forth pacing hence, at midnight dark,
The rampart seek, whose circling crown
Crests the ascent of yonder down:
A southern entrance shalt thou find;
There halt, and there thy bugle wind,
And trust thine elfin foe to see,
In guise of thy worst enemy:
Couch then thy lance, and spur thy steed—
Upon him! and Saint George to speed!
If he go down, thou soon shalt know
Whate'er these airy sprites can show;
If thy heart fail thee in the strife,
I am no warrant for thy life.'

XXIII

"Soon as the midnight bell did ring,
Alone, and arm'd, forth rode the King
To that old camp's deserted round:

Sir Knight, you well might mark the mound,
Left hand the town,—the Pictish race,
The trench, long since, in blood did trace;
The moor around is brown and bare,
The space within is green and fair.
The spot our village children know,
For there the earliest wild-flowers grow;
But woe betide the wandering wight,
That treads its circle in the night!
The breadth across, a bowshot clear,
Gives ample space for full career:
Opposed to the four points of heaven,
By four deep gaps are entrance given.
The southernmost our Monarch past,
Halted, and blew a gallant blast;
And on the north, within the ring,
Appear'd the form of England's King,
Who then, a thousand leagues afar,
In Palestine wag'd holy war:
Yet arms like England's did he wield,
Alike the leopards in the shield,
Alike his Syrian courser's frame,
The rider's length of limb the same:
Long afterwards did Scotland know,
Fell Edward was her deadliest foe.

XXIV

"The vision made our Monarch start,
But soon he mann'd his noble heart,
And in the first career they ran,
The Elfin Knight fell, horse and man;
Yet did a splinter of his lance
Through Alexander's visor glance,
And razed the skin—a puny wound.
The King, light leaping to the ground,
With naked blade his phantom foe
Compell'd the future war to show.
Of Largs he saw the glorious plain,
Where still gigantic bones remain,
    Memorial of the Danish war;
Himself he saw, amid the field,
On high his brandish'd war-axe wield,
    And strike proud Haco from his car,
While all around the shadowy Kings
Denmark's grim ravens cower'd their wings.
'Tis said, that, in that awful night,

Remoter visions met his sight,
Foreshowing future conquests far,
When our sons' sons wage northern war;
A royal city, tower and spire,
Redden'd the midnight sky with fire,
And shouting crews her navy bore,
Triumphant, to the victor shore.
Such signs may learned clerks explain,
They pass the wit of simply swain.

XXV

"The joyful King turn'd home again,
Headed his host, and quell'd the Dane;
But yearly, when return'd the night
Of his strange combat with the sprite,
    His wound must bleed and smart;
Lord Gifford then would gibing say,
'Bold as ye were, my liege, ye pay
    The penance of your start.'
Long since, beneath Dunfermline's nave,
King Alexander fills his grave;
    Our Lady give him rest!
Yet still the knightly spear and shield
The Elfin Warrior doth wield,
    Upon the brown hill's breast;
And many a knight hath prov'd his chance,
In the charm'd ring to break a lance,
    But all have foully sped;
Save two, as legends tell, and they
Were Wallace wight, and Gilbert Hay.
    Gentles, my tale is said."

XXVI

The quaighs were deep, the liquor strong,
And on the tale the yeoman-throng
Had made a comment sage and long,
    But Marmion gave a sign:
And, with their lord, the squires retire;
The rest, around the hostel fire,
    Their drowsy limbs recline;
For pillow, underneath each head,
The quiver and the targe were laid.
Deep slumbering on the hostel floor,
Oppress'd with toil and ale, they snore:
The dying flame, in fitful change,
Threw on the group its shadows strange.

XXVII

Apart, and nestling in the hay
Of a waste loft, Fitz-Eustace lay;
Scarce, by the pale moonlight, were seen
The foldings of his mantle green:
Lightly he dreamt, as youth will dream,
Of sport by thicket, or by stream;
Of hawk or hound, of ring or glove,
Or, lighter yet, of lady's love.
A cautious tread his slumber broke,
And, close beside him, when he woke,
In moonbeam half, and half in gloom,
Stood a tall form, with nodding plume;
But, ere his dagger Eustace drew,
His master Marmion's voice he knew.

XXVIII

"Fitz-Eustace! rise, I cannot rest;
Yon churl's wild legend haunts my breast,
And graver thoughts have chafed my mood:
The air must cool my feverish blood;
And fain would I ride forth, to see
The scene of elfin chivalry.
Arise, and saddle me my steed;
And, gentle Eustace, take good heed
Thou dost not rouse these drowsy slaves;
I would not, that the prating knaves
Had cause for saying, o'er their ale,
That I could credit such a tale."
Then softly down the steps they slid,
Eustace the stable door undid,
And, darkling, Marmion's steed array'd,
While, whispering, thus the Baron said:—

XXIX

"Didst never, good my youth, hear tell,
  That on the hour when I was born,
Saint George, who graced my sire's chapelle,
Down from his steed of marble fell,
  A weary wight forlorn?
The flattering chaplains all agree,
The champion left his steed to me.
I would, the omen's truth to show,
That I could meet this Elfin Foe!
Blithe would I battle, for the right
To ask one question at the sprite:

Vain thought! for elves, if elves there be,
An empty race, by fount or sea,
To dashing waters dance and sing,
Or round the green oak wheel their ring."
Thus speaking, he his steed bestrode,
And from the hostel slowly rode.

XXX

Fitz-Eustace followed him abroad,
And mark'd him pace the village road,
   And listen'd to his horse's tramp,
     Till, by the lessening sound,
   He judg'd that of the Pictish camp
     Lord Marmion sought the round.
Wonder it seem'd, in the squire's eyes,
That one, so wary held, and wise,—
Of whom 'twas said he scarce received
For gospel what the church believed,—
   Should, stirr'd by idle tale,
Ride forth in silence of the night,
As hoping half to meet a sprite,
   Array'd in plate and mail.
For little did Fitz-Eustace know,
That passions, in contending flow,
   Unfix the strongest mind;
Wearied from doubt to doubt to flee,
We welcome fond credulity,
   Guide confident, though blind.

XXXI

Little for this Fitz-Eustace car'd,
But, patient, waited till he heard,
At distance, prick'd to utmost speed,
The foot-tramp of a flying steed,
   Come town-ward rushing on;
First, dead, as if on turf it trode,
Then, clattering on the village road;—
In other pace than forth he yode,
   Return'd Lord Marmion.
Down hastily he sprung from selle,
And, in his haste, wellnigh he fell;
To the squire's hand the rein he threw,
And spoke no word as he withdrew:
But yet the moonlight did betray,
The falcon-crest was soil'd with clay;
And plainly might Fitz-Eustace see,

By stains upon the charger's knee,
And his left side, that on the moor
He had not kept his footing sure.
Long musing on these wondrous signs,
At length to rest the squire reclines,
Broken and short; for still, between,
Would dreams of terror intervene.
Eustace did ne'er so blithely mark
The first notes of the morning lark.

Canto Fourth THE CAMP

I

Eustace, I said, did blithely mark
The first notes of the merry lark.
The lark sang shrill, the cock he crew,
And loudly Marmion's bugles blew,
And with their light and lively call
Brought groom and yeoman to the stall.
  Whistling they came, and free of heart,
    But soon their mood was chang'd;
  Complaint was heard on every part,
    Of something disarrang'd.
Some clamour'd loud for armour lost;
Some brawl'd and wrangled with the host;
"By Becket's bones," cried one, "I fear,
That some false Scot has stolen my spear!"
Young Blount, Lord Marmion's second squire,
Found his steed wet with sweat and mire;
Although the rated horse-boy sware,
Last night he dress'd him sleek and fair.
While chaf'd the impatient squire, like thunder
Old Hubert shouts in fear and wonder—
"Help, gentle Blount! help, comrades all!
Bevis lies dying in his stall:
To Marmion who the plight dare tell,
Of the good steed he loves so well?"
Gaping for fear and ruth, they saw
The charger panting on his straw;
Till one, who would seem wisest, cried—
"What else but evil could betide,
With that cursed Palmer for our guide?
Better we had through mire and bush
Been lantern-led by Friar Rush."

II

Fitz-Eustace, who the cause but guess'd,
    Nor wholly understood,
His comrades' clamourous plaints suppress'd,—
    He knew Lord Marmion's mood.
Him, ere he issu'd forth, he sought,
And found deep plung'd in gloomy thought,
    And did his tale display
Simply as if he knew of nought
    To cause such disarray.
Lord Marmion gave attention cold,
Nor marvell'd at the wonders told,—
Pass'd them as accidents of course,
And bade his clarions sound to horse.

III

Young Henry Blount, meanwhile, the cost
Had reckon'd with their Scottish host;
And, as the charge he cast and paid,
"Ill thou deserv'st thy hire," he said;
"Dost see, thou knave, my horse's plight?
Fairies have ridden him all the night,
    And let him in a foam!
I trust that soon a conjuring band,
With English cross, and blazing brand,
Shall drive the devils from this land,
    To their infernal home:
For in this haunted den, I trow,
All night they trample to and fro."
The laughing host look'd on the hire,—
"Gramercy, gentle southern squire,
And if thou comest among the rest,
With Scottish broadsword to be blest,
Sharp be the brand, and sure the blow,
And short the pang to undergo."
Here stay'd their talk,—for Marmion
Gave now the signal to set on.
The Palmer showing forth the way,
They journey'd all the morning day.

IV

The green-sward way was smooth and good,
Through Humbie's and through Saltoun's wood;
A forest glade, which, varying still,
Here gave a view of dale and hill,
There narrower clos'd, till over head

A vaulted screen the branches made.
"A pleasant path," Fitz-Eustace said;
"Such as where errant-knights might see
Adventures of high chivalry;
Might meet some damsel flying fast,
With hair unbound, and looks aghast;
And smooth and level course were here,
In her defence to break a spear.
Here, too, are twilight nooks and dells;
And oft, in such, the story tells,
The damsel kind, from danger freed,
Did grateful pay her champion's meed."
He spoke to cheer Lord Marmion's mind:
Perchance to show his lore design'd;
   For Eustace much had por'd
Upon a huge romantic tome,
In the hall window of his home,
Imprinted at the antique dome
   Of Caxton, or De Worde.
Therefore he spoke,—but spoke in vain,
For Marmion answer'd nought again.

   V
Now sudden, distant trumpets shrill,
In notes prolong'd by wood and hill,
   Were heard to echo far;
Each ready archer grasp'd his bow,
But by the flourish soon they know,
   They breath'd no point of war.
Yet cautious, as in foeman's land,
Lord Marmion's order speeds the band,
   Some opener ground to gain;
And scarce a furlong had they rode,
When thinner trees, receding, show'd
   A little woodland plain.
Just in that advantageous glade,
The halting troop a line had made,
As forth from the opposing shade
   Issu'd a gallant train.

   VI
First came the trumpets, at whose clang
So late the forest echoes rang;
On prancing steeds they forward press'd,
With scarlet mantle, azure vest;
Each at his trump a banner wore,

Which Scotland's royal scutcheon bore:
Heralds and pursuivants, by name
Bute, Islay, Marchmount, Rothsay, came,
In painted tabards, proudly showing
Gules, Argent, Or, and Azure glowing,
  Attendant on a King-at-arms,
Whose hand the armorial truncheon held,
That feudal strife had often quell'd,
  When wildest its alarms.

VII

He was a man of middle age;
In aspect manly, grave, and sage,
  As on King's errand come;
But in the glances of his eye,
A penetrating, keen, and sly
  Expression found its home;
The flash of that satiric rage,
Which, bursting on the early stage,
Branded the vices of the age,
  And broke the keys of Rome.
On milk-white palfrey forth he pac'd;
His cap of maintenance was grac'd
  With the proud heron-plume.
From his steed's shoulder, loin, and breast,
  Silk housings swept the ground,
With Scotland's arms, device, and crest,
  Embroider'd round and round.
The double tressure might you see,
  First by Achaius borne,
The thistle and the fleur-de-lis,
  And gallant unicorn.
So bright the King's armorial coat,
That scarce the dazzled eye could note,
In living colours, blazon'd brave,
The Lion, which his title gave.
A train, which well beseem'd his state,
But all unarm'd, around him wait.
  Still is thy name in high account,
    And still thy verse has charms,
  Sir David Lindesay of the Mount,
    Lord Lion King-at-arms!

VIII

Down from his horse did Marmion spring,
Soon as he saw the Lion-King;

For well the stately Baron knew
To him such courtesy was due,
Whom royal James himself had crown'd,
And on his temples plac'd the round
  Of Scotland's ancient diadem:
And wet his brow with hallow'd wine,
And on his finger given to shine
  The emblematic gem.
Their mutual greetings duly made,
The Lion thus his message said:—
"Though Scotland's King hath deeply swore
Ne'er to knit faith with Henry more,
And strictly hath forbid resort
From England to his royal court;
Yet, for he knows Lord Marmion's name,
And honours much his warlike fame,
My liege hath deem'd it shame, and lack
Of courtesy, to turn him back;
And, by his order, I, your guide,
Must lodging fit and fair provide,
Till finds King James meet time to see
The flower of English chivalry."

    IX
Though inly chaf'd at this delay,
Lord Marmion bears it as he may.
The Palmer, his mysterious guide,
Beholding thus his place supplied,
  Sought to take leave in vain:
Strict was the Lion-King's command,
That none who rode in Marmion's band,
  Should sever from the train:
"England has here enow of spies
In Lady Heron's witching eyes:"
To Marchmount thus, apart, he said,
But fair pretext to Marmion made.
The right-hand path they now decline,
And trace against the stream the Tyne.

    X
At length up that wild dale they wind,
  Where Crichtoun Castle crowns the bank;
For there the Lion's care assign'd
  A lodging meet for Marmion's rank.
That Castle rises on the steep
  Of the green vale of Tyne:

And far beneath, where slow they creep,
From pool to eddy, dark and deep,
Where alders moist, and willows weep,
　　You hear her streams repine.
The towers in different ages rose;
Their various architecture shows
　　The builders' various hands;
A mighty mass, that could oppose,
When deadliest hatred fir'd its foes,
　　The vengeful Douglas bands.

　　　　XI
Crichtoun! though now thy miry court
　　But pens the lazy steer and sheep,
　　Thy turrets rude, and totter'd Keep,
Have been the minstrel's lov'd resort.
Oft have I trac'd, within thy fort,
　　Of mouldering shields the mystic sense,
　　Scutcheons of honour, or pretence,
Quarter'd in old armorial sort,
　　Remains of rude magnificence;
Nor wholly yet had time defac'd
　　Thy lordly gallery fair;
Nor yet the stony cord unbrac'd,
Whose twisted knots, with roses lac'd,
　　Adorn thy ruin'd stair.
Still rises unimpair'd below,
The court-yard's graceful portico;
Above its cornice, row and row
　　Of fair hewn facets richly show
　　　　Their pointed diamond form,
　　Though there but houseless cattle go
　　　　To shield them from the storm.
　　And, shuddering, still may we explore,
　　　　Where oft whilom were captives pent,
　　The darkness of thy Massy More;
　　　　Or, from thy grass-grown battlement,
May trace, in undulating line,
The sluggish mazes of the Tyne.

　　　　XII
Another aspect Crichtoun show'd,
As through its portal Marmion rode;
But yet 'twas melancholy state
Received him at the outer gate;
For none were in the Castle then,

But women, boys, or aged men.
With eyes scarce dried, the sorrowing dame
To welcome noble Marmion came;
Her son, a stripling twelve years old,
Proffer'd the Baron's rein to hold;
For each man that could draw a sword
Had march'd that morning with their lord,
Earl Adam Hepburn,—he who died
On Flodden, by his sovereign's side.
Long may his Lady look in vain!
She ne'er shall see his gallant train,
Come sweeping back through Crichtoun-Dean.
'Twas a brave race, before the name
Of hated Bothwell stain'd their fame.

XIII

And here two days did Marmion rest,
   With every rite that honour claims
Attended as the King's own guest:—
   Such the command of Royal James,
Who marshall'd then his land's array,
Upon the Borough-moor that lay.
Perchance he would not foeman's eye
Upon his gathering host should pry,
Till full prepar'd was every band
To march against the English land.
Here while they dwelt, did Lindesay's wit
Oft cheer the Baron's moodier fit;
And, in his turn, he knew to prize
Lord Marmion's powerful mind, and wise,—
Train'd in the lore of Rome and Greece,
And policies of war and peace.

XIV

It chanc'd, as fell the second night,
   That on the battlements they walk'd,
And, by the slowly fading light,
   Of varying topics talk'd;
And, unaware, the Herald-bard
Said Marmion might his toil have spar'd,
   In travelling so far;
For that a messenger from heaven
In vain to James had counsel given
   Against the English war;
And, closer question'd, thus he told

A tale which chronicles of old
In Scottish story have enroll'd:—

XV

SIR DAVID LINDESAY'S TALE

"Of all the palaces so fair,
  Built for the royal dwelling,
In Scotland, far beyond compare
  Linlithgow is excelling;
And in its park in jovial June,
How sweet the merry linnet's tune,
  How blithe the blackbird's lay!
The wild-buck bells from ferny brake,
The coot dives merry on the lake;
The saddest heart might pleasure take
  To see all nature gay.
But June is to our sovereign dear
The heaviest month in all the year:
Too well his cause of grief you know,
June saw his father's overthrow.
Woe to the traitors, who could bring
The princely boy against his King!
Still in his conscience burns the sting.
In offices as strict as Lent,
King James's June is ever spent.

XVI

"When last this ruthful month was come
And in Linlithgow's holy dome
  The King, as wont, was praying;
While, for his royal father's soul,
The chanters sung, the bells did toll,
  The Bishop mass was saying—
For now the year brought round again
The day the luckless king was slain—
  In Katharine's aisle the Monarch knelt,
  With sackcloth-shirt, and iron belt,
    And eyes with sorrow streaming;
Around him in their stalls of state,
The Thistle's Knight-Companions sate,
  Their banners o'er them beaming.
I too was there, and, sooth to tell,
Bedeafen'd with the jangling knell,
Was watching where the sunbeams fell,
  Through the stain'd casement gleaming;

But, while I mark'd what next befell,
   It seem'd as I were dreaming.
Stepp'd from the crowd a ghostly wight,
In azure gown, with cincture white;
His forehead blad, his head was bare,
Down hung at length his yellow hair.
Now, mock me not, when, good my lord,
I pledge to you my knightly word,
That, when I saw his placid grace,
His simple majesty of face,
His solemn bearing, and his pace
   So stately gliding on,
Seem'd to me ne'er did limner paint
So just an image of the Saint
Who propp'd the Virgin in her faint,
   The loved Apostle John!

XVII

"He stepp'd before the Monarch's chair,
And stood with rustic plainness there,
   And little reverence made;
Nor head, nor body, bow'd nor bent,
But on the desk his arm he leant,
   And words like these he said,
In a low voice, but never tone
So thrill'd through vein, and nerve, and bone:
'My mother sent me from afar,
Sir King, to warn thee not to war;
   Woe waits on thine array;
If war thou wilt, of woman fair,
Her witching wiles and wanton snare,
James Stuart, doubly warn'd, beware:
   God keep thee as he may!'
   The wondering Monarch seem'd to seek
      For answer, and found none;
   And when he rais'd his head to speak,
      The monitor was gone.
The Marshal and myself had cast
To stop him as he outward pass'd;
   But, lighter than the whirlwind's blast,
      He vanish'd from our eyes,
   Like sunbeam on the billow cast,
      That glances but, and dies."

XVIII

While Lindesay told his marvel strange,
   The twilight was so pale,

He mark'd not Marmion's colour change,
   While listening to the tale;
But, after a suspended pause,
The Baron spoke: "Of Nature's laws
   So strong I held the force,
That never superhuman cause
   Could e'er control their course,
And, three days since, had judg'd your aim
Was but to make your guest your game.
But I have seen, since past the Tweed,
What much has chang'd my sceptic creed,
And made me credit aught." He staid;
And seem'd to wish his words unsaid:
But, by that strong emotion press'd,
Which prompts us to unload our breast,
   Even when discovery's pain,
To Lindesay did at length unfold
The tale his village host had told,
   At Gifford, to his train.
Nought of the Palmer says he there,
And nought of Constance, or of Clare;
The thoughts, which broke his sleep, he seems
To mention but as feverish dreams.

    XIX
"In vain," said he, "to rest I spread
My burning limbs, and couch'd my head:
   Fantastic thoughts return'd;
And, by their wild dominion led,
   My heart within me burn'd.
So sore was the delirious goad,
I took my steed, and forth I rode,
And, as the moon shone bright and cold,
Soon reach'd the camp upon the wold.
The southern entrance I pass'd through,
And halted, and my bugle blew.
Methought an answer met my ear;
Yet was the blast so low and drear,
So hollow, and so faintly blown,
It might be echo of my own.

    XX
"Thus judging, for a little space
I listen'd, ere I left the place;
   But scarce could trust my eyes,
Nor yet can think they serv'd me true
When sudden in the ring I view,

In form distinct of shape and hue,
  A mounted champion rise.
I've fought, Lord-Lion, many a day,
In single fight, and mix'd affray,
And ever, I myself may say,
  Have borne me as a knight;
But when this unexpected foe
Seem'd starting from the gulf below—
I care not though the truth I show—
  I trembled with affright;
And as I plac'd in rest my spear,
My hand so shook for very fear,
  I scarce could couch it right.

XXI

"Why need my tongue the issue tell?
We ran our course,—my charger fell;
What could he 'gainst the shock of hell?
  I roll'd upon the plain.
High o'er my head, with threatening hand,
The spectre shook his naked brand;
  Yet did the worst remain:
My dazzled eyes I upward cast,—
Not opening hell itself could blast
  Their sight, like what I saw!
Full on his face the moonbeam strook,—
A face could never be mistook!
I knew the stern vindictive look,
  And held my breath for awe.
I saw the face of one who, fled
To foreign climes, has long been dead,—
  I well believe the last;
For ne'er, from vizor rais'd, did stare
A human warrior, with a glare
  So grimly and so ghast.
Thrice o'er my head he shook the blade;
But when to good Saint George I pray'd,
(The first time ere I ask'd his aid)
  He plung'd it in the sheath;
And, on his courser mounting light,
He seem'd to vanish from my sight:
The moonbeam droop'd, and deepest night
  Sunk down upon the heath.
  'Twere long to tell what cause I have
    To know his face, that met me there,
  Call'd by his hatred from the grave,

> To cumber upper air:
> Dead or alive, good cause had he
> To be my mortal enemy."

XXII

Marvell'd Sir David of the Mount;
Then, learn'd in story, 'gan recount
   Such chance had happ'd of old,
When once, near Norham, there did fight,
A spectre fell of fiendish might,
In likeness of a Scottish knight,
   With Brian Bulmer bold,
And train'd him nigh to disallow
The aid of his baptismal vow.
"And such a phantom, too, 'tis said,
With Highland broadsword, targe, and plaid,
   And fingers, red with gore,
Is seen in Rothiemurcus glade,
Or where the sable pine-trees shade
Dark Tomantoul, and Auchnaslaid,
   Dromouchty, or Glenmore.
And yet, whate'er such legends say,
Of warlike demon, ghost, or fay,
   On mountain, moor, or plain,
Spotless in faith, in bosom bold,
True son of chivalry should hold,
   These midnight terrors vain;
For seldom have such spirits power
To harm, save in the evil hour,
When guilt we meditate within,
Or harbour unrepented sin."
Lord Marmion turn'd him half aside,
And twice to clear his voice he tried,
   Then press'd Sir David's hand,—
But nought, at length, in answer said;
And here their farther converse staid,
   Each ordering that his band
Should bowne them with the rising day,
To Scotland's camp to take their way.
   Such was the King's command.

XXIII

Early they took Dun-Edin's road;
And I could trace each step they trode:
Hill, brook, nor dell, nor rock, nor stone,
Lies on the path to me unknown.

Much might it boast of **storied lore;**
But, passing such digression **o'er,**
Suffice it that the route was **laid**
Across the furzy hills of Braid.
They pass'd the glen and scanty rill,
And climb'd the opposing bank, until
They gain'd the top of Blackford Hill.

XXIV

Blackford! on whose uncultur'd breast,
  Among the broom, and thorn, and whin,
A truant-boy, I sought the nest,
Or listed, as I lay at rest,
  While rose, on breezes thin,
The murmur of the city crowd,
And, from his steeple jangling loud,
  Saint Giles's mingling din.
Now, from the summit to the plain,
Waves all the hill with yellow grain;
  And o'er the landscape as I look,
Nought do I see unchang'd remain,
  Save the rude cliffs and chiming brook.
To me they make a heavy moan,
Of early friendships past and gone.

XXV

But different far the change has been,
  Since Marmion, from the crown
Of Blackford, saw that martial scene
  Upon the bent so brown:
Thousand pavilions, white as snow,
Spread all the Borough-moor below,
  Upland, and dale, and down—
A thousand did I say? I ween,
Thousands on thousands there were seen,
That chequer'd all the heath between
  The streamlet and the town;
In crossing ranks extending far,
Forming a camp irregular;
Oft giving way, where still there stood
Some relics of the old oak wood,
That darkly huge did intervene,
And tam'd the glaring white with green:
In these extended lines there lay
A martial kingdom's vast array.

XXVI

For from Hebudes, dark with rain,
To eastern Lodon's fertile plain,
And from the southern Redswire edge,
To farthest Rosse's rocky ledge;
From west to east, from south to north,
Scotland sent all her warriors forth.
Marmion might hear the mingled hum
Of myriads up the mountain come;
The horses' tramp, and tingling clank,
Where chiefs review'd their vassal rank,
 And charger's shrilling neigh;
And see the shifting lines advance,
While frequent flash'd, from shield and lance,
 The sun's reflected ray.

XXVII

Thin curling in the morning air,
The wreaths of failing smoke declare
To embers now the brands decay'd,
Where the night-watch their fires had made.
They saw, slow rolling on the plain,
Full many a baggage-cart and wain,
And dire artillery's clumsy car,
By sluggish oxen tugg'd to war;
And there were Borthwick's Sisters Seven,
And culverins which France had given.
Ill-omen'd gift! the guns remain
The conqueror's spoil on Flodden plain.

XXVIII

Nor mark'd they less, where in the air
A thousand streamers flaunted fair;
 Various in shape, device, and hue,
 Green, sanguine, purple, red, and blue,
Broad, narrow, swallow-tail'd, and square,
Scroll, pennon, pensil, bandrol, there
 O'er the pavilions flew.
Highest and midmost, was descried
The royal banner floating wide;
 The staff, a pine-tree, strong and straight,
Pitch'd deeply in a massive stone,
Which still in memory is shown,
 Yet bent beneath the standard's weight
  Whene'er the western wind unroll'd,
  With toil, the huge and cumbrous fold,

And gave to view the dazzling field,
Where, in proud Scotland's royal shield,
   The ruddy lion ramp'd in gold.

XXIX

Lord Marmion view'd the landscape bright,
He view'd it with a chief's delight,
  Until within him burn'd his heart,
  And lightning from his eye did part,
    As on the battle-day;
  Such glance did falcon never dart,
    When stooping on his prey.
"Oh! well, Lord-Lion, hast thou said,
Thy King from warfare to dissuade
  Were but a vain essay;
For, by St. George, were that host mine,
Not power infernal nor divine,
Should once to peace my soul incline,
Till I had dimm'd their armour's shine
  In glorious battle-fray!"
Answer'd the Bard, of milder mood:
"Fair is the sight,—and yet 'twere good,
  That kings would think withal,
When peace and wealth their land has bless'd,
'Tis better to sit still at rest,
  Than rise, perchance to fall."

XXX

Still on the spot Lord Marmion stay'd,
For fairer scene he ne'er survey'd.
  When sated with the martial show
  That peopled all the plain below,
  The wandering eye could o'er it go,
  And mark the distant city glow
    With gloomy splendour red;
  For on the smoke-wreaths, huge and slow,
  That round her sable turrets flow,
    The morning beams were shed,
  And ting'd them with a lustre proud,
  Like that which streaks a thunder-cloud.
Such dusky grandeur cloth'd the height,
Where the huge Castle holds its state,
  And all the steep slope down,
Whose ridgy back heaves to the sky,
Pil'd deep and massy, close and high,
  Mine own romantic town!

But northward far, with purer blaze,
On Ochil mountains fell the rays,
And as each heathy top they kiss'd,
It gleam'd a purple amethyst.
Yonder the shores of Fife you saw;
Here Preston Bay and Berwick-Law:
   And, broad between them roll'd,
The gallant Frith the eye might note,
Whose islands on its bosom float,
   Like emeralds chas'd in gold.
Fitz-Eustace' heart felt closely pent;
As if to give his rapture vent,
The spur he to his charger lent,
   And rais'd his bridle hand,
And, making demi-volte in air,
Cried "Where's the coward that would not dare
   To fight for such a land!"
The Lindesay smil'd his joy to see;
Nor Marmion's frown repress'd his glee.

    XXXI
Thus while they look'd, a flourish proud,
Where mingled trump, and clarion loud,
   And fife, and kettle-drum,
And sackbut deep, and psaltery,
And war-pipe with discordant cry,
And cymbal clattering to the sky,
Making wild music bold and high,
   Did up the mountain come;
The whilst the bells, with distant chime,
Merrily toll'd the hour of prime,
   And thus the Lindesay spoke:
"Thus clamour still the war-notes when
The king to mass his way has ta'en,
Or to St. Katharine's of Sienne,
   Or Chapel of Saint Rocque.
To you they speak of martial fame;
But me remind of peaceful game,
   When blither was their cheer,
Thrilling in Falkland-woods the air,
In signal none his steed should spare,
But strive which foremost might repair
   To the downfall of the deer.

    XXXII
"Nor less," he said, "when looking forth,
I view yon Empress of the North

Sit on her hilly throne;
Her palace's imperial bowers,
Her castle, proof to hostile powers,
Her stately halls and holy towers—
   Nor less," he said, "I moan,
To think what woe mischance may bring,
And how these merry bells may ring
The death-dirge of our gallant king;
   Or with the larum call
The burghers forth to watch and ward,
'Gainst southern sack and fires to guard
   Dun-Edin's leaguer'd wall.
But not for my presaging thought
Dream conquest sure, or cheaply bought!
   Lord Marmion, I say nay:
God is the guider of the field,
He breaks the champion's spear and shield,—
   But thou thyself shalt say,
When joins yon host in deadly stowre,
That England's dames must weep in bower,
   Her monks the death-mass sing;
For never saw'st thou such a power
   Led on by such a King."
And now, down-winding to the plain,
The barriers of the camp they gain,
   And there they made a stay.
There stays the Minstrel, till he fling
His hand o'er every Border string,
And fit his harp the pomp to sing,
Of Scotland's ancient Court and King,
   In the succeeding lay.

Canto Fifth THE COURT

I

The train has left the hills of Braid;
The barrier guard have open made
(So Lindesay bade) the palisade,
   That closed the tented ground;
Their men the warders backward drew,
And carried pikes, as they rode through
   Into its ample bound.

Fast ran the Scottish warriors there,
Upon the Southern band to stare,
And envy with their wonder rose,
To see such well-appointed foes;
Such length of shafts, such mighty bows,
So huge, that many simply thought
But for a vaunt such weapons wrought;
And little deem'd their force to feel,
Through links of mail, and plates of steel,
When rattling upon Flodden vale,
The cloth-yard arrows flew like hail.

II

Nor less did Marmion's skilful view
Glance every line and squadron through;
And much he marvell'd one small land
Could marshal forth such various band:
    For men-at-arms were here,
Heavily sheath'd in mail and plate,
Like iron towers for strength and weight,
On Flemish steeds of bone and height,
    With battle-axe and spear.
Young knights and squires, a lighter train,
Practis'd their chargers on the plain,
By aid of leg, of hand, and rein,
    Each warlike feat to show,
To pass, to wheel, the croupe to gain,
And high curvett, that not in vain
The sword sway might descend amain
    On foeman's casque below.
He saw the hardy burghers there
March arm'd, on foot, with faces bare,
    For vizor they wore none,
Nor waving plume, nor crest of knight;
But burnish'd were their corslets bright,
Their brigantines, and gorgets light,
    Like very silver shone.
Long pikes they had for standing fight,
    Two-handed swords they wore,
And many wielded mace of weight,
    And bucklers bright they bore.

III

On foot the yeoman too, but dress'd
In his steel-jack, a swarthy vest,
    With iron quilted well;

Each at his back (a slender store)
His forth days' provision bore,
  As feudal statutes tell.
His arms were halbert, axe, or spear,
A crossbow there, a hagbut here,
  A dagger-knife, and brand.
Sober he seem'd, and sad of cheer,
As loth to leave his cottage dear,
  And march to foreign strand;
Or musing, who would guide his steer
  To till the fallow land.
Yet deem not in his thoughtful eye
Did aught of dastard terror lie;
  More dreadful far his ire,
Than theirs, who, scorning danger's name,
In eager mood to battle came,
Their valour like light straw on flame,
  A fierce but fading fire.

IV

Not so the Borderer: bred to war,
He knew the battle's din afar,
  And joy'd to hear it swell.
His peaceful day was slothful ease;
Nor harp, nor pipe, his ear could please
  Like the loud slogan yell.
On active steed, with lance and blade,
The light-arm'd pricker plied his trade,—
  Let nobles fight for fame;
Let vassals follow where they lead,
Burghers to guard their townships bleed,
  But war's the Borderer's game.
Their gain, their glory, their delight,
To sleep the day, maraud the night,
  O'er mountain, moss, and moor;
Joyful to fight they took their way,
Scarce caring who might win the day,
  Their booty was secure.
These, as Lord Marmion's train pass'd by,
Look'd on at first with careless eye,
Nor marvell'd aught, well taught to know
The form and force of English bow.
But when they saw the lord array'd
In splendid arms and rich brocade,
Each Borderer to his kinsman said,—
  "Hist, Ringan! seest thou there?

Canst guess which road they'll homeward ride?
O! could we but on Border side,
By Eusedale glen, or Liddell's tide,
  Beset a prize so fair!
That fangless Lion, too, their guide,
Might chance to lose his glistering hide;
Brown Maudlin, of that doublet pied,
  Could make a kirtle rare."

V

Next, Marmion mark'd the Celtic race,
Of different language, form, and face,
  A various race of man;
Just then the Chiefs their tribes array'd,
And wild and garish semblance made,
The chequer'd trews, and belted plaid,
And varying notes the war-pipes bray'd,
  To every varying clan;
Wild through their red or sable hair
Look'd out their eyes with savage stare,
  On Marmion as he pass'd;
Their legs above the knee were bare;
Their frame was sinewy, short, and spare,
  And harden'd to the blast;
Of taller race, the chiefs they own
Were by the eagle's plumage known.
The hunted red-deer's undress'd hide
Their hairy buskins well supplied;
The graceful bonnet deck'd their head:
Back from their shoulders hung the plaid;
A broadsword of unwieldy length,
A dagger proved for edge and strength,
  A studded targe they wore,
And quivers, bows, and shafts,—but, O!
Short was the shaft, and weak the bow,
  To that which England bore.
The Isles-men carried at their backs
The ancient Danish battle-axe.
They raised a wild and wondering cry,
As with his guide rode Marmion by.
Loud were their clamouring tongues, as when
The clanging sea-fowl leave the fen,
And, with their cries discordant mix'd,
Grumbled and yell'd the pipes betwixt.

VI

Thus through the Scottish camp they pass'd,
And reach'd the City gate at last,
Where all around, a wakeful guard,
Arm'd burghers kept their watch and ward.
Well had they cause of jealous fear,
When lay encamp'd, in field so near,
The Borderer and the Mountaineer.
As through the bustling streets they go,
All was alive with martial show:
At every turn, with dinning clang,
The armourer's anvil clash'd and rang;
Or toil'd the swarthy smith, to wheel
The bar that arms the charger's heel;
Or axe, or falchion, to the side
Of jarring grindstone was applied.
Page, groom, and squire, with hurrying pace,
Through street, and lane, and market-place,
    Bore lance, or casque, or sword;
While burghers, with important face,
    Describ'd each new-come lord,
Discuss'd his lineage, told his name,
His following, and his warlike fame.
The Lion led to lodging meet,
Which high o'erlook'd the crowded street;
    There must the Baron rest,
Till past the hour of vesper tide,
And then to Holy-Rood must ride,—
    Such was the King's behest.
Meanwhile the Lion's care assigns
A banquet rich, and costly wines,
    To Marmion and his train;
And when the appointed hour succeeds,
The Baron dons his peaceful weeds,
And following Lindesay as he leads
    The palace-halls they gain.

VII

Old Holy-Rood rung merrily,
That night, with wassell, mirth, and glee:
King James within her princely bower,
Feasted the Chiefs of Scotland's power,
Summon'd to spend the parting hour;
For he had charged, that his array
Should southward march by break of day.

Well lov'd that splendid monarch aye
  The banquet and the song,
By day the tourney, and by night
The merry dance, trac'd fast and light,
The maskers quaint, the pageant bright,
  The revel loud and long.
This feat outshone his banquets past,
It was his blithest—and his last.
The dazzling lamps, from gallery gay,
Cast on the Court a dancing ray;
Here to the harp did minstrels sing;
There ladies touch'd a softer string;
With long-ear'd cap, and motley vest,
The licensed fool retail'd his jest;
His magic tricks the juggler plied;
At dice and draughts the gallants vied;
While some, in close recess apart,
Courted the ladies of their heart,
  Nor courted them in vain;
For often, in the parting hour,
Victorious Love asserts his power
  O'er coldness and disdain;
And flinty is her heart, can view
To battle march a lover true,
Can hear, perchance, his last adieu,
  Nor own her share of pain.

    VIII
Through this mix'd crowd of glee and game,
The King to greet Lord Marmion came,
  While, reverent, all made room.
An easy task it was, I trow,
King James's manly form to know,
Although, his courtesy to show,
He doff'd, to Marmion bending low,
  His broider'd cap and plume.
For royal was his garb and mien,
  His cloak, of crimson velvet pil'd,
  Trimm'd with the fur of marten wild;
His vest of changeful satin sheen,
  The dazzled eye beguil'd;
His gorgeous collar hung adown,
Wrought with the badge of Scotland's crown,
The thistle brave, of old renown:
His trusty blade, Toledo right,
Descended from a baldric bright;

White were his buskins, on the heel
His spurs inlaid of gold and steel;
His bonnet, all of crimson fair,
Was button'd with a ruby rare:
And Marmion deem'd he ne'er had seen
A prince of such a noble mien.

IX

The Monarch's form was middle size;
For feat of strength, or exercise,
  Shaped in proportion fair;
And hazel was his eagle eye,
And auburn of the darkest dye,
  His short curl'd beard and hair.
Light was his footstep in the dance,
  And firm his stirrup in the lists;
And, oh! he had that merry glance
  That seldom lady's heart resists.
Lightly from fair to fair he flew,
And lov'd to plead, lament, and sue,
Suit lightly won, and short-liv'd pain,
For monarchs seldom sigh in vain.
  I said he joy'd in banquet bower;
But, 'mid his mirth, 'twas often strange,
How suddenly his cheer would change,
  His look o'ercast and lower,
If, in a sudden turn, he felt
The pressure of his iron belt,
That bound his breast in penance pain,
In memory of his father slain.
Even so 'twas strange how, evermore,
Soon as the passing pang was o'er,
Forward he rush'd, with double glee,
Into the stream of revelry;
Thus, dim-seen object of affright
Startles the courser in his flight,
And half he halts, half springs aside;
But feels the quickening spur applied,
And, straining on the tighten'd rein,
Scours doubly swift o'er hill and plain.

X

O'er James's heart, the courtiers say,
Sir Hugh the Heron's wife held sway:
  To Scotland's Court she came,
To be a hostage for her lord,

Who Cessford's gallant heart had gor'd,
And with the King to make accord,
    Had sent his lovely dame.
Nor to that lady free alone
Did he gay King allegiance own;
    For the fair Queen of France
Sent him a turquois ring and glove,
And charg'd him, as her knight and love,
    For her to break a lance;
And strike three strokes with Scottish brand,
And march three miles on Southron land,
And bid the banners of his band
    In English breezes dance.
    And thus for France's Queen he drest
    His manly limbs in mailed vest;
    And thus admitted English fair
    His inmost counsels still to share;
    And thus, for both, he madly plann'd
    The ruin of himself and land!
        And yet, the sooth to tell,
Nor England's fair, nor France's Queen,
Were worth one pearl-drop, bright and sheen,
        From Margaret's eyes that fell,—
His own Queen Margaret, who, in Lithgow's bower,
All lonely sat, and wept the weary hour.

    XI
    The Queen sits lone in Lithgow pile,
        And weeps the weary day
    The war against her native soil,
    Her Monarch's risk in battle broil:—
    And in gay Holy-Rood, the while,
    Dame Heron rises with a smile
        Upon the harp to play.
    Fair was her rounded arm, as o'er
        The strings her fingers flew;
    And as she touch'd and tuned them all,
    Ever her bosom's rise and fall
        Was plainer given to view;
    For, all for heat, was laid aside
    Her wimple, and her hood untied.
    And first she pitch'd her voice to sing,
    Then glanced her dark eye on the King,
    And then around the silent ring;
    And laugh'd, and blush'd, and oft did say
    Her pretty oath, by Yea, and Nay,

She could not, would not, durst not play!
At length, upon the harp, with glee,
Mingled with arch simplicity,
A soft, yet lively, air she rung,
While thus the wily lady sung:

XII

LOCHINVAR

"O, young Lochinvar is come out of the west,
Through all the wide Border his steed was the best;
And save his good broadsword he weapons had none,
He rode all unarm'd, and he rode all alone.
So faithful in love, and so dauntless in war,
There never was knight like the young Lochinvar.

"He staid not for brake, and he stopp'd not for stone,
He swam the Eske river where ford there was none;
But ere he alighted at Netherby gate,
The bride had consented, the gallant came late:
For a laggard in love, and a dastard in war,
Was to wed the fair Ellen of brave Lochinvar.

"So boldly he enter'd the Netherby Hall,
Among bride's-men, and kinsmen, and brothers, and all:
Then spoke the bride's father, his hand on his sword,
(For the poor craven bridegroom said never a word)
'O come ye in peace here, or come ye in war,
Or to dance at our bridal, young Lord Lochinvar?'

" 'I long woo'd your daughter, my suit you denied;—
Love swells like the Solway, but ebbs like its tide—
And now am I come, with this lost love of mine,
To lead but one measure, drink one cup of wine.
There are maidens in Scotland more lovely by far,
That would gladly be bride to the young Lochinvar.'

"The bride kiss'd the goblet: the knight took it up,
He quaff'd off the wine, and he threw down the cup.
She look'd down to blush, and she look'd up to sigh,
With a smile on her lips, and a tear in her eye.
He took her soft hand, ere her mother could bar,—
'Now tread we a measure!' said young Lochinvar.

"So stately his form, and so lovely her face,

That never a hall such a galliard did grace;
While her mother did fret, and her father did fume,
And the bridegroom stood dangling his bonnet and plume;
And the bride-maidens whisper'd, ' 'Twere better by far,
To have match'd our fair cousin with young Lochinvar.'

"One touch to her hand, and one word in her ear,
When they reach'd the hall-door, and the charger stood near;
So light to the croupe the fair lady he swung,
So light to the saddle before her he sprung!
'She is won! we are gone, over bank, bush, and scaur;
They'll have fleet steeds that follow,' quoth young Lochinvar.

"There was mounting 'mong Graemes of the Netherby clan;
Forsters, Fenwicks, and Musgraves, they rode and they ran:
There was racing and chasing on Cannobie Lee,
But the lost bride of Netherby ne'er did they see.
So daring in love, and so dauntless in war,
Have ye e'er heard of gallant like young Lochinvar?"

XIII

The Monarch o'er the siren hung
And beat the measure as she sung;
And, pressing closer, and more near,
He whisper'd praises in her ear.
In loud applause the courtiers vied;
And ladies wink'd, and spoke aside.
  The witching dame to Marmion threw
    A glance, where seem'd to reign
  The pride that claims applauses due,
  And of her royal conquest too,
    A real or feign'd disdain:
Familiar was the look, and told,
Marmion and she were friends of old.
The King observ'd their meeting eyes,
With something like displeas'd surprise;
For monarchs ill can rivals brook,
Even in a word, or smile, or look.
Straight took he forth the parchment broad,
Which Marmion's high commission show'd:
"Our Borders sack'd by many a raid,
Our peaceful liege-men robb'd," he said:
"On day of truce our Warden slain,
Stout Barton kill'd, his vessels ta'en—
Unworthy were we here to reign,
Should these for vengeance cry in vain;

Our full defiance, hate, and scorn,
Our herald has to Henry borne."

XIV

He paus'd, and led where Douglas stood,
And with stern eye the pageant view'd:
I mean that Douglas, sixth of yore,
Who coronet of Angus bore,
And, when his blood and heart were high,
Did the third James in camp defy,
And all his minions led to die
  On Lauder's dreary flat:
Princes and favourites long grew tame
And trembled at the homely name
  Of Archibald Bell-the-Cat;
The same who left the dusky vale
Of Hermitage in Liddisdale,
  Its dungeons, and its towers,
Where Bothwell's turrets brave the air,
And Bothwell bank is blooming fair,
  To fix his princely bowers.
Though now, in age, he had laid down
His armour for the peaceful gown,
  And for a staff his brand,
Yet often would flash forth the fire,
That could, in youth, a monarch's ire
  And minion's pride withstand;
And even that day, at council board,
  Unapt to soothe his sovereign's mood,
  Against the war had Angus stood,
And chaf'd his royal lord.

XV

His giant-form, like ruin'd tower,
Though fall'n its muscles' brawny vaunt,
Huge-bon'd, and tall and grim, and gaunt,
  Seem'd o'er the gaudy scene to lower:
His locks and beard in silver grew;
His eyebrows kept their sable hue.
Near Douglas when the Monarch stood,
His bitter speech he thus pursued:
"Lord Marmion, since these letters say
That in the North you needs must stay
  While slightest hopes of peace remain,
Uncourteous speech it were, and stern,
To say—Return to Lindisfarne

Until my herald come again.
Then rest you in Tantallon Hold;
Your host shall be the Douglas bold,—
A chief unlike his sires of old.
He wears their motto on his blade,
Their blazon o'er his towers display'd;
Yet loves his sovereign to oppose,
More than to face his country's foes.
And, I bethink me, by St. Stephen,
    But e'en this morn to me was given
A prize, the first fruits of the war,
Ta'en by a galley from Dunbar,
    A bevy of the maids of Heaven.
Under your guard, these holy maids
Shall safe return to cloister shades,
And, while they at Tantallon stay,
Requiem for Cochran's soul may say."
And, with the slaughter'd favourite's name,
Across the Monarch's brow there came
A cloud of ire, remorse, and shame.

XVI

In answer nought could Angus speak;
His proud heart swell'd wellnigh to break:
He turn'd aside, and down his cheek
    A burning tear there stole,
His hand the Monarch sudden took,
That sight his kind heart could not brook:
    "Now by the Bruce's soul,
Angus, my hasty speech forgive!
For sure as doth his spirit live,
As he said of the Douglas old,
    I well may say of you,
That never king did subject hold,
In speech more free, in war more bold,
    More tender and more true:
Forgive me, Douglas, once again."
And, while the King his hand did strain,
The old man's tears fell down like rain.
To seize the moment Marmion tried,
And whisper'd to the King aside:
"Oh! let such tears unwonted plead
For respite short from dubious deed!
A child will weep a bramble's smart,
A maid to see her sparrow part,
A stripling for a woman's heart:

But woe awaits a country, when
She sees the tears of bearded men.
Then oh! what omen, dark and high,
When Douglas wets his manly eye!"

XVII

Displeas'd was James, that stranger view'd
And tamper'd with his changing mood.
"Laugh those that can, weep those that may,"
Thus did the fiery Monarch say,
"Southward I march by break of day;
And if within Tantallon strong
The good Lord Marmion tarries long,
Perchance our meeting next may fall
At Tamworth, in his castle-hall."
The haughty Marmion felt the taunt,
And answer'd, grave, the royal vaunt:
"Much honour'd were my humble home
If in its halls King James should come;
But Nottingham has archers good,
And Yorkshire men are stern of mood;
Northumbrian prickers wild and rude.
On Derby Hills the paths are steep;
In Ouse and Tyne the fords are deep;
And many a banner will be torn,
And many a knight to earth be borne,
And many a sheaf of arrows spent,
Ere Scotland's King shall cross the Trent:
Yet pause, brave Prince, while yet you may!"
The Monarch lightly turn'd away,
And to his nobles loud did call,—
"Lords, to the dance! a hall! a hall!"
Himself his cloak and sword flung by,
And led Dame Heron gallantly;
And minstrels, at the royal order,
Rung out "Blue Bonnets o'er the Border."

XVIII

Leave we these revels now, to tell
What to Saint Hilda's maids befell,
Whose galley, as they sail'd again
To Whitby, by a Scot was ta'en.
Now at Dun-Edin did they bide,
Till James should of their fate decide;
     And soon, by his command,
Were gently summon'd to prepare

To journey under Marmion's care,
As escort honour'd, safe, and fair,
　　Again to English land.
The Abbess told her chaplet o'er,
Now knew which saint she should implore;
For, when she thought of Constance, sore
　　She fear'd Lord Marmion's mood.
And judge what Clara must have felt!
The sword that hung in Marmion's belt
　　Had drunk De Wilton's blood.
Unwittingly, King James had given,
　　As guard to Whitby's shades,
The man most dreaded under Heaven
　　By these defenceless maids:
Yet what petition could avail,
Or who would listen to the tale
Of women, prisoner, and nun,
'Mid bustle of a war begun?
They deem'd it hopeless to avoid
The convoy of their dangerous guide.

XIX

Their lodging, so the King assign'd,
To Marmion's, as their guardian, join'd;
And thus it fell, that, passing nigh,
The Palmer caught the Abbess' eye,
　　Who warn'd him by a scroll,
She had a secret to reveal,
That much concern'd the Church's weal,
　　And health of sinner's soul;
And, with deep charge of secrecy,
　　She named a place to meet,
Within an open balcony,
That hung from dizzy pitch, and high,
　　Above the stately street;
To which, as common to each home,
At night they might in secret come.

XX

At night, in secret, there they came,
The Palmer and the holy Dame.
The moon among the clouds rose high,
And all the city hum was by.
Upon the street, where late before
Did din of war and warriors roar,
　　You might have heard a pebble fall,

A beetle hum, a cricket sing,
An owlet flap his boding wing
  On Gi‘es’s steeple tall.
The antique buildings, climbing high,
Whose Gothic frontlets sought the sky,
  Were here wrapt deep in shade;
There on their brows the moonbeam broke,
Through the faint wreaths of silvery smoke,
   And on the casements play’d.
   And other light was none to see,
    Save torches gliding far,
  Before some chieftain of degree,
  Who left the royal revelry
    To bowne him for the war.
A solemn scene the Abbess chose,
A solemn hour, her secret to disclose.

XXI

“O holy Palmer!” she began,
“For sure he must be sainted man,
Whose blessed feet have trod the ground
Where the Redeemer’s tomb is found,
For His dear Church’s sake, my tale
Attend, nor deem of light avail,
Though I must speak of worldly love,
How vain to those who wed above!
De Wilton and Lord Marmion woo’d
Clara de Clare, of Gloster’s blood—
(Idle it were of Whitby’s dame,
To say of that same blood I came);
And once, when jealous rage was high,
Lord Marmion said despiteously
Wilton was traitor in his heart,
And had made league with Martin Swart
When he came here on Simnel’s part,
And only cowardice did restrain
His rebel aid on Stokefield’s plain,—
And down he threw his glove:—the thing
Was tried, as wont, before the King;
Where frankly did De Wilton own,
That Swart in Gueldres he had known;
And that between them then there went
Some scroll of courteous compliment.
For this he to his castle sent;
But when his messenger return’d,
Judge how De Wilton’s fury burn’d!

For in his packet there was laid
Letters that claim'd disloyal aid,
And proved King Henry's cause betray'd.
His fame, thus blighted, in the field
He strove to clear, by spear and shield;—
To clear his fame in vain he strove,
For wondrous are His ways above!
Perchance some form was unobserv'd;
Perchance in prayer, or faith, he swerv'd;
Else how could guiltless champion quail,
Or how the blessed ordeal fail?

XXII

"His squire, who now De Wilton saw
As recreant doom'd to suffer law,
   Repentant, own'd in vain,
That, while he had the scrolls in care,
A stranger maiden, passing fair,
Had drench'd him with a beverage rare;
   His words no faith could gain.
With Clare alone he credence won,
Who, rather than wed Marmion,
Did to Saint Hilda's shrine repair,
To give our house her livings fair
And die a vestal vot'ress there.
The impulse from the earth was given,
But bent her to the paths of heaven.
A purer heart, a lovelier maid,
Ne'er shelter'd her in Whitby's shade,
No, not since Saxon Edelfled;
   Only one trace of earthly strain,
      That for her lover's loss
   She cherishes a sorrow vain,
      And murmurs at the cross.
   And then her heritage;—it goes
      Along the banks of Tame;
   Deep fields of grain the reaper mows,
   In meadows rich the heifer lows,
   The falconer and huntsman knows
      Its woodlands for the game.
Shame were it to Saint Hilda dear,
And I, her humble vot'ress here,
   Should do a deadly sin,
Her temple spoil'd before mine eyes,
If this false Marmion such a prize
   By my consent should win;

Yet hath our boisterous monarchs sworn
That Clare shall from our house be torn,
And grievous cause have I to fear,
Such mandate doth Lord Marmion bear.

XXIII

"Now, prisoner, helpless, and betray'd
To evil power, I claim thine aid,
  By every step that thou hast trod
To holy shrine and grotto dim;
By every martyr's tortur'd limb,
By angel, saint, and seraphim,
  And by the Church of God!
For mark:—When Wilton was betray'd,
And with his squire forg'd letters laid,
She was, alas! that sinful maid,
  By whom the deed was done;
O! shame and horror to be said—
  She was a perjur'd nun!
No clerk in all the land, like her,
Traced quaint and varying character.
Perchance you may a marvel deem,
  That Marmion's paramour
(For such vile thing she was) should scheme
  Her lover's nuptial hour;
But o'er him thus she hop'd to gain,
As privy to his honour's stain,
  Illimitable power:
For this she secretly retain'd
  Each proof that might the plot reveal,
  Instructions with his hand and seal;
And thus Saint Hilda deign'd,
  Through sinner's perfidy impure,
  Her house's glory to secure,
And Clare's immortal weal.

XXIV

" 'Twere long, and needless, here to tell
How to my hand these papers fell;
  With me they must not stay.
Saint Hilda keep her Abbess true!
Who knows what outrage he might do,
  While journeying by the way?
O blessed Saint, if e'er again
I venturous leave thy calm domain,
To travel or by land or main,

Deep penance may I pay!
Now, saintly Palmer, mark my prayer:
I give this packet to thy care,
For thee to stop they will not dare;
    And O! with cautious speed,
To Wolsey's hand the papers bring,
That he may show them to the King:
    And, for thy well-earn'd meed,
Thou holy man, at Whitby's shrine
A weekly mass shall still be thine,
    While priests can sing and read.
What ail'st thou? Speak!" For as he took
The charge, a strong emotion shook
    His frame; and, ere reply,
They heard a faint, yet shrilly tone,
Like distant clarion feebly blown,
    That on the breeze did die;
And loud the Abbess shriek'd in fear,
"Saint Withold, save us! What is here?
    Look at yon City Cross!
See on its battled tower appear
Phantoms, that scutcheons seem to rear,
    And blazon'd banners toss!"

        XXV
Dun-Edin's Cross, a pillar'd stone,
Rose on a turret octagon;
(But now is razed that monument,
    Whence royal edict rang,
And voice of Scotland's law was sent
    In glorious trumpet-clang.
O! be his tomb as lead to lead,
Upon its dull destroyer's head!—
A minstrel's malison is said.)
Then on its battlements they saw
A vision, passing Nature's law,
    Strange, wild, and dimly seen;
Figures that seem'd to rise and die,
Gibber and sign, advance and fly,
While nought confirm'd could ear or eye
    Discern of sound or mien.
Yet darkly did it seem, as there
Heralds and Pursuivants prepare,
With trumpet sound and blazon fair,
    A summons to proclaim;
But indistinct the pageant proud,

As fancy forms of midnight cloud,
When flings the moon upon her shroud
    A wavering tinge of flame;
It flits, expands, and shifts, till loud,
From midmost of the spectre crowd,
    This awful summons came:—

XXVI

"Prince, prelate, potentate, and peer,
    Whose names I now shall call,
Scottish, or foreigner, give ear;
Subjects of him who sent me here,
At his tribunal to appear,
    I summon one and all:
I cite you by each deadly sin,
That e'er hath soil'd your hearts within:
I cite you by each brutal lust,
That e'er defil'd your earthly dust,—
    By wrath, by pride, by fear,
By each o'ermastering passion's tone,
By the dark grave, and dying groan!
When forty days are pass'd and gone,
I cite you, at your Monarch's throne,
    To answer and appear."
Then thunder'd forth a roll of names:
The first was thine, unhappy James!
    Then all thy nobles came.
Crawford, Glencairn, Montrose, Argyle,
Ross, Bothwell, Forbes, Lennox, Lyle—
Why should I tell their separate style?
    Each chief of birth and fame,
Of Lowland, Highland, Border, Isle,
Foredoom'd to Flodden's carnage pile,
    Was cited there by name;
And Marmion, Lord of Fontenaye,
Of Lutterward, and Scrivelbaye;
De Wilton, erst of Aberley,
The self-same thundering voice did say.
    But then another spoke:
"Thy fatal summons I deny,
And thine infernal Lord defy,
Appealing me to Him on High,
    Who burst the sinner's yoke."
At that dread accent, with a scream,
Parted the pageant like a dream,
    The summoner was gone.

Prone on her face the Abbess fell,
And fast, and fast, her beads did tell;
Her nuns came, startled by the yell,
    And found her there alone.
She mark'd not, at the scene aghast,
What time, or how, the Palmer pass'd.

    XXVII

Shift we the scene. The camp doth move,
    Dun-Edin's streets are empty now,
Save when, for weal of those they love,
    To pray the prayer, and vow the vow,
The tottering child, the anxious fair,
The grey-hair'd sire, with pious care,
To chapels and to shrines repair—
Where is the Palmer now? and where
The Abbess, Marmion, and Clare?
Bold Douglas! to Tantallon fair
    They journey in thy charge:
Lord Marmion rode on his right hand.
The Palmer still was with the band;
Angus, like Lindesay, did command,
    That none should roam at large.
But in that Palmer's alter'd mien
A wondrous change might now be seen;
    Freely he spoke of war,
Of marvels wrought by single hand,
When lifted for a native land;
And still look'd high, as if he plann'd
    Some desperate deed afar.
His courser would he feed and stroke,
And, tucking up his sable frocke,
Would first his mettle bold provoke,
    Then soothe or quell his pride.
Old Hubert said that never one
He saw, except Lord Marmion,
    A steed so fairly ride.

    XXVIII

Some half-hour's march behind, there came,
    By Eustace govern'd fair,
A troop escorting Hilda's Dame,
    With all her nuns, and Clare.
No audience had Lord Marmion sought;
    Ever he fear'd to aggravate
    Clara de Clare's suspicious hate;

And safer 'twas, he thought,
   To wait till, from the nuns remov'd,
   The influence of kindsmen lov'd,
   And suit by Henry's self approv'd,
Her slow consent had wrought.
   His was no flickering flame, that dies
   Unless when fann'd by looks and sighs,
   And lighted oft at lady's eyes;
   He long'd to stretch his wide command
   O'er luckless Clara's ample land:
   Besides, when Wilton with him vied,
   Although the pang of humbled pride
   The place of jealousy supplied,
Yet conquest by that meanness won
He almost loath'd to think upon,
Led him, at times, to hate the cause,
Which made him burst through honour's laws.
If e'er he lov'd, 'twas her alone,
Who died within that vault of stone.

    XXIX

And now, when close at hand they saw
North Berwick's town, and lofty Law,
Fitz-Eustace bade them pause a while,
Before a venerable pile,
   Whose turrets view'd, afar,
The lofty Bass, the Lambie Isle,
   The ocean's peace or war.
At tolling of a bell, forth came
The convent's venerable Dame,
And pray'd Saint Hilda's Abbess rest
With her, a loved and honour'd guest,
Till Douglas should a bark prepare
To waft her back to Whitby fair.
Glad was the Abbess, you may guess,
And thank'd the Scottish Prioress;
And tedious were to tell, I ween,
The courteous speech that pass'd between.
   O'erjoy'd the nuns their palfreys leave;
But when fair Clara did intend,
Like them, from horseback to descend,
   Fitz-Eustace said—"I grieve,
Fair lady, grieve e'en from my heart,
Such gentle company to part;
   Think not discourtesy;
But lords' commands must be obey'd;

And Marmion and the Douglas said,
   That you must wend with me.
Lord Marmion hath a letter broad,
Which to the Scottish Earl he show'd,
Commanding, that, beneath his care,
Without delay, you shall repair
To your good kinsman, Lord Fitz-Clare."

    XXX

The startled Abbess loud exclaim'd;
But she, at whom the blow was aim'd,
Grew pale as death, and cold as lead;
She deem'd she heard her death-doom read.
"Cheer thee, my child!" the Abbess said,
"They dare not tear thee from my hand,
To ride alone with armed band."
   "Nay, holy mother, nay,"
Fitz-Eustace said; "the lovely Clare
Will be in Lady Angus' care,
   In Scotland while we stay;
And, when we move, an easy ride
Will bring us to the English side,
Female attendance to provide
   Befitting Gloster's heir:
Nor thinks nor dreams my noble lord
By slightest look or act or word
   To harass Lady Clare.
Her faithful guardian he will be,
Nor sue for slightest courtesy
   That e'en to stranger falls,
Till he shall place her, safe and free,
   Within her kinsman's halls."
He spoke, and blush'd with earnest grace;
His faith was painted on his face,
   And Clare's worst fear reliev'd.
The Lady Abbess loud exclaim'd
On Henry, and the Douglas blam'd,
   Entreated, threaten'd, griev'd;
To martyr, saint, and prophet pray'd,
Against Lord Marmion inveigh'd,
And call'd the Prioress to aid,
To curse with candle, bell, and book.
Her head the grave Cistertian shook:
"The Douglas, and the King," she said,
"In their commands will be obey'd;

Grieve not, nor dream that harm can fall
The maiden in Tantallon hall."

XXXI

The Abbess, seeing strife was vain,
Assumed her wonted state again—
  For much of state she had—
Compos'd her veil, and rais'd her head,
And "Bid," in solemn voice she said,
  "They master, bold and bad,
The records of his house turn o'er,
  And, when he shall there written see,
  That one of his own ancestry
  Drove the Monks forth of Coventry,
Bid him his fate explore!
  Prancing in pride of earthly trust,
  His charger hurl'd him to the dust,
  And, by a base plebeian thrust,
He died his band before.
  God judge 'twixt Marmion and me;
  He is a Chief of high degree,
And I a poor recluse:
  Yet oft, in holy writ, we see
  Even such weak minister as me
May the oppressor bruise:
  For thus, inspir'd, did Judith slay
    The mighty in his sin,
  And Jael thus, and Deborah"——
  Here hasty Blount broke in:
"Fitz-Eustace, we must march our band:
Saint Anton' fire thee! wilt thou stand
All day, with bonnet in thy hand,
  To hear the Lady preach?
By this good light! if thus we stay,
Lord Marmion, for our fond delay,
  Will sharper sermon teach.
Come, don thy cap, and mount thy horse;
The Dame must patience take perforce."

XXXII

"Submit we then to force," said Clare,
"But let this barbarous lord despair
  His purpos'd aim to win;
Let him take living, land, and life;
But to be Marmion's wedded wife

In me were deadly sin:
And if it be the King's decree,
That I must find no sanctuary,
In that inviolable dome,
Where even a homicide might come,
   And safely rest his head,
Though at its open portals stood,
Thirsting to pour forth blood for blood,
   The kindsmen of the dead;
Yet one asylum is my own
   Against the dreaded hour;
A low, a silent, and a lone,
   Where kings have little power.
One victim is before me there.
Mother, your blessing, and in prayer
Remember your unhappy Clare!"
Loud weeps the Abbess, and bestows
   Kind blessings many a one:
Weeping and wailing loud arose,
Round patient Clare, the clamorous woes
   Of every simple nun.
His eyes the gentle Eustace dried,
And scarce rude Blount the sight could bide.
   Then took the squire her rein,
And gently led away her steed,
And, by each courteous word and deed,
   To cheer her strove in vain.

XXXIII

But scant three miles the band had rode,
   When o'er a height they pass'd,
And, sudden, close before them show'd
   His towers, Tantallon vast;
Broad, massive, high, and stretching far,
And held impregnable in war.
On a projecting rock they rose,
And round three sides the ocean flows,
The fourth did battled walls enclose,
   And double mound and fosse.
By narrow drawbridge, outworks strong,
Through studded gates, an entrance long,
   To the main court they cross.
It was a wide and stately square:
Around were lodgings, fit and fair,
   And towers of various form,
Which on the court projected far,

And broke its lines quadrangular.
Here was square keep, there turret high,
Or pinnacle that sought the sky,
Whence oft the Warder could descry
    The gathering ocean-storm.

XXXIV

Here did they rest. The princely care
Of Douglas, why should I declare,
Or say they met reception fair?
    Or why the tidings say,
Which, varying, to Tantallon came,
By hurrying posts or fleeter fame,
    With every varying day?
And, first they heard King James had won
    Etall, and Wark, and Ford; and then,
    That Norham Castle strong was ta'en.
At that sore marvell'd Marmion;—
And Douglas hop'd his Monarch's hand
Would soon subdue Northumberland
    But whisper'd news there came,
That, while his host inactive lay,
And melted by degrees away,
King James was dallying off the day
    With Heron's wily dame.
Such acts to chronicles I yield;
    Go seek them there, and see:
Mine is a tale of Flodden Field,
    And not a history.
At length they heard the Scottish host
On that high ridge had made their post,
    Which frowns o'er Millfield Plain;
And that brave Surrey many a band
Had gather'd in the Southern land,
And march'd into Northumberland,
    And camp at Wooler ta'en.
Marmion, like charger in the stall,
That hears, without, the trumpet-call,
    Began to chafe, and swear—
"A sorry thing to hide my head
In castle, like a fearful maid,
    When such a field is near!
Needs must I see this battle-day:
Death to my fame if such a fray
Were fought, and Marmion away!
The Douglas, too, I wot not why,

Hath 'bated of his courtesy:
No longer in his halls I'll stay."
Then bade his band they should array
For march against the dawning day.

Canto Sixth   THE BATTLE

I

While great events were on the gale,
And each hour brought a varying tale,
And the demeanour, changed and cold,
Of Douglas, fretted Marmion bold,
And, like the impatient steed of war,
He snuff'd the battle from afar;
And hopes were none, that back again
Herald should come from Terouenne,
Where England's King in leaguer lay,
Before decisive battle-day;
Whilst these things were, the mournful Clare
Did in the Dame's devotions share:
For the good Countess ceaseless pray'd
To Heaven and Saints, her sons to aid,
And, with short interval, did pass
From prayer to book, from book to mass,
And all in high Baronial pride,—
A life both dull and dignified;
Yet as Lord Marmion nothing press'd
Upon her intervals of rest,
Dejected Clara well could bear
The formal state, the lengthen'd prayer,
Though dearest to her wounded heart
The hours that she might spend apart.

II

I said Tantallon's dizzy steep
Hung o'er the margin of the deep.
Many a rude tower and rampart there
Repell'd the insult of the air,
Which, when the tempest vex'd the sky,
Half breeze, half spray, came whistling by.
Above the rest, a turret square
Did o'er its Gothic entrance bear,

Of sculpture rude, a stony shield;
The Bloody Heart was in the Field,
And in the chief three mullets stood,
The cognizance of Douglas blood.
The turret held a narrow stair,
Which, mounted, gave you access where
A parapet's embattled row
Did seaward round the castle go.
Sometimes in dizzy steps descending,
Sometimes in narrow circuit bending,
Sometimes in platform broad extending,
Its varying circle did combine
Bulwark, and bartizan, and line,
And bastion, tower, and vantage-coign;
Above the booming ocean leant
The far-projecting battlement;
The billows burst, in ceaseless flow,
Upon the precipice below.
Where'er Tantallon faced the land,
Gate-works, and walls, were strongly mann'd;
No need upon the sea-girt side;
The steepy rock, the frantic tide,
Approach of human step denied;
And thus these lines and ramparts rude
Were left in deepest solitude.

III

And, for they were so lonely, Clare
Would to these battlements repair,
And muse upon her sorrows there,
   And list the sea-bird's cry;
Or slow, like noontide ghost, would glide
Along the dark-grey bulwarks' side,
And ever on the heaving tide
   Look down with weary eye.
Oft did the cliff and swelling main
Recall the thoughts of Whitby's fane,—
A home she ne'er might see again;
   For she had laid adown,
So Douglas bade, the hood and veil,
And frontlet of the cloister pale,
   And Benedictine gown:
It were unseemly sight, he said,
A novice out of convent shade.
Now her bright locks, with sunny glow,
Again adorn'd her brow of snow;

Her mantle rich, whose borders, round,
A deep and fretted broidery bound,
In golden foldings sought the ground;
Of holy ornament, alone
Remain'd a cross with ruby stone;
   And often did she look
On that which in her hand she bore,
With velvet bound, and broider'd o'er,
   Her breviary book.
In such a place, so lone, so grim,
At dawning pale, or twilight dim,
   It fearful would have been
To meet a form so richly dress'd,
With book in hand, and cross on breast,
   And such a woeful mien.
Fitz-Eustace, loitering with his bow,
To practise on the gull and crow,
Saw her, at distance, gliding slow,
   And did by Mary swear
Some love-lorn Fay she might have been,
Or, in Romance, some spell-bound Queen;
For ne'er, in work-day world, was seen
   A form so witching fair.

   IV
Once walking thus, at evening tide,
It chanced a gliding sail she spied,
And, sighing, thought—"The Abbess, there,
Perchance, does to her home repair;
Her peaceful rule, where Duty, free,
Walks hand in hand with Charity;
Where oft Devotion's tranced glow
Can such a glimpse of heaven bestow,
That the enraptur'd sisters see
High vision and deep mystery;
The very form of Hilda fair,
Hovering upon the sunny air,
And smiling on her votaries' prayer.
O! wherefore, to my duller eye,
Did still the Saint her form deny!
Was it, that, sear'd by sinful scorn,
My heart could neither melt nor burn?
Or lie my warm affections low,
With him, that taught them first to glow?
Yet, gentle Abbess, well I knew,
To pay thy kindness grateful due,

And well could brook the mild command,
That ruled thy simple maiden band.
How different now! condemn'd to bide
My doom from this dark tyrant's pride.
But Marmion has to learn, ere long,
That constant mind, and hate of wrong,
Descended to a feeble girl,
From Red De Clare, stout Gloster's Earl:
Of such a stem, a sapling weak
He ne'er shall bend, although he break.

V

"But see! what makes this armour here?"—
    For in her path there lay
Targe, corslet, helm; she view'd them near.
"The breastplate pierc'd!—Ay, much I fear,
Weak fence wert thou 'gainst foeman's spear,
That hath made fatal entrance here,
    As these dark blood-gouts say.
Thus Wilton—oh! not corslet's warp,
Not truth, as diamond pure and hard,
Could be thy manly bosom's guard,
    On yon disastrous day!"
She raised her eyes in mournful mood,—
WILTON himself before her stood!
It might have seem'd his passing ghost,
For every youthful grace was lost;
And joy unwonted, and surprise,
Gave their strange wildness to his eyes.
Expect not, noble dames and lords,
That I can tell such scene in words:
What skilful limner e'er would choose
To paint the rainbow's varying hues,
Unless to mortal it were given
To dip his brush in dyes of heaven?
Far less can my weak line declare
    Each changing passion's shade;
Brightening to rapture from despair,
Sorrow, surprise, and pity there,
And joy, with her angelic air,
And hope, that paints the future fair,
    Their varying hues display'd:
Each o'er its rival's ground extending,
Alternate conquering, shifting, blending,
Till all, fatigued, the conflict yield,
And mighty Love retains the field.

Shortly I tell what then he said,
By many a tender word delay'd,
And modest blush, and bursting sigh,
And question kind, and fond reply:—

VI

DE WILTON'S HISTORY

"Forget we that disastrous day,
When senseless in the lists I lay.
 Thence dragg'd,—but how I cannot know,
  For sense and recollection fled,—
 I found me on a pallet low,
  Within my ancient beadsman's shed.
 Austin,—remember'st thou, my Clare,
How thou didst blush, when the old man,
When first our infant love began,
 Said we would make a matchless pair?—
Menials, and friends, and kinsmen fled
From the degraded traitor's bed,—
He only held my burning head,
And tended me for many a day,
While wounds and fever held their sway.
But far more needful was his care,
When sense return'd to wake despair;
 For I did tear the closing wound,
 And dash me frantic on the ground,
If e'er I heard the name of Clare.
At length, to calmer reason brought,
Much by his kind attendance wrought,
 With him I left my native strand,
And, in a palmer's weeds array'd,
My hated name and form to shade,
 I journey'd many a land;
No more a lord of rank and birth,
But mingled with the dregs of earth.
 Oft Austin for my reason fear'd,
When I would sit, and deeply brood
On dark revenge, and deeds of blood,
 Or wild mad schemes uprear'd.
My friend at length fell sick, and said,
 God would remove him soon:
And, while upon his dying bed,
 He begg'd of me a boon—
If e'er my deadliest enemy

Beneath my brand should conquer'd lie,
Even then my mercy should awake,
And spare his life for Austin's sake.

VII

"Still restless as a second Cain,
To Scotland next my route was ta'en,
    Full well the paths I knew.
Fame of my fate made various sound,
That death in pilgrimage I found,
That I had perish'd of my wound,—
    None cared which tale was true:
And living eye could never guess
De Wilton in his Palmer's dress;
For now that sable slough is shed,
And trimm'd my shaggy beard and head,
I scarcely know me in the glass.
A chance most wondrous did provide,
That I should be that Baron's guide—
    I will not name his name!
Vengeance to God alone belongs;
But, when I think on all my wrongs,
    My blood is liquid flame!
And ne'er the time shall I forget,
When, in a Scottish hostel set,
    Dark looks we did exchange:
What were his thoughts I cannot tell;
But in my bosom muster'd Hell
    Its plans of dark revenge.

VIII

"A word of vulgar augury,
That broke from me, I scarce knew why,
    Brought on a village tale;
Which wrought upon his moody sprite,
And sent him armed forth by night.
    I borrow'd steed and mail,
And weapons, from his sleeping band;
    And, passing from a postern door,
We met, and 'counter'd hand to hand,—
    He fell on Gifford moor.
For the death-stroke my brand I drew,
(O then my helmed head he knew,
    The Palmer's cowl was gone)
Then had three inches of my blade
The heavy debt of vengeance paid;

My hand the thought of Austin staid;
  I left him there alone.
O good old man! even from the grave
Thy spirit could thy master save:
If I had slain my foeman, ne'er
Had Whitby's Abbess, in her fear,
Given to my hand this packet dear,
Of power to clear my injured fame,
And vindicate De Wilton's name.
Perchance you heard the Abbess tell
Of the strange pageantry of Hell,
    That broke our secret speech—
It rose from the infernal shade,
Or featly was some juggle play'd,
    A tale of peace to teach.
Appeal to Heaven I judged was best,
When my name came among the rest.

    IX
"Now here, within Tantallon Hold,
To Douglas late my tale I told,
To whom my house was known of old.
Won by my proofs, his falchion bright
This eve anew shall dub me knight.
These were the arms that once did turn
The tide of fight on Otterburne,
And Harry Hotspur forced to yield,
When the Dead Douglas won the field.
These Angus gave—his armourer's care,
Ere morn shall every breach repair;
For nought, he said, was in his halls,
But ancient armour on the walls,
And aged chargers in the stalls,
And women, priests, and grey-hair'd men,
The rest were all in Twisel glen.
And now I watch my armour here,
By law of arms, till midnight's near;
Then, once again a belted knight,
Seek Surrey's camp with dawn of light.

    X
"There soon again we meet, my Clare!
This Baron means to guide thee there:
Douglas reveres his King's command,
Else would he take thee from his band.
And there thy kinsman, Surrey, too,

Will give De Wilton justice due.
Now meeter far for martial broil,
Firmer my limbs, and strung by toil,
Once more"——"O Wilton! must we then
Risk new-found happiness again,
    Trust fate of arms once more?
And is there not an humble glen,
    Where we, content and poor,
Might build a cottage in the shade,
A shepherd thou, and I to aid
    Thy task on dale and moor?
That reddening brow!—too well I know,
Not even thy Clare can peace bestow
    While falsehood stains thy name.
Go then to fight! Clare bids thee go.
Clare can a warrior's feelings know,
    And weep a warrior's shame,
Can Red Earl Gilbert's spirit feel,
Buckle the spurs upon thy heel,
And belt thee with thy brand of steel,
    And send thee forth to fame!"

                    XI
That night, upon the rocks and bay,
The midnight moonbeam slumbering lay,
And pour'd its silver light, and pure,
Through loop-hole, and through embrazure,
    Upon Tantallon tower and hall;
But chief where arched windows wide
Illuminate the chapel's pride,
    The sober glances fall.
Much was there need; though, seam'd with scars,
Two veterans of the Douglas' wars,
    Though two grey priests were there,
And each a blazing torch held high,
You could not by their blaze descry
    The chapel's carving fair.
Amid that dim and smoky light,
Chequering the silver moonshine bright,
    A bishop by the altar stood,
    A noble lord of Douglas blood,
With mitre sheen, and rocquet white.
Yet show'd his meek and thoughtful eye
But little pride of prelacy;
More pleas'd that, in a barbarous age,
He gave rude Scotland Virgil's page,

Than that beneath his rule he held
The bishopric of fair Dunkeld.
Beside him ancient Angus stood,
Doff'd his furr'd gown, and sable hood:
O'er his huge form and visage pale,
He wore a cap and shirt of mail;
And lean'd his large and wrinkled hand
Upon the huge and sweeping brand
Which wont of yore, in battle fray,
His foeman's limbs to shred away,
As wood-knife lops the sapling spray.
 He seem'd as, from the tombs around
  Rising at judgment-day,
 Some giant Douglas may be found
  In all his old array;
So pale his face, so huge his limb,
So old his arms, his look so grim.

XII

Then at the altar Wilton kneels,
And Clare the spurs bound on his heels;
And think what next he must have felt,
At buckling of the falchion belt!
 And judge how Clara changed her hue,
While fastening to her lover's side
A friend, which, though in danger tried,
 He once had found untrue!
Then Douglas struck him with his blade:
"Saint Michael and Saint Andrew aid,
  I dub thee knight.
Arise, Sir Ralph, De Wilton's heir!
For King, for Church, for Lady fair,
  See that thou fight."
And Bishop Gawain, as he rose,
Said—"Wilton! grieve not for thy woes,
  Disgrace, and trouble;
For He, who honour best bestows,
  May give thee double."
De Wilton sobb'd, for sob he must—
"Where'er I meet a Douglas, trust
  That Douglas is my brother!"
"Nay, nay," old Angus said, "not so:
To Surrey's camp thou now must go,
  Thy wrongs no longer smother.
I have two sons in yonder field;
And, if thou meet'st them under shield,

Upon them bravely—do thy worst;
And foul fall him that blenches first!"

XIII

Not far advanc'd was morning day,
When Marmion did his troop array
 To Surrey's camp to ride;
He had safe conduct for his band,
Beneath the royal seal and hand,
 And Douglas gave a guide:
The ancient Earl, with stately grace,
Would Clara on her palfrey place,
And whisper'd in an under tone,
"Let the hawk stoop, his prey is flown."
The train from out the castle drew,
But Marmion stopp'd to bid adieu:—
 "Though something I might 'plain," he said,
"Of cold respect to stranger guest,
Sent hither by your King's behest,
 While in Tantallon's towers I staid;
Part we in friendship from your land,
And, noble Earl, receive my hand."
But Douglas round him drew his cloak,
Folded his arms, and thus he spoke:
"My manors, halls, and bowers, shall still
Be open, at my Sovereign's will,
To each one whom he lists, howe'er
Unmeet to be the owner's peer.
My castles are my King's alone,
From turret to foundation-stone—
The hand of Douglas is his own;
And never shall in frendly grasp
The hand of such as Marmion clasp."

XIV

Burn'd Marmion's swarthy cheek like fire,
And shook his very frame for ire,
 And "This to me!" he said;
"An 'twere not for thy hoary beard,
Such hand as Marmion's had not spar'd
 To cleave the Douglas' head!
And, first, I tell thee, haughty Peer,
He, who does England's message here,
Although the meanest in her state,
May well, proud Angus, be thy mate:
And, Douglas, more I tell thee here,

Even in thy pitch of pride,
Here in thy hold, thy vassals near—
(Nay, never look upon your lord,
And lay your hands upon your sword!)
    I tell thee, thou'rt defied!
And if thou said'st I am not peer
To any lord in Scotland here,
Lowland or Highland, far or near,
    Lord Angus, thou hast lied!"
On the Earl's cheek the flush of rage
O'ercame the ashen hue of age:
Fierce he broke forth, "And dar'st thou then
To beard the lion in his den,
    The Douglas in his hall?
And hop'st thou hence unscathed to go.
No, by Saint Bride of Bothwell, no!
Up drawbridge, grooms—what, warder, ho!
    Let the portcullis fall."
Lord Marmion turn'd,—well was his need,
And dash'd the rowels in his steed,
Like arrow through the archway sprung,
The ponderous grate behind him rung:
To pass there was such scanty room,
The bars, descending, razed his plume.

        XV
The steed along the drawbirdge flies,
Just as it trembled on the rise;
Nor lighter does the swallow skim
Along the smooth lake's level brim:
And when Lord Marmion reach'd his band,
He halts, and turns with clenched hand,
And shout of loud defiance pours,
And shook his gauntlet at the towers.
"Horse! horse!" the Douglas cried, "and chase!"
But soon he rein'd his fury's pace:
"A royal messenger he came,
Though most unworthy of the name.
A letter forged! Saint Jude to speed!
Did ever knight so foul a deed!
At first in heart it liked me ill,
When the King prais'd his clerkly skill.
Thanks to Saint Bothan, son of mine,
Save Gawain, ne'er could pen a line:
So swore I, and I swear it still,

Let my boy-bishop fret his fill.
Saint Mary mend my fiery mood!
Old age ne'er cools the Douglas blood,
I thought to slay him where he stood.
'Tis pity of him too," he cried:
"Bold can he speak, and fairly ride,
I warrant him a warrior tried."
With this his mandate he recalls,
And slowly seeks his castle halls.

XVI

The day in Marmion's journey wore;
Yet, ere his passion's gust was o'er,
They cross'd the heights of Stanrig-moor.
His troop more closely there he scann'd,
And miss'd the Palmer from the band.
"Palmer or not," young Blount did say,
"He parted at the peep of day;
Good sooth, it was in strange array."
"In what array?" said Marmion, quick.
"My Lord, I ill can spell the trick;
But all night long, with clink and bang,
Close to my couch did hammers clang;
At dawn the falling drawbridge rang,
And from a loop-hole while I peep,
Old Bell-the-Cat came from the keep,
Wrapp'd in a gown of sables fair,
As fearful of the morning air;
Beneath, when that was blown aside,
A rusty shirt of mail I spied,
By Archibald won in bloody work,
Against the Saracen and Turk:
Last night it hung not in the hall;
I thought some marvel would befall.
And next I saw them saddled lead
Old Cheviot forth, the Earl's best steed,
A matchless horse, though something old,
Prompt in his paces, cool and bold.
I heard the Sheriff Sholto say,
The Earl did much the Master pray
To use him on the battle-day;
But he preferr'd"——"Nay, Henry, cease!
Thou sworn horse-courser, hold they peace.
Eustace, thou bear'st a brain—I pray,
What did Blount see at break of day?"

XVII

"In brief, my lord, we both descried
(For then I stood by Henry's side)
The Palmer mount, and outwards ride,
    Upon the Earl's own favourite steed:
All sheath'd he was in armour bright,
And much resembled that same knight,
Subdu'd by you in Cotswold fight:
    Lord Angus wish'd him speed."
The instant that Fitz-Eustace spoke,
A sudden light on Marmion broke;—
"Ah! dastard fool, to reason lost!"
He mutter'd; " 'twas nor fay nor ghost
I met upon the moonlight wold,
But living man of earthly mould.
    O dotage blind and gross!
Had I but fought as wont, one thrust
Had laid De Wilton in the dust,
    My path no more to cross.
How stand we now?—he told his tale
To Douglas; and with some avail;
    'Twas therefore gloom'd his rugged brow.
Will Surrey dare to entertain,
'Gainst Marmion, charge disproved and vain?
    Small risk of that, I trow.
Yet Clare's sharp questions must I shun,
Must separate Constance from the Nun—
O what a tangled web we weave,
When first we practise to deceive!
A Palmer too!—no wonder why
I felt rebuk'd beneath his eye:
I might have known there was but one,
Whose look could quell Lord Marmion."

XVIII

Stung with these thoughts, he urg'd to speed
His troop, and reach'd at eve the Tweed,
Where Lennel's convent clos'd their march;
(There now is left but one frail arch,
    Yet mourn thou not its cells;
Our time a fair exchange has made;
Hard by, in hospitable shade,
    A reverend pilgrim dwells,
Well worth the whole Bernadine brood.
That e'er wore sandal, frock, or hood.)
Yet did Saint Bernard's Abbot there

Give Marmion entertainment fair,
And lodging for his train and Clare.
Next morn the Baron climb'd the tower,
To view afar the Scottish power,
   Encamp'd on Flodden edge:
The white pavilions made a show,
Like remnants of the winter snow,
   Along the dusky ridge.
Long Marmion look'd: at length his eye
Unusual movement might descry
   Amid the shifting lines:
The Scottish host drawn out appears,
For, flashing on the hedge of spears
   The eastern sunbeam shines.
Their front now deepening, now extending;
Their flank inclining, wheeling, bending,
Now drawing back, and now descending,
The skilful Marmion well could know
They watch'd the motions of some foe,
Who travers'd on the plain below.

   XIX
Even so it was. From Flodden ridge
   The Scots beheld the English host
   Leave Barmore-wood, their evening post,
   And heedful watch'd them as they cross'd
The Till by Twisel Bridge.
   High sight it is, and haughty, while
   They dive into the deep defile;
   Beneath the cavern'd cliff they fall,
   Beneath the castle's airy wall;
By rock, by oak, by hawthorn-tree,
   Troop after troop are disappearing;
   Troop after troop their banners rearing,
Upon the eastern bank you see;
Still pouring down the rocky den,
   Where flows the sullen Till,
And rising from the dim-wood glen.
Standards on standards, men on men,
   In slow succession still,
And, sweeping o'er the Gothic arch,
And pressing on, in ceaseless march,
   To gain the opposing hill.
That morn, to many a trumpet clang,
Twisel! thy rock's deep echo rang;
And many a chief of birth and rank,

Saint Helen! at thy fountain drank.
Thy hawthorn glade, which now we see
In spring-tide bloom so lavishly,
Had then from many an axe its doom,
To give the marching columns room.

XX

And why stands Scotland idly now,
Dark Flodden! on thy airy brow,
Since England gains the pass the while,
And struggles through the deep defile?
What checks the fiery soul of James?
Why sits that champion of the dames
   Inactive on his steed,
And sees, between him and his land,
Between him and Tweed's southern strand,
   His host Lord Surrey lead?
What 'vails the vain knight-errant's brand?
O, Douglas, for thy leading wand!
   Fierce Randolph, for thy speed!
O for one hour of Wallace wight,
Or well-skill'd Bruce, to rule the fight,
And cry "Saint Andrew and our right!"
Another sight had seen that morn,
From Fate's dark book a leaf been torn,
And Flodden had been Bannock-bourne!
The precious hour has pass'd in vain,
And England's host has gain'd the plain;
Wheeling their march, and circling still,
Around the base of Flodden hill.

XXI

Ere yet the bands met Marmion's eye
Fitz-Eustace shouted loud and high,
"Hark! hark! my lord, an English drum!
And see ascending squadrons come
   Between Tweed's river and the hill,
Foot, horse, and cannon: hap what hap,
My basnet to a prentice cap,
   Lord Surrey's o'er the Till!
Yet more! yet more!—how far array'd
They file from out the hawthorn shade,
   And sweep so gallant by!
With all their banners bravely spread,
   And all their armour flashing high,
Saint George might waken from the dead,

To see fair England's standards fly."
"Stint in thy prate," quoth Blount, "thou'dst best,
And listen to our lord's behest."
With kindling brow Lord Marmion said,
"This instant be our band array'd;
The river must be quickly cross'd,
That we may join Lord Surrey's host.
If fight King James,—as well I trust,
That fight he will, and fight he must,—
The Lady Clare behind our lines
Shall tarry, while the battle joins."

XXII

Himself he swift on horseback threw,
Scarce to the Abbot bade adieu;
Far less would listen to his prayer
To leave behind the helpless Clare.
Down to the Tweed his band he drew,
And mutter'd as the flood they view,
"The pheasant in the falcon's claw,
He scarce will yield to please a daw:
Lord Angus may the Abbot awe,
  So Clare shall bide with me."
Then on that dangerous ford, and deep,
Where to the Tweed Leat's eddies creep,
  He ventured desperately:
And not a moment will he bide,
Till squire, or groom, before him ride;
Headmost of all he stems the tide,
  And stems it gallantly.
Eustace held Clare upon her horse,
  Old Hubert led her rein,
Stoutly they brav'd the current's course,
And, though far downward driven per force,
  The southern bank they gain;
Behind them, straggling, came to shore,
  As best they might, the train:
Each o'er his head his yew-bow bore,
  A caution not in vain;
Deep need that day that every string,
By wet unharm'd, should sharply ring.
A moment then Lord Marmion staid,
And breath'd his steed, his men array'd,
  Then forward mov'd his band,
Until, Lord Surrey's rear-guard won,
He halted by a Cross of Stone,

That, on a hillock standing lone,
   Did all the field command,

XXIII

Hence might they see the full array
Of either host, for deadly fray;
Their marshall'd lines stretch'd east and west,
   And fronted north and south,
And distant salutation pass'd
   From the loud cannon mouth;
Not in the close successive rattle,
That breathes the voice of modern battle,
   But slow and far between.
The hillock gain'd, Lord Marmion staid:
"Here, by this Cross," he gently said,
   "You well may view the scene.
Here shalt thou tarry, lovely Clare:
O! think of Marmion in thy prayer!
Thou wilt not?—well, no less my care
Shall, watchful, for thy weal prepare.
You, Blount and Eustace, are her guard,
   With ten pick'd archers of my train;
With England if the day go hard,
   To Berwick speed amain.
But if we conquer, cruel maid,
My spoils shall at your feet be laid,
   When here we meet again."
He waited not for answer there,
And would not mark the maid's despair,
   Nor heed the discontented look
From either squire; but spurr'd amain,
And, dashing through the battle plain,
   His way to Surrey took.

XXIV

"The good Lord Marmion, by my life!
   Welcome to danger's hour!
Short greeting serves in time of strife:
   Thus have I rang'd my power:
Myself will rule this central host,
   Stout Stanley fronts their right,
My sons command the vaward post,
   With Brian Tunstall, stainless knight;
   Lord Dacre, with his horsemen light,
   Shall be in rearward of the fight,
And succour those that need it most.

Now, gallant Marmion, well I know
    Would gladly to the vanguard go;
Edmund, the Admiral, Tunstall there,
With thee their charge will blithely share;
There fight thine own retainers too,
Beneath De Burg, thy steward true."
"Thanks, noble Surrey!" Marmion said,
Nor farther greeting there he paid;
But, parting like a thunderbolt,
First in the vanguard made a halt,
    Where such a shout there rose
Of Marmion! Marmion! that the cry,
Up Flodden mountain shrilling high,
Startled the Scottish foes.

XXV

Blount and Fitz-Eustace rested still
With Lady Clare upon the hill!
On which (for the day was spent),
The western sunbeams now were bent.
The cry they heard, its meaning knew,
Could plain their distant comrades view:
Sadly to Blount did Eustace say,
"Unworthy office here to stay!
No hope of gilded spurs to-day.
But see! look up—on Flodden bent
The Scottish foe has fired his tent."
    And sudden, as he spoke,
From the sharp ridges of the hill,
All downward to the banks of Till,
    Was wreath'd in sable smoke.
Volum'd and fast, and rolling far,
The cloud envelop'd Scotland's war,
    As down the hill they broke;
Nor martial shout, nor minstrel tone,
Announc'd their march; their tread alone,
At times one warning trumpet blown,
    At times a stifled hum,
Told England, from his mountain-throne
    King James did rushing come.
Scarce could they hear, or see their foes,
    Until at weapon-point they close.
They close, in clouds of smoke and dust,
With sword-sway, and with lance's thrust;
    And such a yell was there,
Of sudden and portentous birth,

As if men fought upon the earth,
  And fiends in upper air;
O life and death were in the shout,
Recoil and rally, charge and rout,
  And triumph and despair.
Long look'd the anxious squires; their eye
Could in the darkness nought descry.

    XXVI

At length the freshening western blast
Aside the shroud of battle cast;
And, first, the ridge of mingled spears
Above the brightening cloud appears;
And in the smoke the pennons flew,
As in the storm the white sea-mew.
Then mark'd they, dashing broad and far,
The broken billows of the war,
And plumed crests of chieftains brave,
Floating like foam upon the wave;
  But nought distinct they see:
Wide rag'd the battle on the plain;
Spears shook, the falchions flash'd amain;
Fell England's arrow-flight like rain;
Crests rose, and stoop'd, and rose again,
  Wild and disorderly.
Amid the scene of tumult, high
They saw Lord Marmion's falcon fly:
And stainless Tunstall's banner white,
And Edmund Howard's lion bright,
Still bear them bravely in the fight:
  Although against them come,
Of gallant Gordons many a one,
And many a stubborn Badenoch-man,
And many a rugged Border clan,
  With Huntly, and with Home.

    XXVII

Far on the left, unseen the while,
Stanley broke Lennox and Argyle;
Though there the western mountaineer
Rush'd with bare bosom on the spear,
And flung the feeble targe aside,
And with both hands the broadsword plied.
'Twas vain:—But Fortune, on the right,
With fickle smile, cheer'd Scotland's fight.
Then fell that spotless banner white,

The Howard's lion fell;
Yet still Lord Marmion's falcon flew
With wavering flight, while fiercer grew
　　Around the battle-yell.
The Border slogan rent the sky!
A Home! a Gordon! was the cry:
　　Loud, were the clanging blows;
Advanc'd, forc'd back, now low, now high,
　　The pennon sunk and rose;
As bends the bark's mast in the gale,
When rent are rigging, shrouds, and sail,
　　It waver'd 'mid the foes.
No longer Blount the view could bear:
"By Heaven, and all its saints! I swear
　　I will not see it lost!
Fitz-Eustace, you with Lady Clare
May bid your beads, and patter prayer,—
　　I gallop to the host."
And to the gray he rode amain,
Follow'd by all the archer train.
The fiery youth, with desperate charge,
Made, for a space, an opening large,
　　The rescued banner rose,
But darkly clos'd the war around,
Like pine-tree, rooted from the ground,
　　It sunk among the foes.
Then Eustace mounted too:—yet staid
As loath to leave the helpless maid,
　　When, fast as shaft can fly,
Bloodshot his eyes, his nostrils spread,
The loose rein dangling from his head,
Housing and saddle bloody red,
　　Lord Marmion's steed rush'd by;
And Eustace, maddening at the sight,
　　A look and sign to Clara cast
　　To mark he would return in haste,
Then plung'd into the fight.

　　　XXVIII
As me not what the maiden feels,
　　Left in that dreadful hour alone:
Perchance her reason stoops, or reels;
　　Perchance a courage, not her own,
　　Braces her mind to desperate tone.
The scatter'd van of England wheels;
　　She only said, as loud in air

The tumult roar'd, "Is Wilton there?"
  They fly, or, madden'd by despair,
  Fight but to die,—"Is Wilton there?"
With that, straight up the hill there rode
  Two horsemen drench'd with gore,
And in their arms, a helpless load,
  A wounded knight they bore.
His hand still strain'd the broken brand;
His arms were smear'd with blood and sand:
Dragg'd from among the horses' feet,
With dinted shield, and helmet beat,
The falcon-crest and plumage gone,
Can that be haughty Marmion!
Young Blount his armour did unlace,
And, gazing on his ghastly face,
  Said "By Saint George, he's gone!
That spear-wound has our master sped,
And see the deep cut on his head!
  Good-night to Marmion."
"Unnurtur'd Blount! thy brawling cease:
He opes his eyes," said Eustace; "peace!"

XXIX

When, doff'd his casque, he felt free air,
Around 'gan Marmion wildly stare:—
"Where's Harry Blount? Fitz-Eustace where?
Linger ye here, ye hearts of hare!
Redeem my pennon,—charge again!
Cry 'Marmion to the rescue!'—Vain!
Last of my race, on battle-plain
That shout shall ne'er be heard again!
Yet my last thought is England's; fly,
  To Dacre bear my signet-ring:
  Tell him his squadrons up to bring.
Fitz-Eustace, to Lord Surrey hie;
  Tunstall lies dead upon the field,
  His life-blood stains the spotless shield:
  Edmund is down:—my life is reft;
  The Admiral alone is left.
  Let Stanley charge with spur of fire,—
  With Chester charge, and Lancashire,
  Full upon Scotland's central host,
  Or victory and England's lost.
  Must I bid twice?—hence, varlets! fly!
  Leave Marmion here alone—to die."

They parted, and alone he lay;
  Clare drew her from the sight away,
Till pain wrung forth a lowly moan,
And half he murmur'd, "Is there none,
  Of all my halls have nurst,
Page, squire, or groom, one cup to bring
Of blessed water from the spring,
  To slake my dying thirst!"

XXX

O Woman! in our hours of ease,
Uncertain, coy, and hard to please,
And variable as the shade
By the light quivering aspen made;
When pain and anguish wring the brow,
A ministering angel thou!
Scarce were the piteous accents said,
When, with the Baron's casque, the maid
  To the nigh streamlet ran:
Forgot were hatred, wrongs, and fears;
The plaintive voice alone she hears,
  Sees but the dying man.
She stoop'd her by the runnel's side,
  But in abhorrence backward drew;
For, oozing from the mountains side,
Where raged the war, a dark-red tide
  Was curdling in the streamlet blue.
Where shall she turn?—behold her mark
  A little fountain cell,
Where water, clear as diamond-spark,
  In a stone basin fell.
Above, some half-worn letters say,
Drink . weary . pilgrim . drink . and . pray .
For . the . kind . soul . of . Sybil . Grey .
  Who . built . this . cross . and . well.
She fill'd the helm, and back she hied,
And with surprise and joy espied
  A monk supporting Marmion's head:
A pious man, whom duty brought
To dubious verge of battle fought,
  To shrieve the dying, bless the dead.

XXXI

Deep drank Lord Marmion of the wave,
And, as she stoop'd his brow to lave—

"Is it the hand of Clare," he said,
"Or injur'd Constance, bathes my head?"
   Then, as remembrance rose,—
"Speak not to me of shrift or prayer!
   I must redress her woes.
Short space, few words, are mine to spare:
Forgive and listen, gentle Clare!"
"Alas!" she said, "the while,—
O, think of your immortal weal!
In vain for Constance is your zeal;
   She—died at Holy Isle."
Lord Marmion started from the ground,
As light as if he felt no wound;
Tough in the action burst the tide,
In torrents, from his wounded side.
"Then it was truth," he said; "I knew
That the dark presage must be true.
I would the Fiend, to whom belongs
The vengeance due to all her wrongs,
   Would spare me but a day!
For wasting fire, and dying groan,
And priests slain on the altar stone,
   Might bribe him for delay.
It may not be! this dizzy trance—
Curse on yon base marauder's lance,
And doubly curs'd my failing brand!
A sinful heart makes feeble hand."
Then, fainting, down on earth he sunk,
Supported by the trembling Monk.

XXXII

With fruitless labour, Clara bound,
And strove to stanch the gushing wound:
The Monk, with unavailing cares,
Exhausted all the Church's prayers.
Ever, he said, that, close and near,
A lady's voice was in his ear,
And that the priest he could not hear;
   For that she ever sung,
"In the lost battle, borne down by the flying,
Where mingles war's rattle with groans of the dying!"
   So the notes rung;—
"Avoid thee, Fiend! with cruel hand,
Shake not the dying sinner's sand!
O, look, my son, upon yon sign
Of the Redeemer's grace divine;

O, think on faith and bliss!
By many a death-bed I have been,
And many a sinner's parting seen,
   But never aught like this."
The war, that for a space did fail,
Now trebly thundering swell'd the gale,
   And—STANLEY! was the cry
A light on Marmion's visage spread,
   And fired his glazing eye:
With dying hand, above his head,
He shook the fragment of his blade,
   And shouted "Victory!
Charge, Chester, charge! On, Stanley, on!"
Were the last words of Marmion.

XXXIII

By this though deep the evening fell,
Still rose the battle's deadly swell,
For still the Scots, around their King,
Unbroken, fought in desperate ring.
Where's now their victor vaward wing,
   Where Huntly, and where Home?—
O, for a blast of that dread horn,
On Fontarabian echoes borne,
   That to King Charles did come,
When Rowland brave, and Olivier,
And every paladin and peer,
   On Roncesvalles died!
Such blast might warn them, not in vain,
To quit the plunder of the slain,
And turn the doubtful day again,
   While yet on Flodden side,
Afar, the Royal Standard flies,
And round it toils, and bleeds, and dies,
   Our Caledonian pride!
In vain the wish—for far away,
While spoil and havoc mark their way,
Near Sybil's Cross the plunderers stray.
"O, Lady," cried the Monk, "away!"
   And plac'd her on her steed,
And led her to the chapel fair,
   Of Tilmouth upon Tweed.
There all the night they spent in prayer,
And at the dawn of morning, there
She met her kinsman, Lord Fitz-Clare.

XXXIV

But as they left the dark'ning heath,
More desperate grew the strife of death.
The English shafts in volleys hail'd,
In headlong charge their horse assail'd;
Front, flank, and rear, the squadrons sweep
To break the Scottish circle deep,
   That fought around their King.
But yet, though thick the shafts as snow,
Though charging knights like whirlwinds go,
Though bill-men ply the ghastly blow,
   Unbroken was the ring;
The stubborn spear-men still made good
Their dark impenetrable wood,
Each stepping where his comrade stood,
   The instant that he fell.
No thought was there of dastard flight;
Link'd in the serried phalanx tight,
Groom fought like noble, squire like knight,
   As fearlessly and well;
Till utter darkness closed her wing
O'er their thin host and wounded King.
Then skilful Surrey's sage commands
Led back from strife his shatter'd bands;
   And from the charge they drew,
As mountain-waves, from wasted lands,
   Sweep back to ocean blue.
Then did their loss his foemen know;
Their King, their Lords, their mightiest low,
They melted from the field as snow,
When streams were swoln and south winds blow,
   Dissolves in silent dew.
Tweed's echoes heard the ceaseless plash,
   While many a broken band,
Disorder'd, through her currents dash,
   To gain the Scottish land;
To town and tower, to town and dale,
To tell red Flodden's dismal tale,
And raise the universal wail.
Tradition, legend, tune, and song,
Shall many an age that wail prolong:
Still from the sire the son shall hear
Of the stern strife, and carnage drear,
   Of Flodden's fatal field,
Where shiver'd was fair Scotland's spear,
   And broken was her shield!

XXXV

Day dawns upon the mountain's side:
There, Scotland! lay thy bravest pride,
Chiefs, knights, and nobles, many a one:
The sad survivors all are gone.
View not that corpse mistrustfully,
Defac'd and mangled though it be;
Nor to yon Border castle high,
Look northward with upbraiding eye;
   Nor cherish hope in vain,
That, journeying far on foreign strand,
The Royal Pilgrim to his land
   May yet return again.
He saw the wreck his rashness wrought;
Reckless of life, he desperate fought,
   And fell on Flodden plain:
And well in death his trusty brand,
Firm clench'd within his manly hand,
   Beseem'd the monarch slain.
But, O! how changed since yon blithe night!
Gladly I turn me from the sight,
   Unto my tale again.

XXXVI

Short is my tale: Fitz-Eustace' care
A pierc'd and mangled body bare
To moated Lichfield's lofty pile;
And there, beneath the southern aisle
A tomb, with Gothic sculpture fair,
Did long Lord Marmion's image bear.
(Now vainly for its sight you look;
'Twas levell'd when fanatic Brook
The fair cathedral storm'd and took;
But, thanks to Heaven and good Saint Chad,
A guerdon meet the spoiler had!)
There erst was martial Marmion found,
His feet upon a couchant hound,
   His hands to heaven uprais'd;
And all around, on scutcheon rich,
And tablet carv'd, and fretted niche,
   His arms and feats were blaz'd.
And yet, though all was carv'd so fair,
And priest for Marmion breath'd the prayer,
The last Lord Marmion lay not there.
From Ettrick woods a peasant swain
Follow'd his lord to Flodden plain,—

One of those flowers, whom plaintive lay
In Scotland mourns as "wede away:"
Sore wounded, Sybil's Cross he spied,
And dragg'd him to its foot, and died,
Close by the noble Marmion's side.
The spoilers stripp'd and gash'd the slain,
And thus their corpses were mista'en;
And thus, in the proud Baron's tomb,
The lowly woodsman took the room.

XXXVII

Less easy task it were, to show
Lord Marmion's nameless grave, and low.
They dug his grave e'en where he lay,
    But every mark is gone;
Time's wasting hand has done away
The simple Cross of Sybil Grey,
    And broke her font of stone:
But yet from out the little hill
Oozes the slender springlet still;
    Oft halts the stranger there,
For thence may best his curious eye
The memorable field descry;
    And shepherd boys repair
To seek the water-flag and rush,
And rest them by the hazel bush,
    And plait their garlands fair;
Nor dream they sit upon the grave,
That holds the bones of Marmion brave.
When thou shalt find the little hill,
With thy heart commune, and be still.
If ever, in temptation strong,
Thou left'st the right path from the wrong;
If every devious step, thus trod,
Still led thee farther from the road;
Dread thou to speak presumptuous doom
On noble Marmion's lowly tomb;
But say, "He died a gallant knight,
With sword in hand, for England's right."

XXXVIII

I do not rhyme to that dull elf,
Who cannot image to himself,
That all through Flodden's dismal night,
Wilton was foremost in the fight;
That, when brave Surrey's steed was slain,
'Twas Wilton mounted him again;

'Twas Wilton's brand that deepest hew'd,
Amid the spearmen's stubborn wood:
Unnam'd by Hollinshed or Hall,
He was the living soul of all:
That, after fight, his faith made plain,
He won his rank and lands again;
And charg'd his old paternal shield
With bearings won on Flodden Field.
Nor sing I to that simple maid,
To whom it must in terms be said,
That King and kinsmen did agree,
To bless fair Clara's constancy;
Who cannot, unless I relate,
Paint to her mind the bridal's state;
That Wolsey's voice the blessing spoke,
More, Sands, and Denny, pass'd the joke:
That bluff King Hal the curtain drew,
And Catherine's hand the stocking threw;
And afterwards, for many a day,
That it was held enough to say,
In blessing to a wedded pair,
"Love they like Wilton and like Clare!"

L'ENVOY

Why then a final note prolong,
Or lengthen out a closing song,
Unless to bid the gentles speed,
Who long have listed to my rede?
To Statesmen grave, if such may deign
To read the Minstrel's idle strain,
Sound head, clean hand, and piercing wit,
And patriotic heart—as PITT!
A garland for the hero's crest,
And twin'd by her he loves the best;
To every lovely lady bright,
What can I wish but faithful knight?
To every faithful lover too,
What can I wish but lady true?
And knowledge to the studious sage;
And pillow to the head of sage.
To thee, dear schoolboy, whom my lay
Has cheated of thy hour of play,
Light task, and merry holiday!
To all, to each, a fair good-night,
And pleasing dreams, and slumbers light!

Thomas the Rhymer

Part I (ANCIENT)

True Thomas lay on Huntlie bank;
  A ferlie he spied wi' his ee;
And there he saw a ladye bright
  Come riding down by the Eildon-tree.

Her shirt was o' the grass-green silk,
  Her mantle o' the velvet fyne;
At ilka tett of her horse's mane,
  Hung fifty siller bells and nine.

True Thomas he pull'd aff his cap,
  And louted low down to his knee,
"All hail, thou mighty Queen of Heaven!
  For thy peer on earth I never did see."

"O no, O no, Thomas," she said,
  "That name does not belang to me;
I am but the Queen of fair Elfland,
  That am hither come to visit thee.

"Harp and carp, Thomas," she said,
  "Harp and carp along wi' me;
And if ye dare to kiss my lips,
  Sure of your bodie I will be."

"Betide me weal, betide me woe,
  That weird shall never daunton me;"
Syne he has kiss'd her rosy lips
  All underneath the Eildon-tree.

"Now ye maun go wi' me," she said,
  "True Thomas, ye maun go wi' me;
And ye maun serve me seven years,
  Thro' weal or woe as may chance to be."

She mounted on her milk-white steed.
  She's ta'en true Thomas up behind:
And aye, whene'er her bridle rung,
  The steed flew swifter than the wind.

O they rade on, and farther on;
   The steed gaed swifter than the wind;
Until they reach'd a desert wide,
   And living land was left behind.

"Light down, light down now, true Thomas,
   And lean your head upon my knee;
Abide and rest a little space,
   And I will show you ferlies three.

"O see ye not yon narrow road,
   So thick beset with thorns and briers?
That is the path of righteousness,
   Though after it but few inquires.

"And see ye not that braid braid road,
   That lies across that lily leven?
That is the path of wickedness,
   Though some call it the road to heaven.

"And see ye not that bonny road,
   That winds about the fernie brae?
That is the road to fair Elfland,
   Where thou and I this night maun gae.

"But, Thomas, ye maun hold your tongue,
   Whatever ye may hear or see;
For, if ye speak word in Elfyn land,
   Ye'll ne'er get back to your ain countrie."

O they rade on, and farther on,
   And they waded through rivers aboon the knee,
And they saw neither sun nor moon,
   But they heard the roaring of the sea.

It was mirk mirk night, and there was nae stern light,
   And they waded through red blude to the knee;
For a' the blude that's shed on earth
   Rins through the springs o' that countrie.

Syne they came on to a garden green,
   And she pu'd an apple frae a tree—
"Take this for thy wages, true Thomas;
   It will give thee the tongue that can never lie."

"My tongue is mine ain," true Thomas said;
   "A gudely gift ye wad gie to me!

I neither dought to buy nor sell,
  At fair or tryst where I may be.

"I dought neither speak to prince or peer,
  Nor ask of grace from fair ladye."
"Now hold thy peace!" the lady said,
  "For as I say, so must it be."

He has gotten a coat of the even cloth,
  And a pair of shoes of velvet green;
And till seven years were gane and past
  True Thomas on earth was never seen.

Part II (*MODERNIZED FROM THE PROPHECIES*)

When seven years were come and gane,
  The sun blink'd fair on pool and stream;
And Thomas lay on Huntlie bank,
  Like one awaken'd from a dream.

He heard the trampling of a steed,
  He saw the flash of armour flee,
And he beheld a gallant knight
  Come riding down by the Eildon-tree.

He was a stalwart knight, and strong;
  Of giant make he 'pear'd to be:
He stirr'd his horse, as he were wode,
  Wi' gilded spurs, of faushion free.

Says "Well met, well met, true Thomas!
  Some uncouth ferlies show to me."
Says "Christ thee save, Corspatrick brave!
  Thrice welcome, good Dunbar, to me!

"Light down, light down, Corspatrick brave!
  And I will show thee curses three,
Shall gar fair Scotland greet and grane,
  And change the green to the black livery.

"A storm shall roar this very hour,
  From Ross's hills to Solway sea."
"Ye lied, ye lied, ye warlock hoar!
  For the sun shines sweet on fauld and lee."

He put his hand on the Earlie's head;
  He show'd him a rock beside the sea,
Where a king lay stiff beneath his steed,
  And steel-dight nobles wiped their ee.

"The neist curse lights on Branxton hills:
   By Flodden's high and heathery side,
Shall wave a banner red as blude,
   And chieftains throng wi' meikle pride.

"A Scottish King shall come full keen,
   The ruddy lion beareth he;
A feather'd arrow sharp, I ween,
   Shall make him wink and warre to see.

"When he is bloody, and all to-bledde,
   Thus to his men he still shall say—
'For God's sake, turn ye back again,
   And give yon southern folk a fray!
Why should I lose? the right is mine!
   My doom is not to die this day.'

"Yet turn ye to the eastern hand,
   And woe and wonder ye sall see;
How forty thousand spearmen stand,
   Where yon rank river meets the sea.

"There shall the lion lose the gylte,
   And the libbards bear it clean away;
At Pinkyn Cleuch there shall be split
   Much gentil bluid that day."

"Enough, enough, of curse and ban;
   Some blessings show thou now to me,
Or, by the faith o' my bodie," Corspatrick said,
   "Ye shall rue the day ye e'er saw me!"

"The first of blessings I shall thee show,
   Is by a burn* that's call'd of bread;
Where Saxon men shall tine the bow,
   And find their arrows lack the head.

"Beside that brigg, out-ower that burn,
   Where the water bickereth bright and sheen,
Shall many a fallen courser spurn,
   And knights shall die in battle keen.

"Beside a headless cross of stone,
   The libbards there shall lose the gree:
The raven shall come, the erne shall go,
   And drink the Saxon bluid sae free.

* Bannock-burn.

The cross of stone they shall not know,
   So thick the corses there shall be."

"But tell me now," said brave Dunbar,
   "True Thomas, tell now unto me,
What man shall rule the isle Britain,
   Even from the north to the southern sea?"

"A French Queen shall bear the son,
   Shall rule all Britain to the sea;
He of the Bruce's blood shall come,
   As near as in the ninth degree.

"The waters worship shall his race;
   Likewise the waves of the farthest sea;
For they shall ride over ocean wide,
   With hempen bridles, and horse of tree."

Part III (*MODERN*)

When seven years more were come and gone,
   Was war through Scotland spread,
And Ruberslaw show'd high Dunyon
   His beacon blazing red.

Then all by bonny Caldingknow,
   Pitch'd palliouns took their room,
And crested helms, and spears a-rowe,
   Glanced gaily through the broom.

The Leader, rolling to the Tweed,
   Resounds the ensenzie;
They roused the deer from Caddenhead,
   To distant Torwoodlee.

The feast was spread in Ercildoune,
   In Learmont's high and ancient hall:
And there were knights of great renown,
   And ladies laced in pall.

Nor lacked they, while they sat at dine,
   The music nor the tale,
Nor goblets of the blood-red wine,
   Nor mantling quaighs of ale.
True Thomas rose with harp in hand.
   When as the feast was done:
(In minstrel strife in Fairy Land
   The elfin harp he won.)

Hush'd were the throng, both limb and tongue,
    And harpers for envy pale;
And armed lords lean'd on their swords,
    And hearken'd to the tale.

In number high, the witching tale
    The prophet pour'd along;
No after bard might e'er avail
    Those numbers to prolong.

Yet fragments of the lofty strain
    Float down the tide of years,
As, buoyant on the stormy main,
    A parted wreck appears.

He sung King Arthur's Table Round:
    The Warrior of the Lake;
How courteous Gawaine met the wound,
    And bled for ladies' sake.

But chief, in gentle Tristrem's praise,
    The notes melodious swell;
Was none excell'd in Arthur's days,
    The knight of Lionelle.

For Marke, his cowardly uncle's right,
    A venom'd wound he bore;
When fierce Morholde he slew in fight
    Upon the Irish shore.

No art the poison might withstand;
    No medicine could be found,
Till lovely Isolde's lily hand
    Had probed the rankling wound.

With gentle hand and soothing tongue
    She bore the leech's part;
And, while she o'er his sick-bed hung,
    He paid her with his heart.

O fatal was the gift, I ween!
    For, doom'd in evil tide,
The maid must be rude Cornwall's queen,
    His cowardly uncle's bride.

Their loves, their woes, the gifted bard
    In fairy tissue wove;
Where lords and knights and ladies bright
    In gay confusion strove.

The Garde Joyeuse amid the tale
  High rear'd its glittering head;
And Avalon's enchanted vale
  In all its wonders spread.

Brangwain was there, and Segramore,
  And fiend-born Merlin's gramarye;
Of that famed wizard's mighty lore,
  O who could sing but he?

Through many a maze the winning song
  In changeful passion led,
Till bent at length the listening throng
  O'er Tristrem's dying bed.

His ancient wounds their scars expand,
  With agony his heart is wrung:
O where is Isolde's lilye hand,
  And where her soothing tongue?

She comes! she comes! like a flash of flame
  Can lovers' footsteps fly;
She comes! she comes! she only came
  To see her Tristrem die.

She saw him die; her latest sigh
  Join'd in a kiss his parting breath;
The gentlest pair that Britain bare
  United are in death.

There paused the harp: its lingering sound
  Died slowly on the ear;
The silent guests still bent around,
  For still they seem'd to hear.

Then woe broke forth in murmurs weak:
  Nor ladies heaved alone the sigh;
But, half ashamed, the rugged cheek
  Did many a gauntlet dry.

On Leader's stream and Learmont's tower
  The mists of evening close;
In camp, in castle, or in bower
  Each warrior sought repose.

Lord Douglas in his loft tent
  Dream'd o'er the woeful tale;
When footsteps light across the bent
  The warrior's ears assail.

He starts, he wakes: "What, Richard, ho!
    Arise, my page, arise!
What venturous wight at dead of night
    Dare step where Douglas lies?"

Then forth they rush'd: by Leader's tide,
    A selcouth sight they see—
A hart and hind pace side by side,
    As white as snow on Fairnalie.

Beneath the moon with gesture proud
    They stately move and slow;
Nor scare they at the gathering crowd,
    Who marvel as they go.

To Learmont's tower a message sped,
    As fast as page might run;
And Thomas started from his bed,
    And soon his clothes did on.

First he woxe pale, and then woxe red!
    Never a word he spake but three;—
"My sand is run; my thread is spun;
    This sign regardeth me."

The elfin harp his neck around,
    In minstrel guise, he hung;
And on the wind in doleful sound
    Its dying accents rung.

Then forth he went; yet turn'd him oft
    To view his ancient hall:
On the grey tower in lustre soft
    The autumn moonbeams fall;

And Leader's waves like silver sheen
    Danced shimmering in the ray;
In deepening mass, at distance seen,
    Broad Soltra's mountains lay.

"Farewell, my father's ancient tower!
    A long farewell," said he:
"The scene of pleasure, pomp, or power
    Thou never more shalt be.

"To Learmont's name no foot of earth
    Shall here again belong,
And on thy hospitable hearth
    The hare shall leave her young.

"Adieu! adieu!" again he cried,
  All as he turn'd him roun'—
"Farewell to Leader's silver tide!
  Farewell to Ercildoune!"

The hart and hind approach'd the place,
  As lingering yet he stood;
And there, before Lord Douglas' face,
  With them he cross'd the flood.

Lord Douglas leap'd on his berry-brown steed,
  And spurr'd him the Leader o'er;
But, though he rode with lightning speed,
  He never saw them more.

Some said to hill, and some to glen,
  Their wondrous course had been;
But ne'er in haunts of living men
  Again was Thomas seen.

From *Minstrelsy of the Scottish Border.*

Glenfinlas; or, Lord Ronald's Coronach

For them the viewless forms of air obey,
   Their bidding heed, and at their beck repair;
They know what spirit brews the stormful day,
   And heartless oft, like moody madness stare,
To see the phantom-train their secret work prepare.
COLLINS

O hone a rie'! O hone a rie'!
   The pride of Albin's line is o'er,
And fall'n Glenartney's stateliest tree;
   We ne'er shall see Lord Ronald more!

O, sprung from great Macgillianore,
   The chief that never fear'd a foe,
How matchless was thy broad claymore,
   How deadly thine unerring bow!

Well can the Saxon widows tell,
   How on the Teith's resounding shore
The boldest Lowland warriors fell,
   As down from Lenny's pass you bore.

But o'er his hills, in festal day,
   How blazed Lord Ronald's beltane-tree,
While youths and maids the light strathspey
   So nimbly danced with Highland glee!

Cheer'd by the strength of Ronald's shell,
   E'en age forgot his tresses hoar;
But now the loud lament we swell,
   O ne'er to see Lord Ronald more!

From distant isles a chieftain came,
   The joys of Ronald's halls to find,
And chase with him the dark-brown game,
   That bounds o'er Albin's hills of wind.

'Twas Moy; whom in Columba's isle
   The seer's prophetic spirit found,
As, with a minstrel's fire the while,
   He waked his harp's harmonious sound.

Full many a spell to him was known,
  Which wandering spirits shrink to hear;
And many a lay of potent tone,
  Was never meant for mortal ear.

For there, 'tis said, in mystic mood,
  High converse with the dead they hold,
And oft espy the fated shroud,
  That shall the future corpse enfold.

O so it fell, that on a day,
  To rouse the red deer from their den,
The Chiefs have ta'en their distant way,
  And scour'd the deep Glenfinlas glen.

No vassals wait their sports to aid,
  To watch their safety, deck their board;
Their simple dress the Highland plaid,
  Their trusty guard the Highland sword.

Three summer days, through brake and dell,
  Their whistling shafts successful flew;
And still, when dewy evening fell,
  The quarry to their hut they drew.

In grey Glenfinlas' deepest nook
  The solitary cabin stood,
Fast by Moneira's sullen brook,
  Which murmurs through that lonely wood.

Soft fell the night, the sky was calm,
  When three successive days had flown;
And summer mist in dewy balm
  Steep'd heathy bank and mossy stone.

The moon, half-hid in silvery flakes,
  Afar her dubious radiance shed,
Quivering on Katrine's distant lakes,
  And resting on Benledi's head.

Now in their hut, in social guise,
  Their silvan fare the Chiefs enjoy;
And pleasure laughs in Ronald's eyes,
  As many a pledge he quaffs to Moy.

"What lack we here to crown our bliss,
  While thus the pulse of joy beats high?
What, but fair woman's yielding kiss,
  Her panting breath and melting eye?

"To chase the deer of yonder shades,
    This morning left their father's pile
The fairest of our mountain maids,
    The daughters of the proud Glengyle.

"Long have I sought sweet Mary's heart,
    And dropp'd the tear, and heaved the sigh:
But vain the lover's wily art,
    Beneath a sister's watchful eye.

"But thou mayst teach that guardian fair,
    While far with Mary I have flown,
Of other hearts to cease her care,
    And find it hard to guard her own.

"Touch but thy harp—thou soon shalt see
    The lovely Flora of Glengyle,
Unmindful of her charge and me,
    Hang on thy notes 'twixt tear and smile.

"Or, if she choose a melting tale,
    All underneath the greenwood bough,
Will good Saint Oran's rule prevail,
    Stern huntsman of the rigid brow?"

"Since Enrick's fight, since Morna's death,
    No more on me shall rapture rise,
Responsive to the panting breath,
    Or yielding kiss, or melting eyes.

"E'en then, when o'er the heath of woe,
    Where sunk my hopes of love and fame,
I bade my harp's wild wailings flow,
    On me the Seer's sad spirit came.

"The last dread curse of angry heaven,
    With ghastly sights and sounds of woe,
To dash each glimpse of joy, was given;
    The gift—the future ill to know.

"The bark thou saw'st yon summer morn
    So gaily part from Oban's bay,
My eye beheld her dash'd and torn,
    Fra on the rocky Colonsay.

"They Fergus too, thy sister's son,—
    Thou saw'st with pride the gallant's power,
As marching 'gainst the Lord of Downe
    He left the skirts of huge Benmore.

"Thou only saw'st their tartans wave,
  As down Benvoirlich's side they wound,
Heard'st but the pibroch answering brave
  To many a target clanking round.

"I heard the groans, I mark'd the tears,
  I saw the wound his bosom bore,
When on the serried Saxon spears
  He pour'd his clan's resistless roar.

"And thou who bidst me think of bliss,
  And bidst my heart awake to glee,
And court like thee the wanton kiss—
  That heart, O Ronald, bleeds for thee!

"I see the death-damps chill thy brow;
  I hear thy Warning Spirit cry;
The corpse-lights dance! they're gone! and now—
  No more is given to gifted eye!"

"Alone enjoy thy dreary dreams,
  Sad prophet of the evil hour!
Say, should we scorn joy's transient beams,
  Because to-morrow's storm may lour?

"Or false or sooth they words of woe,
  Clangillian's Chieftain ne'er shall fear;
His blood shall bound at rapture's glow,
  Though doom'd to stain the Saxon spear.

"E'en now, to meet me in yon dell,
  My Mary's buskins brush the dew."
He spoke, nor bade the Chief farewell,
  But called his dogs, and gay withdrew.

Within an hour return'd each hound;
  In rush'd the rousers of the deer;
They howl'd in melancholy sound,
  Then closely couch'd beside the Seer.

No Ronald yet—though midnight came,
  And sad were Moy's prophetic dreams,
As, bending o'er the dying flame,
  He fed the watch-fire's quivering gleams.

Sudden the hounds erect their ears,
  And sudden cease their moaning howl;
Close press'd to Moy, they mark their fears
  By shivering limbs and stifled growl.

Untouch'd, the harp began to ring,
  As softly, slowly, oped the door;
And shook responsive every string,
  As, light, a footstep press'd the floor.

And by the watch-fire's glimmering light,
  Close by the minstrel's side was seen
An huntress maid in beauty bright,
  All dropping wet her robes of green.

All dropping wet her garments seem;
  Chill'd was her cheek, her bosom bare,
As, bending o'er the dying gleam,
  She wrung the moisture from her hair.

With maiden blush, she softly said,
  "O gentle huntsman, hast thou seen,
In deep Glenfinlas' moonlight glade,
  A lovely maid in vest of green:

"With her a Chief in Highland pride;
  His shoulders bear the hunter's bow,
The mountain dirk adorns his side,
  Far on the wind his tartans flow?"

"And who art thou? and who are they?"
  All ghastly gazing, Moy replied:
"And why, beneath the moon's pale ray,
  Dare ye thus roam Glenfinlas' side?"

"Where wild Loch Katrine pours her tide,
  Blue, dark, and deep, round many an isle,
Our father's towers o'erhang her side,
  The castle of the bold Glengyle.

"To chase the dun Glenfinlas deer
  Our woodland course this morn we bore,
And haply met, while wandering here,
  The son of great Macgillianore.

"O aid me, then, to seek the pair,
  Whom, loitering in the woods, I lost;
Alone, I dare not venture there,
  Where walks, they say, the shrieking ghost."

"Yes, many a shrieking ghost walks there;
  Then, first, my own sad vow to keep,
Here will I pour my midnight prayer,
  Which still must rise when mortals sleep."

"O first, for pity's gentle sake,
 Guide a lone wanderer on her way!
For I must cross the haunted brake,
 And reach my father's towers ere day."

"First, three times tell each Ave-bead,
 And thrice a Pater-noster say,
Then kiss with me the holy rede;
 So shall we safely wend our way."

"O shame to knighthood, strange and foul!
 Go, doff the bonnet from thy brow,
And shroud thee in the monkish cowl,
 Which best befits thy sullen vow.

"Not so, by high Dunlathmon's fire,
 They heart was froze to love and joy,
When gaily rung thy raptured lyre
 To wanton Morna's melting eye."

Wild stared the minstrel's eyes of flame,
 And high his sable locks arose,
And quick his colour went and came,
 As fear and rage alternate rose.

"And thou! when by the blazing oak
 I lay, to her and love resign'd,
Say, rode ye on the eddying smoke,
 Or sail'd ye on the midnight wind?

"Not thine a race of mortal blood,
 Nor old Glengyle's pretended line;
Thy dame, the Lady of the Flood—
 They sire, the Monarch of the Mine."

He mutter'd thrice Saint Oran's rhyme,
 And thrice Saint Fillan's powerful prayer;
Then turn'd him to the eastern clime,
 And sternly shook his coal-black hair.

And, bending o'er his harp, he flung,
 His wildest witch-notes on the wind;
And loud and high and strange they rung,
 As many a magic change they find.

Tall wax'd the Spirit's altering form,
 Till to the roof her stature grew;
Then, mingling with the rising storm,
 With one wild yell away she flew.

Rain beats, hail rattles, whirlwinds tear:
　The slender hut in fragments flew;
But not a lock of Moy's loose hair
　Was waved by wind, or wet by dew.

Wild mingling with the howling gale,
　Loud bursts of ghastly laughter rise;
High o'er the minstrel's head they sail,
　And die amid the northern skies.

The voice of thunder shook the wood,
　As ceased the more than mortal yell;
And, spattering foul, a shower of blood
　Upon the hissing firebrands fell.

Next dropp'd from high a mangled arm;
　The fingers strain'd an half-drawn blade:
And last, the life-blood streaming warm,
　Torn from the trunk, a gasping head.

Oft o'er that head, in battling field,
　Stream'd the proud crest of high Benmore;
That arm the broad claymore could wield,
　Which dyed the Teith with Saxon gore.

Woe to Moneira's sullen rills!
　Woe to Glenfinlas' dreary glen!
There never son of Albin's hills
　Shall draw the hunter's shaft agen!

E'en the tired pilgrim's burning feet
　At noon shall shun that sheltering den,
Lest, journeying in their rage, he meet
　The wayward Ladies of the Glen.

And we—behind the Chieftain's shield
　No more shall we in safety dwell;
None leads the people to the field—
　And we the loud lament must swell.

O hone a rie'! O hone a rie'!
　The pride of Albin's line is o'er!
And fall'n Glenartney's stateliest tree;
　We ne'er shall see Lord Ronald more!

From *Minstrelsy of the Scottish Border.*

The Eve of Saint John

The Baron of Smaylho'me rose with day,
  He spurr'd his courser on,
Without stop or stay, down the rocky way,
  That leads to Brotherstone.

He went not with the bold Buccleuch,
  His banner broad to rear;
He went not 'gainst the English yew
  To lift the Scottish spear.

Yet his plate-jack was braced, and his helmet was laced,
  And his vaunt-brace of proof he wore;
At his saddle-gerthe was a good steel sperthe,
  Full ten pound weight and more.

The Baron return'd in three days' space,
  And his looks were sad and sour;
And weary was his courser's pace,
  As he reach'd his rocky tower.

He came not from where Ancram Moor
  Ran red with English blood;
Where the Douglas true and the bold Buccleuch
  'Gainst keen Lord Evers stood.

Yet was his helmet hack'd and hew'd,
  His acton pierced and tore,
His axe and his dagger with blood imbrued,—
  But it was not English gore.

He lighted at the Chapellage,
  He held him close and still;
And he whistled thrice for his little foot-page,
  His name was English Will.

"Come thou hither, my little foot-page,
  Come hither to my knee;
Though thou art young, and tender of age,
  I think thou art true to me.

"Come, tell me all that thou hast seen,
  And look thou tell me true!

Since I from Smaylho'me tower have been,
  What did thy lady do?"

"My lady each night sought the lonely light
  That burns on the wild Watchfold;
For, from height to height, the beacons bright
  Of the English foremen told.

"The bittern clamour'd from the moss,
  The wind blew loud and shrill;
Yet the craggy pathway she did cross
  To the eiry Beacon Hill.

"I watch'd her steps, and silent came
  Where she sat her on a stone;
No watchman stood by the dreary flame,
  It burned all alone.

"The second night I kept her in sight
  Till to the fire she came,
And, by Mary's might! an armed Knight
  Stood by the lonely flame.

"And many a word that warlike lord
  Did speak to my lady there;
But the rain fell fast, and loud blew the blast,
  And I heard not what they were.

"The third night there the sky was fair,
  And the mountain-blast was still,
As again I watch'd the secret pair
  On the lonesome Beacon Hill.

"And I heard her name the midnight hour,
  And name this holy eve,
And say 'Come this might to thy lady's bower;
  Ask no bold Baron's leave.

" 'He lifts his spear with the bold Buccleuch;
  His lady is all alone;
The door she'll undo to her knight so true
  On the eve of good Saint John.'

" 'I cannot come, I must not come,
  I dare not come to thee;
On the eve of Saint John I must wander alone,
  In thy bower I may not be.'

" 'Now out on thee, fainthearted knight!
  Thou shouldst not say me nay;

For the eve is sweet, and when lovers meet
   Is worth the whole summer's day.

" 'And I'll chain the blood-hound, and the wander shall not
      sound,
   And rushes shall be strew'd on the stair;
So, by the black rood-stone, and by holy Saint John,
   I conjure thee, my love, to be there!'

" 'Though the blood-hound be mute, and the rush beneath my
      foot,
   And the warder his bugle should not blow,
Yet there sleepeth a priest in the chamber to the east,
   And my footstep he would know.'

" 'O fear not the priest, who sleepeth to the east,
   For to Dryburgh the way he has ta'en;
And there to say mass, till three days do pass,
   For the soul of a knight that is slayne.'

"He turn'd him around, and grimly he frown'd,
   Then he laugh'd right scornfully—
'He who says the mass-rite for the soul of that knight
   May as well say mass for me.

" 'At the lone midnight hour, when bad spirits have power,
   In thy chamber will I be.'
With that he was gone, and my lady left alone,
   And no more did I see."

Then changed, I trow, was that bold Baron's brow,
   From the dark to the blood-red high—
"Now tell me the mien of the knight thou hast seen,
   For, by Mary, he shall die!"

"His arms shone full bright in the beacon's red light;
   His plume it was scarlet and blue;
On his shield was a hound in a silver leash bound,
   And his crest was a branch of the yew."

"Thou liest, thou liest, thou little foot-page,
   Loud dost thou lie to me!
For that knight is cold, and low laid in the mould,
   All under the Eildon-tree."

"Yet hear but my word, my noble lord!
   For I heard her name his name;
And that lady bright, she called the knight
   Sir Richard of Coldinghame."

The bold Baron's brow then changed, I trow,
　　From high blood-red to pale—
"The grave is deep and dark, and the corpse is stiff and stark,
　　So I may not trust thy tale.

"Where fair Tweed flows round holy Melrose,
　　And Eildon slopes to the plain,
Full three nights ago, by some secret foe,
　　That gay gallant was slain.

"The varying light deceived thy sight,
　　And the wild winds drown'd the name;
For the Dryburgh bells ring and the white monks do sing
　　For Sir Richard of Coldinghame!"

He pass'd the court-gate, and he oped the tower-grate,
　　And he mounted the narrow stair
To the bartizan-seat, where, with maids that on her wait
　　He found his lady fair.

That lady sat in mournful mood,
　　Look'd over hill and vale,
Over Tweed's fair flood and Mertoun's wood
　　And all down Teviotdale.

"Now hail, now hail, thou lady bright!"
　　"Now hail, thou Baron true!
What news, what news from Ancram fight?
　　What news from the bold Buccleuch?"

"The Ancram Moor is red with gore,
　　For many a southron fell;
And Buccleuch has charged us evermore
　　To watch our beacons well."

The lady blush'd red, but nothing she said;
　　Nor added the Baron a word.
Then she stepp'd down the stair to her chamber fair,
　　And so did her moody lord.

In sleep the lady mourn'd, and the Baron toss'd and turn'd,
　　And oft to himself he said,
"The worms around him creep, and his bloody grave is deep—
　　It cannot give up the dead!"

It was near the ringing of matin-bell,
　　The night was wellnigh done,
When a heavy sleep on that Baron fell,
　　On the eve of good Saint John.

The lady look'd through the chamber fair,
  By the light of a dying flame;
And she was aware of a knight stood there—
  Sir Richard of Coldinghame!

"Alas! away, away!" she cried,
  "For the holy Virgin's sake!"
"Lady, know who sleeps by thy side;
  But, lady, he will not awake.

"By Eildon-tree, for long nights three,
  In bloody grave have I lain;
The mass and the death-prayer are said for me,
  But, lady, they are said in vain.

"By the Baron's brand, near Tweed's fair strand,
  Most foully slain I feel;
And my restless sprite on the beacon's height
  For a space is doom'd to dwell.

"At our trysting-place, for a certain space,
  I must wander to and fro;
But I had not had power to come to thy bower
  Had'st thou not conjured me so."

Love master'd fear; her brow she cross'd—
  "How, Richard, hast thou sped?
And art thou saved, or art thou lost?"
  The vision shook his head!

"Who spilleth life shall forfeit life;
  So bid thy lord believe:
That lawless love is guilt above,
  This awful sign receive."

He laid his left palm on an oaken beam,
  His right upon her hand—
The lady shrunk, and fainting sunk,
  For it scorch'd like a fiery brand.

The sable score of fingers four
  Remains on that board impress'd;
And for evermore that lady wore
  A covering on her wrist.

There is a nun in Dryburgh bower,
  Ne'er looks upon the sun;
There is a monk in Melrose tower,
  He speaketh word to none;

That nun who ne'er beholds the day,
    That monk who speaks to none—
That nun was Smaylho'me's Lady gay,
    That monk the bold Baron.

From *Minstrelsy of the Scottish Border.*

The Erl-King

FROM THE GERMAN OF GOETHE

O, who rides by night thro' the woodland so wild?
It is the fond father embracing his child;
And close the boy nestles within his loved arm,
To hold himself fast, and to keep himself warm.

"O father, see yonder! see yonder!" he says;
"My boy, upon what dost thou fearfully gaze?"
"O, 'tis the Erl-King with his crown and his shroud."
"No, my son, it is but a dark wreath of the cloud."

The Erl-King speaks:

"O come and go with me, thou loveliest child;
By many a gay sport shall thy time be beguiled;
My mother keeps for thee full many a fair toy,
And many a fine flower shall she pluck for my boy."

"O father, my father, and did you not hear
The Erl-King whisper so low in my ear?"
"Be still, my heart's darling—my child, be at ease;
It was but the wild blast as it sung thro' the trees."

Erl-King:

"O wilt thou go with me, thou loveliest boy?
My daughter shall tend thee with care and with joy;
She shall bear thee so lightly thro' wet and thro' wild,
And press thee, and kiss thee, and sing to my child."

"O father, my father, and saw you not plain
The Erl-King's pale daughter glide past thro' the rain?"
"O yes, my loved treasure, I knew it full soon;
It was the grey willow that danced to the moon."

Erl-King:

"O come and go with me, no longer delay,
Or else, silly child, I will drag thee away."

"O father! O father! now, now, keep your hold,
The Erl-King has seized me—his grasp is so cold!"

Sore trembled the father; he spurr'd thro' the wild,
Clasping close to his bosom his shuddering child;
He reaches his dwelling in doubt and in dread,
But, clasp'd to his bosom, the infant was dead.

From *Ballads from the German.*

Glossary

acton, a padded jacket worn under armor

angel, an ancient gold coin

argent, silver (heraldry)

baith, both

baldric, a richly ornamented belt

bandrol, a long forked flag

barded, armored

barret-cap, a small cloth cap

bartizan, a turret (for defense)

basnet, a light helmet

beadsman, a man paid to offer prayers for another

Ben-Shie, an evil fairy

bent, a slope; also, aimed (as a bow)

bill, a battle-ax on a long staff

billmen, troops armed with bills

black-jack, a tar-coated leather jug

boune, bowne; make ready

bourne, a stream or rivulet

bowyer, an archer (poetic)

bra' or braw, brave; handsome

bracken, coarse fern

brae, a riverbank

brake, a thicket; bracken

brand, a sword

braw, brave

brigantine, medieval coat of armor

brook, bear; endure

cairn, a pile of stones

caitiff, a captive; an unfortunate man

can, a drinking cup

canna, cannach; cotton grass

casque, a war helmet

chanters, the pipes of the bagpipe

chief, the upper part of a shield (heraldry)

claymore, a large two-edged sword

combust, overpowered by the sun's light (an astrological term) coronach, a dirge

cresset, a hanging lamp

cumber, trouble; harass

cushat-dove, a wood pigeon of
 Europe

daggled, mud-spattered

darkling, in the dark

daw, a jackdaw; a simpleton

deas, a platform

demi-volt, a half-vault (horse-
 manship)

dhu, black

dight, dressed; bedecked

dingle, a hollow; a narrow dale

donjon, the keep of a castle

down, undulating land

draughts, the game of checkers

eiry, eerie

eke, also

emprise, enterprise; endeavor

enow, enough

erne, a European sea eagle

falchion, a broad-bladed sword

fane, a church; a temple

fay, faith; a fairy

featly, cleverly; nimbly

fell, a moor; a down

fieldfare, a thrush

fosse, a ditch; a moat

galliard, a lively French dance

gammon, a leg, a foot, or a
 thigh

ghast, ghastly

glaive, a broadsword

glozing, flattering

gorget, throat armor

gramercy, *grand merci;* many
 thanks

guerdon, reward

gules, red (heraldry)

gyve, a fetter

hackbut; hagbut, a mustket; a
 gun barrel

halberd; halbert, a long spear
 with a battle-ax

hale, haul; drag

haps, happens

heath, evergreen; heather

heath-cock, the male of the
 black grouse

hest, command; behest

hosen, hose

housing, saddlecloth

jack, a leather jacket

jennet, a small Spanish horse

jerkin, a short coat or jacket

keep, a tower in a castle

ken, know; understand

kern, a light-armed foot soldier

kirtle, outer petticoat or short skirt

larum, alarum; alarm

leech, a physician or surgeon

levin, lightning

linn, a waterfall; a pool; a steep ravine

linnet, a small finch

linstock; lintstock, a staff used in firing a cannon

lists, the arena of a tournament

loot, past tense of let

malison, a curse; a malediction

Malvoisie, Malmsey wine

mark, about eight ounces

mavis, the missel thrush

mean, a meadow; a fermented drink of honey and water

meed, a reward; worth

mere, a lake

merle, the European blackbird

mewed, shut up; confined

minion, a favorite; a follower

mitre, bishop's headdress

morion, a high-crested helmet

morrice-pike, a morris pike; a large spear or pike

morricers, performers of a folk dance; morris dancers

mulct, a fine or penalty

mullet, a five-pointed star (heraldry)

or, gold

paladin, a champion; a legendary hero

pale, a perpendicular stripe in an escutcheon (heraldry)

pall, a rich cloth

palmer, a pilgrim to the Holy Land

pardoner, a seller of priestly indulgences

pentacle, a figure or object used as a talisman

pibroch, music for the Scottish Highland bagpipe

pike, variant of pick

pipe, a large cask

pitch, a point or peak

placket, a petticoat

plained, lamented

plate-jack, coat armor

plump, a body of cavalry

pricker, a cavalryman

prore, the prow of a ship

psaltery, an ancient stringed instrument

ptarmigan, a grouse

pursuivant, an attendant on a herald

quaigh, a drinking vessel (usually of wood)

racking, flying like a wind-driven cloud

reave, to split or tear away

reck, to take heed

reft, bereft; despoiled

retrograde, to recede (as a planet)

rochet, a bishop's close-fitting vestment

rood, a cross

rowan, the mountain ash

runnel, a stream

ruth, compassion

sack, a dry white wine

sackbut, an early version of the slide trombone

sall, shall

salvo-shot, an artillery salute

scaur, variant of scar; a rocky eminence

scutcheon, escutcheon; a shield

seamew, a sea gull

selle, a saddle

seneschal, the steward or major-domo of a great feudal lord

sewer, a high-ranking butler

shaw, a thicket or grove of trees

sheen, bright; shining

Shinar, Babylon or Babel

slogan, the war or rallying cry of a Highland clan

snood, a fillet worn around the hair of a maiden

soland, the gannet

sooth, truth; true

sperthe, variant of sparth; a long battle-ax

stark, stalwart

still, always

stowre, variant of stour; tumult; strife

strath, a wide river valley

strathspey, a lively Scottish dance

streight, strait

strook, struck or stricken

stumah, faithful

tabard, a herald's jacket

tables, backgammon

targe, a shield

tartan, woolen plaid cloth worn in the Highlands of Scotland; each clan has its own distinctive tartan.

Tinchel, a ring formed by sportsmen to bag game

toil, trap

tressure, a charge (border) in heraldry

trews, close-fitting breeches and stockings in one piece, worn by the Highlanders

trine, threefold

trow, believe; trust

truncheon, a short staff or cudgel

unrecked, unheeded

unsparred, unbarred

vail, avail

vair, a kind of squirrel fur

vantage-coign, an advantageous position

vaunt-brace, armor for the forearm

vaward, the forefront; the van

vich, son of

wan, won

weal, well-being; prosperity; happiness

weed, an outer garment

ween, expect; suppose

whilom, formerly

whin, gorse; furze

whinyard, a short sword or hunting knife

wight, a human being

wildering, bewildering

wold, an upland plain

woned, dwelt

wot, know

yare, ready

yode, went

zone, belt

OTHER AIRMONT CLASSICS

Complete and Unabridged with Introductions